Frommer's®

W9-BZP-440

Chinese PhraseFinder & Dictionary

1st Edition

WILEY

Wiley Publishing, Inc.

Published by:

Wiley Publishing, Inc.

111 River St.
Hoboken, NJ 07030-5774

ISBN-13: 978-0-470-17838-6

Editor: Wendy Abraham
Series Editor: Maureen Clarke
Photo Editor: Richard H. Fox
Illustrations by Maciek Albrecht

Translation, Copyediting, Proofreading, Production, and Layout by:
Lingo Systems, 15115 SW Sequoia Pkwy, Ste 200, Portland, OR 97224

For information on our other products and services or to obtain technical support,
please contact our Customer Care Department within the U.S. at 800/762-2974, outside the U.S. at 317/572-3993 or fax 317/572-4002.
Wiley also publishes its books in a variety of electronic formats. Some content that
appears in print may not be available in electronic formats.

Manufactured in the United States of America

5   4   3   2   1

Contents

Introduction   vii

1 Survival Chinese (& Grammar Basics)   1

Basic Greetings 1, The Key Questions 3, Numbers & Counting 7, Measurements 10, Time 12, Pronunciations 17, Personal Pronouns 22, Classifiers 23 Adjectives 26, Verbs 26, Aspect Markers 27

2 Getting There & Getting Around   33

At the Airport 33, Renting a Vehicle 44, By Taxi 50, By Train 51, By Bus 53, By Boat or Ship 54, By Subway 55, Considerations for Travelers with Special Needs 56

3 Lodging   58

Room Preferences 58, In-Room Amenities 63, Happy Camping 68

4 Dining   69

Finding a Restaurant 69, Ordering 71, Drinks 75, Settling Up 77, Menu Reader 77, Buying Groceries 82

5 Socializing   87

Greetings 87, Curse Words 89, Getting Personal 90, Topics of Conversation 99, Getting to Know Someone 102

6   **Money & Communications**   **106**

Money 106, Phone Service 108, Internet Access 111,
Getting Mail 112

7   **Culture**   **115**

Cinema 115, Performances 116, Museums,
Galleries & Sights 118

8   **Shopping**   **119**

General Shopping Terms 119, Clothes Shopping 120,
Artisan Market Shopping 123, Bookstore / Newsstand
Shopping 124, Shopping for Electronics 125,
At the Barber / Hairdresser 126

9   **Sports & Fitness**   **129**

Getting Fit 129, Catching a Game 131, Hiking 132,
Boating or Fishing 135, Diving 136, Surfing 136,
Golfing 137

10 **Nightlife**   **139**

Club Hopping 139, Across a Crowded Room 142,
Getting Intimate 144, In the Casino 147

11 **Health & Safety**   **149**

At the Pharmacy 149, At the Doctor's Office 150,
At the Police Station 154

English–Chinese Dictionary   **157**

Chinese–English Dictionary   **205**

An Invitation to the Reader

In researching this book, we discovered many wonderful sayings and terms useful to travelers in Chinese-speaking countries. We're sure you'll find others. Please tell us about them so we can share them with your fellow travelers in upcoming editions. If you were disappointed about any aspect of this book, we'd like to know that, too. Please write to:

Frommer's Chinese PhraseFinder & Dictionary, 1st Edition
Wiley Publishing, Inc.
111 River St. • Hoboken, NJ 07030-5774

An Additional Note

The packager, editors and publisher cannot be held responsible for the experience of readers while traveling. Your safety is important to us, however, so we encourage you to stay alert and aware of your surroundings. Keep a close eye on cameras, purses, and wallets, all favorite targets of thieves and pickpockets.

Frommers.com

Now that you have the language for a great trip, visit our website at **www.frommers.com** for travel information on more than 3,600 destinations. With features updated regularly, we give you instant access to the most current trip-planning information available. At Frommers.com you'll also find the best prices on airfares, accommodations, and car rentals—and you can even book travel online through our travel booking partners. Frommers.com also features:

- Online updates to our most popular guidebooks
- Vacation sweepstakes and contest giveaways
- Newsletter highlighting the hottest travel trends
- Online travel message boards with featured travel discussions

INTRODUCTION: HOW TO USE THIS BOOK

Given China's population of more than 1.3 billion, it is safe to say that close to a quarter of humanity speaks Chinese, primarily in the People's Republic of China (PRC), the Republic of China (ROC, or Taiwan), Hong Kong, and Singapore. A member of the Sino-Tibetan language family, found in East Asia, Chinese is unique in that its written language can be read and understood by all who speak Chinese, whereas its spoken language has literally hundreds of different local and regional dialects—each mutually incomprehensible without the written word that has bound them together for thousands of years. The easiest Chinese dialect to learn is standard Mandarin, based on the northern dialect, which has only four tones (as opposed to other dialects with nine or even eleven tones in several different registers). Mandarin is the official dialect of both the PRC and Taiwan and is the dialect whose pronunciation and tones this book will highlight.

Our intention is not to teach you Chinese; we figure you'll find an audio program for that. Our aim is to provide a portable travel tool that's easy to use. The problem with most phrasebooks is that you practically have to memorize the contents before you know where to look for a term you might need on the spot. This phrasebook is designed for fingertip referencing, so you can whip it out and find the words you need fast. The extensive PhraseFinder dictionary at the back is an additional perk, and one to which we're guessing you'll appreciate having instant access.

Like most phrasebooks, part of this book organizes terms by chapters, like the chapters in a Frommer's guide—getting a room, getting a good meal, etc. Within those sections, we tried to organize phrases intuitively, according to how frequently most readers would be likely to use them. But let's say you're in a cab and you've received the wrong change, and you forget which chapter covers money. With Frommer's PhraseFinder, you can quickly look up "change" in the dictionary, and learn how to say "Sorry, but this isn't the correct change."

To make the best use of this book, we recommend that you spend some time flipping through it before you depart for your trip. Familiarize yourself with the order of the chapters. Read through the pronunciations section in chapter one and practice pronouncing random phrases throughout the book. Try looking up a few phrases in the phrasebook section as well as in the dictionary. This way, you'll be able to locate phrases faster and speak them more clearly when you need them.

What will make this book most practical? What will make it easiest to use? These are the questions we asked ourselves constantly as we assembled these travel terms.

Our immediate goal was to create a phrasebook as indispensable as your passport. Our far-ranging goal, of course, is to enrich your experience of travel. And with that, we wish you: *Yí lù píng an*. (Bon voyage!).

CHAPTER ONE

SURVIVAL CHINESE

If you tire of toting around this phrasebook, tear out this chapter.
You should be able to navigate your destination with only the
terms found in the next 32 pages.

BASIC GREETINGS

For a full list of greetings, see p87.

Hello.	您好。
	nín hǎo。
How are you?	您好吗？
	nín hǎo ma?
I'm fine, thanks.	我很好，谢谢。
	wǒ hěn hǎo, xiè xiè。
And you?	您呢？
	nín ne?
My name is _____.	我叫_____。
	wǒ jiào _____。
And yours?	您呢？
	nín ne?
It's a pleasure to meet you.	见到您很愉快。
	jiàn dào nín hěn yú kuài。
Please.	请。
	qǐng。
Thank you.	谢谢您。
	xiè xiè nín。
Yes.	是的。
	shì de。
No.	不是。
	bù shì。

Okay.	好。
	hǎo。
No problem.	没问题。
	méi wèn tí。
I'm sorry, I don't understand.	很抱歉，我不懂。
	hěn bào qiàn, wǒ bù dǒng。
Would you speak slower please?	您能再说慢点吗？
	nín néng zài shuō màn diǎn ma？
Would you speak louder please?	您能大点声说吗？
	nín néng dà diǎn shēng shuō ma？
Do you speak English?	您说英语吗？
	nín shuō yīng yǔ ma？
Do you speak any other languages?	您说其他语言吗？
	nín shuō qí tā yǔ yán ma？
I speak ____ better than Chinese.	我的_____语说得比汉语好。
	wǒ de _____ yǔ shuō dé bǐ hàn yǔ hǎo。
Would you spell that?	请问它怎么写？
	qǐng wèn tā zěn me xiě？
Would you please repeat that?	请再说一遍好吗？
	qǐng zài shuō yī biàn hǎo ma？
Would you point that out in this dictionary?	您能在这本字典里把它指给我看吗？
	nín néng zài zhè běn zì diǎn lǐ bǎ tā zhǐ gěi wǒ kàn ma？

THE KEY QUESTIONS

With the right hand gestures, you can get a lot of mileage from the following list of single-word questions and answers.

Who?	谁?
	shéi?
What?	什么?
	shuí me?
When?	什么时候?
	shén me shí hou?
Where?	哪里?
	nǎ lǐ?
To where?	到哪里?
	dào nǎ lǐ?
Why?	为什么?
	wéi shén me?
How?	怎么样?
	zěn me yàng?
Which?	哪一个?
	nǎ yī gè?
How many? / How much?	多少?
	duō shǎo?

THE ANSWERS: WHO

For full coverage of pronouns, see p22.

I	我
	wǒ
you	你 / 您 / 你们
(familiar, formal, plural)	*nǐ / nín / nǐ mén*
him	他
	tā
her	她
	tā
us	我们
	wǒ mén
them	他们
	tā mén

THE ANSWERS: WHEN

For full coverage of time, see p12.

now	现在
	xiàn zài
later	稍后
	shāo hòu
in a minute	马上
	mǎ shàng
today	今天
	jīn tiān
tomorrow	明天
	míng tiān
yesterday	昨天
	zuó tiān
in a week	一周内
	yī zhōu nèi
next week	下周
	xià zhōu
last week	上周
	shàng zhōu
next month	下个月
	xià gè yuè
At ____	在_____
	zài _____
ten o'clock this morning.	今天上午十点。
	jīn tiān shàng wǔ shí diǎn。
two o'clock this afternoon.	今天下午两点。
	Jīn tiān xià wǔ liǎng diǎn。
seven o'clock this evening.	今天晚上七点。
	Jīn tiān wǎn shàng qī diǎn。

For full coverage of numbers, see p7.

THE ANSWERS: WHERE

here	这里	*zhè lǐ*
there	那里	*nà lǐ*
near	附近	*fù jìn*
closer	较近	*jiào jìn*
closest	最近	*zuì jìn*
far	远	*yuǎn*
farther	较远	*jiào yuǎn*
farthest	最远	*zuì yuǎn*
across from	在...对面	*zài ... duì miàn*
next to	紧邻	*jǐn lín*
behind	后面	*hòu miàn*
straight ahead	一直向前	*yī zhí xiàng qián*
left	左边	*zuǒ biān*
right	右边	*yòu biān*
up	上边	*shàng biān*
down	下边	*xià biān*
lower	较低	*jiào dī*

higher	较高 *jiào gāo*
forward	前面 *qián miàn*
back	后面 *hòu miàn*
around	周围 *zhōu wéi*
across the street	街对面 *jiē duì miàn*
down the street	沿着街道 *yán zhe jiē dào*
on the corner	在拐角处 *zài guǎi jiǎo chù*
kitty-corner	斜对角 *xié duì jiǎo*
____ blocks from here	离这里_____条街远的地方 *lí zhè lǐ _____ tiáo jiē yuǎn de dì fāng*

For a full list of numbers, see the next page.

THE ANSWERS: WHICH

this one	这个 *zhè gè*
that (that one)	那个 *nà gè*
these	这些 *zhè xiē*
those (those there, close by)	那些 *nà xiē*

NUMBERS & COUNTING

one	一 *yī*		seventeen	十七 *shí qī*
two	二 *èr*		eighteen	十八 *shí bā*
three	三 *sān*		nineteen	十九 *shí jiǔ*
four	四 *sì*		twenty	二十 *èr shí*
five	五 *wǔ*		twenty-one	二十一 *èr shí yī*
six	六 *liù*		thirty	三十 *sān shí*
seven	七 *qī*		forty	四十 *sì shí*
eight	八 *bā*		fifty	五十 *wǔ shí*
nine	九 *jiǔ*		sixty	六十 *liù shí*
ten	十 *shí*		seventy	七十 *qī shí*
eleven	十一 *shí yī*		eighty	八十 *bā shí*
twelve	十二 *shí èr*		ninety	九十 *jiǔ shí*
thirteen	十三 *shí sān*		one hundred	一百 *yī bǎi*
fourteen	十四 *shí sì*		two hundred	二百 *èr bǎi*
fifteen	十五 *shí wǔ*		one thousand	一千 *yī qiān*
sixteen	十六 *shí liù*			

FRACTIONS & DECIMALS

one eighth	八分之一 *bā fēn zhī yī*
one quarter	四分之一 *sì fēn zhī yī*
one third	三分之一 *sān fēn zhī yī*
one half	二分之一 *èr fēn zhī yī*
two thirds	三分之二 *sān fēn zhī èr*
three quarters	四分之三 *sì fēn zhī sān*
double	两倍 *liǎng bèi*
triple	三倍 *sān bèi*
one tenth	十分之一 *shí fēn zhī yī*
one hundredth	百分之一 *bǎi fēn zhī yī*
one thousandth	千分之一 *qiān fēn zhī yī*

MATH

addition	加 *jiā*
2 + 1	二加一 *èr jiā yī*
subtraction	减 *jiǎn*
2 − 1	二减一 *èr jiǎn yī*

multiplication	乘	
	chéng	
2 × 3	二乘以三	
	èr chéng yǐ sān	
division	除	
	chú	
6 ÷ 3	六除以三	
	liù chú yǐ sān	

ORDINAL NUMBERS

first	第一	
	dì yī	
second	第二	
	dì èr	
third	第三	
	dì sān	
fourth	第四	
	dì sì	
fifth	第五	
	dì wǔ	
sixth	第六	
	dì liù	
seventh	第七	
	dì qī	
eighth	第八	
	dì bā	
ninth	第九	
	dì jiǔ	
tenth	第十	
	dì shí	
last	最后	
	zuì hòu	

MEASUREMENTS

Measurements will usually be metric, though you may need a few American measurement terms.

inch	英寸
	yīng cùn
foot	英尺
	yīng chǐ
mile	英里
	yīng lǐ
millimeter	毫米
	háo mǐ
centimeter	分米
	fēn mǐ
meter	米
	mǐ
kilometer	千米
	qiān mǐ
hectare	公顷
	gōng qǐng
squared	平方
	píng fāng
short	短
	duǎn
long	长
	cháng

VOLUME

milliliters	毫升
	háo shēng
liter	升
	shēng
kilo	千
	qiān
ounce	盎司
	àng sī

cup	杯
	bēi
pint	品脱
	pǐn tuō
quart	夸脱
	kuā tuō
gallon	加仑
	jiā lún

QUANTITY

some	一些
	yī xiē
none	一个也没有
	yī gè yě méi yǒu
all	全部
	quán bù
many / much	许多
	xǔ duō
a little bit (can be used for quantity or for time)	一点
	yī diǎn
dozen	一打
	yī dá

SIZE

small	小的
	xiǎo de
the smallest	最小的
	zuì xiǎo de
medium	中等的
	zhōng děng de
big	大的
	dà de
fat	胖的
	pàng de

wide	宽的
	kuān de
narrow	窄的
	zhǎi de

TIME

When the Chinese tell time, the period of the day is stated before the exact hour (early morning, noon, afternoon and evening). All of China is officially on one time zone, despite the great distances from one province to the next.

For full coverage of number terms, see p7.

HOURS OF THE DAY

What time is it?	现在几点钟?
	xiàn zài jǐ diǎn zhōng?
At what time?	在几点钟?
	zài jǐ diǎn zhōng?
For how long?	多长时间?
	duō cháng shí jiān?
It's one o'clock.	现在一点钟。
	xiàn zài yī diǎn zhōng。
It's two o'clock.	现在两点钟。
	xiàn zài liǎng diǎn zhōng。
It's two thirty.	现在两点半。
	xiàn zài liǎng diǎn bàn。
It's two fifteen.	现在两点一刻。
	xiàn zài liǎng diǎn yī kè。
It's a quarter to three.	现在两点四十五分。
	xiàn zài liǎng diǎn sì shí wǔ fēn。
It's noon.	现在是中午。
	xiàn zài shì zhōng wǔ。
It's midnight.	现在是午夜。
	xiàn zài shì wǔ yè。
It's early.	现在还早。
	xiàn zài hái zǎo。

It's late.	现在晚了。
	xiàn zài wǎn le。
in the morning	在上午
	zài shàng wǔ
in the afternoon	在下午
	zài xià wǔ
at night	在晚上
	zài wǎn shàng
dawn	黎明
	lí míng

DAYS OF THE WEEK

Sunday	星期日
	xīng qī rì
Monday	星期一
	xīng qī yī
Tuesday	星期二
	xīng qī èr
Wednesday	星期三
	xīng qī sān
Thursday	星期四
	xīng qī sì
Friday	星期五
	xīng qī wǔ
Saturday	星期六
	xīng qī liù
today	今天
	jīn tiān
tomorrow	明天
	míng tiān
yesterday	昨天
	zuó tiān
the day before yesterday	前天
	qián tiān
one week	一周
	yī zhōu

next week	下周
	xià zhōu
last week	上周
	shàng zhōu

MONTHS OF THE YEAR

January	一月
	yī yuè
February	二月
	èr yuè
March	三月
	sān yuè
April	四月
	sì yuè
May	五月
	wǔ yuè
June	六月
	liù yuè
July	七月
	qī yuè
August	八月
	bā yuè
September	九月
	jiǔ yuè
October	十月
	shí yuè
November	十一月
	shí yī yuè
December	十二月
	shí èr yuè
next month	下个月
	xià gè yuè
last month	上个月
	shàng gè yuè

SEASONS OF THE YEAR

spring	春季
	chūn jì
summer	夏季
	xià jì
autumn	秋季
	qīu jì
winter	冬季
	dōng jì

CHINESE GRAMMAR BASICS

THE ALPHABET

While there is no alphabet in Chinese, each morpheme (the smallest unit of meaning in a language) is represented by one syllable, which in turn consists of an initial sound and a final sound, and which is always uttered in one of the four tones which characterize the Mandarin dialect.

PRONUNCIATION GUIDE
INITIAL SOUNDS

In Chinese, initials are always comprised of consonants, which are much more numerous than the final vowel sounds, and are represented in the pinyin Romanization system as follows:

PINYIN AND CHINA'S WRITTEN LANGUAGE

The official Romanization system of the People's Republic of China (PRC), "pinyin" literally means "to spell the way it sounds." Adopted in the 1950s, it became China's official Romanization system in 1979. While English is not commonly found on street signs or storefronts in China, pinyin is ubiquitous, so boning up on the basics in advance of your trip is well worth the effort. Since Chinese written characters don't necessarily give any indication of pronunciation, the Chinese themselves are taught pinyin in school in addition to the characters. In the Republic of China a mixture of various Romanization systems, including pinyin, is currently used.

As a point of reference, Chinese characters date to the earliest dynasty with archaeological evidence, the Shang (1766–1122 BC), and were originally used for divination purposes.

They can be read left to right, right to left, or top to bottom. The four most common types of characters, reflecting meanings and sounds, include: **pictographs**, which are formed

INITIAL SOUNDS, CONT'D.

Initial	Sound	Pronunciation
b	baw	*bore*
p	paw	*pour*
m	maw	*mourn*
f	faw	*four*
d	duh	*dull*
t	tuh	*ton*
n	nuh	*null*
l	luh	*lull*
g	guh	*gum*
k	kuh	*come*
h	huh	*hum*
j	gee	*gee*

according to the shape of the objects themselves, such as the sun and the moon, and indicate the meaning of the character rather than the sound; **ideographs**, which represent more abstract concepts; **complex ideographs**, which are combinations of simpler characters; and phonetic compounds, also called **logographs**, formed by two elements—one hinting at the meaning of the word and the other giving a clue as to the sound. This last category accounts for over 80% of all Chinese characters.

To simplify the Chinese writing system so that the vast majority of Chinese could attain an adequate level of literacy, which hovered around 15% in 1949 when the PRC was established, the number of strokes required to create many characters was greatly reduced. These are known as "simplified" characters, and are used in the PRC today, where the literacy rate has climbed to 85%. "Traditional" (long form) characters are still taught and used in Taiwan. Using simplified characters in Taiwan can be construed as making a political statement, and would best be avoided if you are having business material translated into Chinese and printed for use in Taiwan.

q	chee	*cheese*
x	she	*she*
z	dzuh	*"ds" as in suds*
c	tsuh	*"ts" as in cuts*
s	suh	*son*
zh	jir	*germ*
ch	chir	*chirp*
sh	shir	*shirt*
r	ir	*"er" as in larger*
w	wuh	*what*
y	yuh	*yum*

FINAL SOUNDS

There are only six vowels sounds in standard Mandarin: a, o, e, i, u, and ü. Pronouncing the vowels in sequence, your mouth will start off very wide and your tongue will start off very low. Vowels can be combined to form compound vowels, listed below:

Final	Sound	Pronunciation
a	ah	*not*
ai	i	*eye*
ao	ow	*chow*
an	ahn	*on*
ang	ahng	*thong*
o	aw	*draw*
ong	oong	*too+ng*
ou	oh	*toe*
e	uh	*bush*
ei	ay	*way*
en	un	*none*
eng	ung	*strung*
er	ar	*star*
i	ee	*bee*
ia	ya	*gotcha*
iao	yaow	*meow*

ie	yeh	*yet*
iu	yo	*leo*
ian	yan	*Cheyenne*
iang	yahng	*y+angst*
in	een	*seen*
ing	eeng	*ping*
iong	yoong	*you+ng*
u	oo	*too*
ua	wa	*suave*
uo	waw	*war*
ui	way	*sway*
uai	why	*why*
uan	wan	*want*
un	one	*won*
uang	wahng	*wan+ng*
ueng	wung	*one+ng*
ü	yew	*ewe*
üe	yweh	*you+eh*
üan	ywan	*you+wan*
ün	yewn	*you+n*

TONES

In the pinyin system of Romanization, Tone marks always appear above the vowel. If there are consecutive vowels, the Tone mark appears above the first vowel in that sequence. The only exception to this is for the vowels iu and ui, where the Tone mark falls on the second vowel.

In a spoken language with a great number of homophones, Tones are the key to understanding the meaning of what is being said. Even so, any given syllable with a specific Tone can also often have more than one meaning. Ultimately only by viewing the written character can the meaning be deduced on the spot. When dealing with spoken Chinese, the meaning must be deduced in large part from the context of what else is being said.

Mandarin has the following four Tones:

First tone: High level. This tone should be as high as your individual pitch range can be, and is indicated by a horizontal line above the vowel: ā

Second tone: Rising. This tone should have your voice going up as if asking a question, and is indicated by a line which rises from left to right above the vowel: á

Third tone: Dipping then rising. This tone starts in the middle level of your voice range and then falls before slightly rising again at the end. It is indicated by a reverse triangle without the horizontal line on top, located above the vowel: ǎ

Fourth tone: Falling. This tone sounds as if you're giving an order, falling from the high pitch level it starts at. It is indicated by a line dropping from left to right above the vowel: à

Other Tonal Rules

Two Consecutive Third Tones: When one third tone is followed by another, the first third tone is spoken like a second tone (rising), and only the second third tone exhibits the characteristics of a full third tone (falling and then rising again).

Half-Third Tones: When one third tone is followed by any other tone, only the first half (the falling half) of the tone is pronounced before the remaining syllables are pronounced with their respective tones. It sounds more like a low, level tone.

Neutral Tones: Although there are four primary tones in Mandarin, a fifth tone exists which is actually toneless, or neutral. There is no tone mark above a fifth tone, and you say it only when you attach it to grammatical particles or the second character of repetitive syllables such as bàba (father) or māma (mother).

Tonal Changes in Yī and Bù

Yī (one) and **bù** (not or no) are unusual in that their tones may change depending on what comes after them. Yī by itself is pronounced with the first tone, but when a first, second or third tone follows it, **yī** is spoken with a fourth tone, such as in **yìzhāng zhǐ** (a piece of paper). If a fourth tone follows yī it automatically becomes a second tone, such as in the word **yíyàng** (the same).

THE MONOSYLLABLE MYTH

Since each Chinese character is pronounced as a single syllable, the myth that Chinese is monosyllabic is often believed to be the case. The truth is that most Chinese words are polysyllabic and are written in clusters of characters. Most words in modern Chinese are two syllables (two characters). For example, míng means "clear, bright" and bái means "white, blank." Put together, míngbái means "understand, clear."

TERMS FOR MANDARIN

Standard Mandarin, the official language of both the PRC and the ROC, is referred to as **pǔtōnghuà** ("the common language") in the PRC, and **guóyǔ** ("national speech") in the ROC.

ELEMENTS OF CHINESE GRAMMAR
SENTENCE STRUCTURE

In general the way to tell how one part of a Chinese sentence relates to another is by the use of particles and the order of the words (syntax) rather than morphology (changes in the form of the word through inflection).

The basic word order of Chinese is exactly the same as in English: Subject-Verb-Object:

Subject	Verb	Object
I **(wǒ)**	love **(xǐ huān)**	spinach **(bōcài)**
You **(nǐ)**	read **(kàn)**	books **(shū)**

While Chinese word order resembles English, most everything else about the language differs. There are no gender-specific nouns in Chinese, no distinction between singular and plural, no verb conjugation, no such thing as first, second, or third person, no such thing as active or passive voices, or even past or present tense. Additionally, one word can function as both subject and object. Context is often the only way one knows when an action may have taken place.

PERSONAL PRONOUNS

English	Pinyin	Pronunciation
I	wǒ	waw
You	nǐ	nee
He / She / It	tā	tah
We	wǒ mén	waw-mun
You (Plural)	nǐ mén	nee-mun
They	tā mén	tah-mun

CLASSIFIERS

Classifiers, also referred to as measure words, help classify particular nouns, and are located in between a number (or a demonstrative pronoun such as "this" or "that") and a noun. They're similar to English words such as a "gaggle" of geese or a "school" of fish. While English doesn't use classifiers nearly as often as Chinese, in Chinese they can be found wherever a number is followed by a noun, or an implied noun. The most common classifier is "ge" (guh), which can safely be used when in doubt.

Classifier	Pinyin	Pronunciation
Printed and bound things (such as books or magazines)	běn	bun
Stick-like things, such as string or blades of grass	gēn	gun
Things with flat surfaces such as tables or beds	zhāng	jahng
Round, tiny things such as pearls	kē	kuh

Subject	Verb	Number	Classifier	Object
I	want	a / one		book
Wǒ	yào	yī	běn	shū
You	buy	three		tables
Nǐ	mǎi	sǎn	zhāng	zhuō zi

THIS & THAT

English	Pinyin	Pronunciation
This	zhè (ge)	jay (guh)
That	nà (ge)	nah (guh)
These	zhè xiē	jay-shyeh
Those	nà xiē	nay-shyeh

DEFINITE VS. INDEFINITE ARTICLES

Equivalents to the English articles "a," "an," and "the" do not exist in Chinese. The only way to tell if something is being referred to specifically (definite) or just generally (indefinite) is by the word order.

Nouns that refer specifically to something are usually found at the beginning of a sentence before the verb:

yǐ zi zài nàr. (The chairs are there.)

hái zi xǐ huān tā. (The child likes him.)

dāo zài zhuō zi shàng. (The knife / knives are on the table.)

Nouns that refer to something more general are usually found at the end of the sentence, after the verb:

nǎ r yǒu shū? (Where are some books? / Where is there a book?)

nà r yǒu shū. (There are some books over there.)

zhè ge yǒu wèn tí. (There's a problem with this. / There are some problems with this.)

EXCEPTIONS TO DEFINITE VS. INDEFINITE ARTICLES

Several exceptions to the above rules on definite vs. indefinite articles exist in Chinese:

- If a noun is at the beginning of a sentence it might refer to something indefinite if the sentence makes a general comment (as opposed to relating an entire story), like when the verb **shì** is part of the comment: **xióng māo shì dòng wù.** (Pandas are animals.)

- If an adjective appears after the noun it might also indicate an indefinite article: **pú tao hěn tián**. (Grapes are very sweet.)

- If an auxiliary verb exists it might also indicate an indefinite article: **māo huì zhuā lǎo shǔ.** (Cats can catch mice.)

- If a verb indicates that the action occurs habitually it may indicate an indefinite article: **niú chī cǎo.** (Cows eat grass.)

- Nouns preceded by a numeral and a classifier are considered definite: **wǔ gè xué sheng dōu hěn cōng ming.** (The five students are all quite smart.)

- If the word **yǒu** (to exist) comes before the noun and is then followed by a verb, it can also indicate an indefinite article: **yǒu shū zài zhuō zi shàng.** (There are books on top of the table.)

- Finally, if the word **zhè** (this) or **nà** (that), plus a classifier is used when a noun comes after the verb, it indicates a definite reference: **wǒ yào mǎi nà zhāng huà.** (I want to buy that painting.)

ADJECTIVES

If an adjective is pronounced with only one syllable it appears immediately in front of the noun it qualifies:

lǜ chá (green tea)

cháng gǔ tóu (long bone)

If the adjective has two syllables, however, the possessive particle de (duh) is placed between it and whatever it qualifies:

gàn jìng de yī fu (clean clothes)

chǎo nào de hái zi (noisy child / children)

If a numeral is followed by a classifier, those should both go in front of the adjective and whatever it qualifies:

yī jiàn xīn yī fu (a [piece of] new clothing)

sì běn yǒu qù de shū (four interesting books)

Finally, when an adjective is also the predicate, appearing at the end of a sentence, it follows the subject or the topic without needing the verb shì (shir; to be):

tā de fáng zi hěn gàn jìng. (His house [is] very clean.)

nà jiàn yī fu tài jiù. (That piece of clothing [is] too old.)

VERBS

There is no conjugation of verbs in Chinese. The verb in the sentence "They eat Chinese food" is said the same way as in the sentence "He eats Chinese food." There are ways to indicate tense in Chinese sentences, but these are noted in the section on "Aspect Markers" below. The verb itself is never inflected. Below are some of the most common verbs in Chinese:

English	Pinyin	Pronunciation
To read	kàn	kahn
I read books.	wǒ kàn shū.	Waw kahn shoo.
To have	yǒu	yo
We have books.	wǒ mén yǒu shū.	Waw mun yo shoo.
To want	yào	yow
She wants cake.	tā yào dàn gāo.	Tah yow dahn gow.
To Be	shì	shir
We are Chinese.	wǒ mén shì zhōng guó rén.	Waw mun shir joong gwaw run.
To study	xué xí	shweh she
You study Chinese.	nǐ xué xí hàn yǔ.	Nee shweh she hahn yew.
To know	zhī dào	jir dow
I know him.	wǒ zhī dào tā.	Waw jir dow tah.

NOTE: The verb **yǒu** (to have) can also be translated as "there is" or "there are." Examples: **yǒu hěn duō hái zi** (There are many children); **wǒ yǒu hěn duō hái zi**. (I have many children.)

ASPECT MARKERS (EXPRESSIONS OF TENSE)

Aspects characterize the Chinese language in place of tense and refer to how a speaker views an event or a state of being. There are only two aspects in Chinese: complete and continuous, as opposed to English, which has many different aspects such as indefinite, continuous, perfect, perfect continuous, etc.

Le

Le indicates an action has been completed if it's used as a suffix to a verb:

English	Pinyin	Pronunciation
You bought many books.	nǐ mǎi le hěn duō shū.	Nee my luh hun dwaw shoo.
He brought his umbrella.	tā dài le tā de yǔ sǎn.	Tah dye luh tah duh yew sahn.

Le in Questions

To turn statements with le into questions, add meiyou at the end of them, which automatically negates the action completed by le:

English	Pinyin	Pronunciation
You bought many books.	nǐ mǎi le hěn duō shū.	Nee my luh hun dwaw shoo.
Did he bring his umbrella?	tā yǒu méi yǒu dài tā de yǔ sǎn?	Tah yo mayo dye tah duh yew sahn?

Guò

Guò indicates that something has been done at one time or another, even though it is not currently happening.

English	Pinyin	Pronunciation
He has been to France.	tā qù guò fǎ guó.	Tah chyew gwaw fah gwaw.
We have eaten French food.	wǒ mén chī guò fǎ guó cài.	Waw mun chir gwaw fah gwaw tsye.

Zài

Zài indicates if an action is currently happening as you speak. You can also add the word **zhèng** in front of it to add emphasis, which can be translated as "to be right in the middle of" doing something.

English	Pinyin	Pronunciation
We are eating.	wǒ mén zài chī fàn.	Waw mun dzye chir fahn.
We're in the middle of eating.	wǒ mén zhèng zài chī fàn.	Waw mun juhng dzye chir fahn.
Your father is cooking.	nǐ bà ba zài zuò fàn.	Nee bah bah dzye dzwaw fahn.
Your father is right in the middle of cooking.	nǐ bà ba zhèng zài zuò fàn.	Nee bah bah juhng dzye dzwaw fahn.

Zhe

To indicate continual action resulting from something else, add the syllable **zhe** to the end of the verb:

English	Pinyin	Pronunciation
He's wearing a red hat.	tā dài zhe yī dǐng hóng mào zi.	Tah dye juh ee deeng hoong maow dzuh.
You're wearing a yellow shirt.	nín chuān zhe yī jiàn huáng chèn shān.	Nee chwahn juh ee jyan hwahng chun shahn.

Zhe can also indicate two actions occurring at the same time:

English	Pinyin	Pronunciation
She's sitting and eating.	tā zài zuò zhe chī fàn.	Tah dzye dzwaw juh chir fahn.
He's singing while he walks.	tā zǒu zhe chàng gē.	Tah dzoe juh chahng guh.

NEGATION

Bù

Bù can negate something done in the past, present or anticipated for the future.

English	Pinyin	Pronunciation
She didn't like to eat spinach when she was young.	tā xiǎo de shí hòu bù xǐ huān chī bō cài.	Tah shyaow duh shir ho boo she hwahn chir baw tsye.
They don't want to sing.	tā men bú yào chàng gē.	Tah mun boo yow chahng guh.
The restaurant won't be open on Friday.	fàn diàn xīng qī wǔ bù kāi mén.	Fahn dyan sheeng chee woo boo kye mun.

Méi yǒu

To negate the verb **yǒu**, the usual negative prefix **bù** cannot be used. Instead you must use the prefix **méi**.

English	Pinyin	Pronunciation
We don't have books.	wǒ mén méi yǒu shū.	Waw mun may yo shoo.
They don't have dogs.	tā mén méi yǒu gǒu.	Tah mun may yo go.

QUESTIONS

The simplest way to ask a question in Chinese is to end any statement with the particle **ma**.

English	Pinyin	Pronunciation
Does he read?	tā kàn shū ma?	Tah kahn shoo mah?
Do you speak English?	nǐ shuō yīng yǔ ma?	Nee shwaw eeng yew mah?

Alternative choice questions

Another way to pose questions is by repeating the verb in its negative form by inserting **bù** in between the repeating verbs. This form can only be used for a yes or no question.

English	Pinyin	Pronunciation
Are you an American?	nǐ shì bù shì měi guó rén?	Nee shir boo shir may gwaw run?
Does she want children?	tā yào bù yào hái zi?	Ta yow boo yow hi dzuh?

Interrogative pronouns

Another way to ask questions in Chinese is by using the following interrogative pronouns:

English	Pinyin	Pronunciation
Who / whom	shéi	shay
Whose	shéi de	shay duh
What	shénme	shummah
Which	nǎ (+ classifier)	nah
Where	nǎr	nar

POSSESSIVES

The particle **de** is attached to the end of a pronoun or other modifier to indicate possession.

English	Pinyin	Pronunciation
My computer has Internet.	wǒ de jì suàn jī yǒu yīn tè wǎng.	Waw duh dyan now yo een tuh wahng.
Does yours?	nǐ de ne?	Nee duh nuh?

CHAPTER TWO

GETTING THERE & GETTING AROUND

This section deals with every form of transportation. Whether you've just reached your destination by plane or you're renting a car to tour the countryside, you'll find the phrases you need in the next 25 pages.

AT THE AIRPORT

I am looking for ____	我在找_____
	wǒ zài zhǎo _____
a porter.	行李搬运工。
	xíng li bān yùn gōng。
the check-in counter.	值机柜台。
	zhí jī guì tái。
the ticket counter.	售票台。
	shòu piào tái。
arrivals.	飞机到达处。
	fēi jī dào dá chù。
departures.	飞机起飞处。
	fēi jī qǐ fēi chù。
gate number ____.	登机口号_____。
	dēng jī kǒu hào _____。

For full coverage of numbers, see p7.

the waiting area.	等候处。
	děng hòu chù。
the men's restroom.	男洗手间。
	nán xǐ shǒu jiān。
the women's restroom.	女洗手间。
	nǚ xǐ shǒu jiān。
the police station.	警察局。
	jǐng chá jú。
a security guard.	保安。
	bǎo ān。

the smoking area.	吸烟区。
	xī yān qū。
the information booth.	问讯台。
	wèn xùn tái。
a public telephone.	公用电话。
	gōng yòng diàn huà。
an ATM.	**ATM。**
	ATM。
baggage claim.	行李领取处。
	xíng li lǐng qǔ chù。
a luggage cart.	行李手推车。
	xíng li shǒu tuī chē。
a currency exchange.	货币兑换处。
	huò bì duì huàn chù。
a café.	咖啡馆。
	kā fēi guǎn。
a restaurant.	饭店。
	fàn diàn。
a bar.	酒吧。
	jiǔ bā。
a bookstore or newsstand.	书店或报亭。
	shū diàn huò bào tíng。
a duty-free shop.	免税商店。
	miǎn shuì shāng diàn。
Is there Internet access here?	这能上网吗?
	zhè néng shàng wǎng ma?
I'd like to page someone.	我想呼叫某人。
	wǒ xiǎng hū jiào mǒu rén。
Do you accept credit cards?	可以用信用卡吗?
	kě yǐ yòng xìn yòng kǎ ma?

CHECKING IN

| I would like a one-way ticket to ____. | 我想要一张到____的单程票。 |
| | *wǒ xiǎng yào yī zhāng dào ____ de dān chéng piào。* |

I would like a round trip ticket to ____.	我想要一张到_____的往返票。 *wǒ xiǎng yào yī zhāng dào _____ de wǎng fǎn piào.*
How much are the tickets?	这些票多少钱? *zhè xiē piào duō shǎo qián?*
Do you have anything less expensive?	有便宜一些的吗? *yǒu pián yi yī xiē de ma?*
How long is the flight?	飞行时间有多长? *fēi xíng shí jiān yǒu duō cháng?*

For full coverage of number terms, see p7.
For full coverage of time, see p12.

What time does flight ____ leave?	_____航班什么时候起飞? *_____ háng bān shén me shí hòu qǐ fēi?*
What time does flight ____ arrive?	_____航班什么时候到达? *_____ háng bān shén me shí hòu dào dá?*
Do I have a connecting flight?	我需要中转航班吗? *wǒ xū yào zhōng zhuǎn háng bān ma?*
Do I need to change planes?	我需要转机吗? *wǒ xū yào zhuǎn jī ma?*
My flight leaves at __:__.	我的航班在__:__起飞。 *wǒ de háng bān zài __:__ qǐ fēi。*

For full coverage of numbers, see p7.

What time will the flight arrive?	航班何时到达? *háng bān hé shí dào dá?*
Is the flight on time?	此次航班准时吗? *cǐ cì háng bān zhǔn shí ma?*
Is the flight delayed?	此次航班延误了吗? *cǐ cì háng bān yán wù le ma?*
From which terminal is flight ____ leaving?	航班_____从哪个航站起飞? *háng bān _____ cóng nǎ gè háng zhàn qǐ fēi?*

Common Airport Signs

飞机进港	Arrivals
飞机出港	Departures
候机楼	Terminal
登机口	Gate
票务	Ticketing
海关	Customs
行李领取处	Baggage Claim
推	Push
拉	Pull
禁止吸烟	No Smoking
入口	Entrance
出口	Exit
男洗手间	Men's
女洗手间	Women's
机场巴士	Shuttle Buses
出租车	Taxis

From which gate is flight ____ leaving?

航班 _____ 从哪个登机口起飞？

háng bān _____ cóng nǎ gè dēng jǐ kǒu qǐ fēi?

How much time do I need for check-in?

我需要花多长时间办理登机手续？

wǒ xū yào huā duō cháng shí jiān bàn lǐ dēng jǐ shǒu xù?

Is there an express check-in line?

是否有快速登机队列？

shì fǒu yǒu kuài sù dēng jǐ duì liè?

Is there electronic check-in?

可以进行电子登机吗？

kě yǐ jìn xíng diàn zǐ dēng jǐ ma?

Seat Preferences

I would like ____ ticket(s) in ____
  first class.

我要买_____张_____票。

wǒ yào mǎi _____ zhāng _____piào.

  头等舱
  tóu děng cāng

business class.	商务舱 *shāng wù cāng*
economy class.	经济舱 *jīng jì cāng*
I would like ____	我想要_____ *wǒ xiǎng yào _____*
Please don't give me ____	请不要给我_____ *qǐng bù yào gěi wǒ _____*
a window seat.	靠窗的座位。 *kào chuāng de zuò wèi。*
an aisle seat.	靠过道的座位。 *kào guò dào de zuò wèi。*
an emergency exit row seat.	靠应急舱门的座位。 *kào yìng jí cāng mén de zuò wèi。*
a bulkhead seat.	第一排靠前挡板的座位。 *dì yī pái kào qián dǎng bǎn de zuò wèi。*
a seat by the restroom.	卫生间旁的座位。 *wèi shēng jiān páng de zuò wèi。*
a seat near the front.	靠前的座位。 *kào qián de zuò wèi。*
a seat near the middle.	靠中间的座位。 *kào zhōng jiān de zuò wèi。*
a seat near the back.	靠后的座位。 *kào hòu de zuò wèi。*
Is there a meal on the flight?	航班上是否供应膳食？ *háng bān shàng shì fǒu gōng yìng shàn shí?*
I'd like to order ____	我想订_____ *wǒ xiǎng dìng _____*
a vegetarian meal.	一套素餐。 *yī tào sù cān。*
a kosher meal.	一套犹太教徒餐。 *yī tào yóu tài jiào tú cān。*
a diabetic meal.	一套糖尿病人餐。 *yī tào táng niào bìng rén cān。*

I am traveling to ____.	我要前往_____。
	wǒ yào qián wǎng _____。
I am coming from ____.	我来自_____。
	wǒ lái zì _____。
I arrived from ____.	我从_____来。
	wǒ cóng _____ lái。

For full coverage of country terms, see English / Chinese dictionary.

I'd like to change / cancel / confirm my reservation.	我想更改 / 取消 / 确认我的预定。
	wǒ xiǎng gēng gǎi / qǔ xiāo / què rèn wǒ de yù dìng。
I have ____ bags to check.	我有 _____ 个旅行袋需要托运。
	wǒ yǒu _____ gè lǚ xíng dài xū yào tuō yùn。

For full coverage of numbers, see p7.

Passengers with Special Needs

Is that wheelchair accessible?	可以使用那个轮椅吗？
	kě yǐ shǐ yòng nà gè lún yǐ ma?
May I have a wheelchair / walker please?	我可以用轮椅 / 助行器吗？
	wǒ kě yǐ yòng lún yǐ / zhù xíng qì ma?
I need some assistance boarding.	我需要登机帮助。
	wǒ xūyào dēng jī bāng zhù。
I need to bring my service dog.	我需要带上我的帮助犬。
	wǒ xū yào dài shàng wǒ de bāng zhù quǎn。
Do you have services for the hearing impaired?	有为听障人士提供的服务吗？
	yǒu wéi tīng zhàng rén shì tí gōng de fú wù ma?
Do you have services for the visually impaired?	有为视障人士提供的服务吗？
	yǒu wéi shì zhàng rén shì tí gōng de fú wù ma?

Trouble at Check-In

How long is the delay?	延误时间有多长？
	yán wù shí jiān yǒu duō cháng?

My flight was late.	我的航班晚点了。
	wǒ de háng bān wǎn diǎn le。
I missed my flight.	我错过了航班。
	wǒ cuò guò le háng bān。
When is the next flight?	下一次航班是什么时间?
	xià yī cì háng bān shì shén me shí jiān?
May I have a meal voucher?	可以给我一张就餐优惠券吗?
	kě yǐ gěi wǒ yī zhāng jiù cān yōu huì
	quàn ma?
May I have a room voucher?	可以给我一张客房优惠券吗?
	kě yǐ gěi wǒ yī zhāng kè fáng yōu huì
	quàn ma?

AT CUSTOMS / SECURITY CHECKPOINTS

I'm traveling with a group.	我随团旅行。
	wǒ suí tuán lǚ xíng。
I'm on my own.	我单独旅行。
	wǒ dān dú lǚ xíng。
I'm traveling on business.	我因公旅行。
	wǒ yīn gōng lǚ xíng。
I'm on vacation.	我在休假。
	wǒ zài xiū jià。
I have nothing to declare.	我没有要申报的东西。
	wǒ méi yǒu yào shēn bào de dōng xi。
I would like to declare _____.	我要申报_____。
	wǒ yào shēn bào _____。
I have some liquor.	我带了一些白酒。
	wǒ dài le yī xiē bái jiǔ。
I have some cigars.	我带了一些雪茄。
	wǒ dài le yī xiē xuě jiā。
They are gifts.	这些都是礼物。
	zhè xiē dōu shì lǐ wù。
They are for personal use.	这些都是个人物品。
	zhè xiē dōu shì gè rén wù pǐn。

That is my medicine.	那是我的药。 *nà shì wǒ de yào.*
I have my prescription.	我有处方。 *wǒ yǒu chǔ fāng.*
My children are traveling on the same passport.	我的孩子与我持同一本护照旅行。 *wǒ de hái zi yǔ wǒ chí tóng yī běn hù zhào lǚ xíng.*
I'd like a male / female officer to conduct the search.	我需要一名男 / 女官员进行搜查。 *wǒ xū yào yī míng nán / nǚ guān yuán jìn xíng sōu chá.*

Trouble at Security

Help me. I've lost ____	帮帮我。我丢了 ____ *bāng bāng wǒ. wǒ diū le* ____
my passport.	我的护照。 *wǒ de hù zhào.*
my boarding pass.	我的登机牌。 *wǒ de dēng jī pái.*

Listen Up: Security Lingo

请脱掉您的鞋。 *qǐng tuō diào nín de xié.*	Please remove your shoes.
脱掉您的上衣 / 毛衣。 *tuō diào nín de shàng yī / máo yī.*	Remove your jacket / sweater.
摘下您的首饰。 *zhāi xià nín de shǒu shì.*	Remove your jewelry.
把您的包放在传送带上。 *bǎ nín de bāo fàng zài chuán sòng dài shàng.*	Place your bags on the conveyor belt.
走到这边。 *zǒu dào zhè biān.*	Step to the side.
我们必须进行手工搜查。 *wǒ mén bì xū jìn xíng shǒu gōng sōu chá.*	We have to do a hand search.

my identification.	我的身份证。
	wǒ de shēn fèn zhèng。
my wallet.	我的钱夹。
	wǒ de qián jiā。
my purse.	我的钱包。
	wǒ de qián bāo。
Someone stole	有人偷了我的钱包 / 钱夹!
my purse / wallet!	*yǒu rén tōu le! wǒ de qián bāo /*
	qián jiā!

IN-FLIGHT

It's unlikely you'll need much Chinese on the plane, but these phrases will help if a bilingual flight attendant is unavailable or if you need to talk to a Chinese-speaking neighbor.

I think that's my seat.	我想这是我的座位。
	wǒ xiǎng shì wǒ de zuò wèi。
May I have _____	可以给我_____
	kě yǐ gěi wǒ _____
water?	水吗?
	shuǐ ma?
sparkling water?	汽水吗?
	qì shuǐ ma?
orange juice?	橙汁吗?
	chéng zhī ma?
soda?	苏打水吗?
	sū dǎ shuǐ ma?
diet soda?	减肥苏打水吗?
	jiǎn féi sū dǎ shuǐ ma?
a beer?	啤酒吗?
	pí jiǔ ma?
wine?	葡萄酒吗?
	pú tao jiǔ ma?

For a complete list of drinks, see p75.

a pillow?	一个枕垫吗?
	yī gè zhěn diàn ma?

a blanket?	一条毯子吗? *yī tiáo tǎn zi ma?*
a hand wipe?	一张手纸帕吗? *yī zhāng shǒu zhǐ pà ma?*
headphones?	耳机吗? *ěr jī ma?*
a magazine or newspaper?	一本杂志或报纸吗? *yī běn zá zhì huò bào zhǐ ma?*
When will the meal be served?	什么时候供餐? *shén me shí hou gòng cān?*
How long until we land?	还有多长时间着陆? *hái yǒu duō cháng shí jiān zhuó lù?*
May I move to another seat?	我可以移到另一个座位吗? *wǒ kě yǐ yí dào lìng yī gè zuò wèi ma?*
How do I turn the light on / off?	我怎样开 / 关灯? *wǒ zěn yàng kāi / guān dēng?*

Trouble In-Flight

These headphones are broken.	这些耳机坏了。 *zhè xiē ěr jī huài le。*
I spilled.	我把___弄洒了。 *wǒ bǎ ___ nòng sǎ le。*
My child spilled.	我的孩子把___弄洒了。 *wǒ de hái zǐ bǎ ___ nòng sǎ le。*
My child is sick.	我的孩子病了。 *wǒ de hái zi bìng le。*
I need an airsickness bag.	我需要一个呕吐袋。 *wǒ xū yào yī gè ǒu tù dài。*
I smell something strange.	我闻到奇怪的味道。 *wǒ wén dào qí guài de wèi dào。*
That passenger is behaving suspiciously.	那个乘客的行为很可疑。 *nà gè chéng kè de xíng wéi hěn kě yí。*

BAGGAGE CLAIM

Where is baggage claim for flight ___?	在哪里领取航班 _____ 的行李？ *zài nǎ lǐ lǐng qǔ háng bān _____ de xíng li?*
Would you please help with my bags?	您能帮我拿一下这些袋子吗？ *nín néng bāng wǒ ná yī xià zhè xiē dài zi ma?*
I am missing ___ bags.	我丢失了一个 _____ 袋子。 *wǒ diū shī le gè _____ dài zi。*

For full coverage of numbers, see p7.

My bag is ___	我的包 _____ *wǒ de bāo _____*
lost.	丢了。 *diū le。*
damaged.	坏了。 *huài le。*
stolen.	被盗了。 *bèi dào le。*
a suitcase.	是一只手提箱。 *shì yī zhī shǒu tí xiāng。*
a briefcase.	是一个公文包。 *shì yī gè gōng wén bāo。*
a carry-on.	是手提行李。 *shì shǒu tí xíng li。*
a suit bag.	是衣服袋。 *shì yī fu dài。*
a trunk.	是大衣箱。 *shì dà yī xiāng。*
golf clubs.	是高尔夫球包。 *shì gāo ěr fū qiú bāo。*

For full coverage of color terms, see English / Chinese Dictionary.

hard.	很硬。 *hěn yìng。*
made out of ___	是用_____ *shì yòng _____*

canvas.

帆布做的。
fān bù zuò de。

vinyl.

乙烯树脂做的。
yǐ xī shù zhī zuò de。

leather.

皮革做的。
pí gé zuò de。

hard plastic.

硬塑料做的。
yìng sù liào zuò de。

aluminum.

铝做的。
lǚ zuò de。

RENTING A VEHICLE

Is there a car rental agency in the airport?

机场有汽车租赁公司吗?
jī chǎng yǒu qì chē zū lìn gōng sī ma?

I have a reservation.

我已预定。
wǒ yǐ yù dìng。

Vehicle Preferences
I would like to rent ____

我要租用____
wǒ yào zū yòng ____

an economy car.

一辆经济型轿车。
yī liàng jīng jì xíng jiào chē。

a midsize car.

一辆中型轿车。
yī liàng zhōng xíng jiào chē。

a sedan.

箱式小轿车。
xiāng shì xiǎo jiào chē。

a convertible.

一辆敞篷汽车。
yī liàng chǎng péng qì chē。

a van.

面包车。
miàn bāo chē。

a sports car.

一辆跑车。
yī liàng pǎo chē。

a 4-wheel-drive vehicle.

一辆四轮驱动汽车。
yī liàng sì lún qū dòng qì chē。

a motorcycle.

一辆摩托车。
yī liàng mó tuō chē。

a scooter.

一辆踏板车。
yī liàng tà bǎn chē.

Do you have one with ____

您的车有_____
nín de chē yǒu _____

air conditioning?

空调吗?
kōng tiáo ma?

a sunroof?

天窗吗?
tiān chuāng ma?

a CD player?

CD 播放器吗?
CD bō fàng qì ma?

satellite radio?

卫星广播吗?
wèi xīng guǎng bō ma?

satellite tracking?

卫星定位吗?
wèi xīng dìng wèi ma?

an onboard map?

车载地图吗?
chē zài dì tú ma?

a DVD player?

DVD 播放器吗?
DVD bō fàng qì ma?

child seats?

儿童座椅吗?
ér tóng zuò yǐ ma?

Do you have a ____

您有_____
nín yǒu _____

smaller car?

小一点的车吗?
xiǎo yī diǎn de chē ma?

bigger car?

大一点的车吗?
dà yī diǎn de chē ma?

cheaper car?

便宜一点的车吗?
pián yi yī diǎn de chē ma?

Do you have a non-smoking car?

您有非吸烟车吗?
nín yǒu fēi xī yān chē ma?

I need an automatic transmission.

我需要带自动变速器的。
wǒ xū yào dài zì dòng biàn sù qì de.

A standard transmission is okay.	有标准变速器就可以了。
	yǒu biāo zhǔn biàn sù qì jiù kě yǐ le.
May I have an upgrade?	我可以要求升级吗？
	wǒ kě yǐ yāo qiú shēng jí ma?

Money Matters

What's the daily / weekly / monthly rate?	日 / 周 / 月租金是多少？
	rì / zhōu / yuè zū jīn shì duō shǎo?
What is the mileage rate?	里程运价费是多少？
	lǐ chéng yùn jià fèi shì duō shǎo?
How much is insurance?	保险是多少？
	bǎo xiǎn shì duō shǎo?
Are there other fees?	还有其他费用吗？
	hái yǒu qí tā fèi yòng ma?
Is there a weekend rate?	有周末价吗？
	yǒu zhōu mò jià ma?

Technical Questions

What kind of fuel does it take?	使用什么汽油？
	shǐ yòng shén me qì yóu?
Do you have the manual in English?	有英语的手册吗？
	yǒu yīng yǔ de shǒu cè ma?
Do you have a booklet in English with the local traffic laws?	有英文的地方交通法规手册吗？
	yǒu yīng wén de dì fāng jiāo tōng fǎ guī shǒu cè ma?

Car Troubles

The ____ doesn't work.	_____坏了。
	_____ *huài le.*

See diagram on p47 for car parts.

It is already dented.	这里已经凹进去了。
	zhè lǐ yǐ jīng āo jìn qù le.
It is scratched.	这里有刮痕。
	zhè lǐ yǒu guā hén.

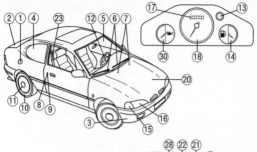

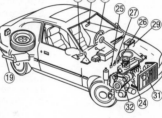

1. 油箱	yóu xiāng		18. 速度计	sù dù jì
2. 行李箱	xíng li xiāng		19. 消声器	xiāo shēng qì
3. 缓冲器	huǎn chōng qì		20. 引擎罩	yǐn qíng zhào
4. 车窗	chē chuāng		21. 方向盘	fāng xiàng pán
5. 挡风玻璃	dǎng fēng bō li		22. 后视镜	hòu shì jìng
6. 风档雨雪刷	fēng dàng yǔ xuě shuā		23. 安全带	ān quán dài
7. 洗涤壶	xǐ dí hú		24. 发动机	fā dòng jī
8. 车门	chē mén		25. 加速器	jiā sù qì
9. 车门锁	chē mén suǒ		26. 离合器	lí hé qì
10. 轮胎	lún tāi		27. 刹车	shā chē
11. 轮毂罩	lún gū zhào		28. 手制动器	shǒu zhì dòng qì
12. 方向盘	fāng xiàng pán		29. 蓄电池	xù diàn chí
13. 应急灯	yìng jí dēng		30. 机油压力表	jī yóu yā lì biǎo
14. 油量计	yóu liàng jì		31. 散热器	sàn rè qì
15. 转弯灯	zhuǎn wān dēng		32. 风扇皮带	fēng shàn pí dài
16. 前灯	qián dēng			
17. 里程表	lǐ chéng biǎo			

Please fill it up with _____.　请帮我加满
qǐng bāng wǒ jiā mǎn

regular.　普通汽油
pǔ tōng qì yóu

unleaded.　无铅汽油
wú qiān qì yóu

diesel.　柴油
chái yóu

The tires look low.　轮胎好像要没气了。
lún tāi hǎo xiàng yào méi qì le

It has a flat tire.　爆胎了。
bào tāi le。

It won't start.　这辆汽车发动不起来。
zhè liàng qì chē fā dòng bù qǐ lái。

It's out of gas.　车没油了。
chē méi yóu le。

The Check Engine light is on.　引擎检验灯是亮的。
yǐn qíng jiǎn yàn dēng shì liàng de。

The oil light is on.　机油灯是亮的。
jī yóu dēng shì liàng de。

The brake light is on.　刹车灯是亮的。
shā chē dēng shì liàng de。

It runs rough.　运转不平稳。
yùn zhuǎn bù píng wěn。

The car is over-heating.　汽车过热。
qì chē guò rè。

Asking for Directions
Excuse me, please.　打扰您一下。
dǎ rǎo nín yī xià。

How do I get to _____?　到_____怎么走?
dào _____ zěn me zǒu?

Go straight.　直走。
zhí zǒu。

Turn left.　向左转。
xiàng zuǒ zhuǎn。

Continue right.	继续向右。
	jì xù xiàng yòu.
It's on the right.	在右侧。
	zài yòu cè.
Can you show me on the map?	您能在地图上指给我看吗?
	nín néng zài dì tú shàng zhǐ gěi wǒ kàn ma?
How far is it from here?	那里离这有多远?
	nà lǐ lí zhè yǒu duō yuǎn?
Is this the right road for ____?	这是到____的路吗?
	zhè shì dào ____ de lù ma?
I've lost my way.	我迷路了。
	wǒ mí lù le.
Would you repeat that?	请您再重复一遍好吗?
	qǐng nín zài chóng fù yī biàn hǎo ma?
Thanks for your help.	谢谢您的帮助。
	xiè xiè nín de bāng zhù.

For full coverage of direction-related terms, see p5.

Road Signs

限速	Speed Limit
停止	Stop
避让	Yield
危险	Danger
无出口	No Exit
单行线	One Way
不准驶入	Do Not Enter
道路封闭	Road Closed
通行费	Toll
只收现金	Cash Only
禁止停车	No Parking
停车费	Parking Fee
停车场	Parking Garage

Sorry, Officer

What is the speed limit?

限速是多少?

xiàn sù shì duō shǎo?

I wasn't going that fast.

我没有开那么快。

wǒ méi yǒu kāi nà me kuài.

How much is the fine?

罚款是多少?

fá kuǎn shì duō shǎo?

Where do I pay the fine?

我在哪里交罚款?

wǒ zài nǎ lǐ jiāo fá kuǎn?

Do I have to go to court?

我必须要上法庭吗?

wǒ bì xū yào shàng fǎ tíng ma?

I had an accident.

我出了事故。

wǒ chū le shì gù.

The other driver hit me.

我被别的车撞了。

wǒ bèi bié de chē zhuàng le.

I'm at fault.

我是过错方。

wǒ shì guò cuò fāng.

BY TAXI

Where is the taxi stand?

出租车站在哪里?

chū zū chē zhàn zài nǎ lǐ?

Is there a limo / bus / van for my hotel?

有豪华大巴 / 公共汽车 / 面包车到宾馆吗?

yǒu háo huá dà bā / gōng gòng qì chē / miàn bāo chē dào bīn guǎn ma?

I need to get to ____.

我要去_____。

wǒ yào qù _____.

How much will that cost?

这需要多少钱?

zhè xū yào duō shǎo qián?

How long will it take?

需要多长时间?

xū yào duō cháng shí jiān?

Can you take me / us to the train / bus station?

您能带我 / 我们到火车 / 公共汽车站吗?

nín néng dài wǒ / wǒ mén dào huǒ chē / gōng gòng qì chē zhàn ma?

Listen Up: Taxi Lingo

请上车！
qǐng shàng chē!

Please get in!

您可以把行李放在这，我来处理。
nín kě yǐ bǎ xíng li fàng zài zhè,
wǒ lái chǔ lǐ.

Leave your luggage here.
I got it.

每个包付 10 元人民币。
měi gè bāo fù shí yuán rén mín bì.

It's 10 RMB for each bag.

多少乘客？
duō shǎo chéng kè?

How many passengers?

您很着急吗？
nín hěn zháo jí ma?

Are you in a hurry?

I am in a hurry.

我很着急。
wǒ hěn zháo jí.

Slow down.

慢点开。
màn diǎn kāi.

Am I close enough to walk?

不用走多远就能到那里吗？
bú yòng zǒu duō yuǎn jiù néng dào
nà lǐ ma?

Let me out here.

我就在这下车。
wǒ jiù zài zhè xià chē.

That's not the correct
change.

找的钱不对。
zhǎo de qián bù duì.

BY TRAIN

How do I get to the train
station?

我怎样到火车站？
wǒ zěn yàng dào huǒ chē zhàn?

Would you take me to the
train station?

可以带我去火车站吗？
kě yǐ dài wǒ qù huǒ
chē zhàn ma?

How long is the trip to _____?

到_____要花多长时间？

dào _____ yào huā duō cháng shí jiān?

When is the next train?

下一班火车是什么时间？

xià yī bān huǒ chē shì shén me shí jiān?

Do you have a schedule / timetable?

您有时刻表吗？

nín yǒu shí kè biǎo ma?

Do I have to change trains?

我需要换车吗？

wǒ xū yào huàn chē ma?

a one-way ticket

单程票

dān chéng piào

a round-trip ticket

往返票

wǎng fǎn piào

Which platform does it leave from?

从哪个站台驶离？

cóng nǎ gè zhàn tái shǐ lí?

Is there a bar car?

有酒吧车吗？

yǒu jiǔ bā chē ma?

Is there a dining car?

有餐车吗？

yǒu cān chē ma?

Which car is my seat in?

我的座位在哪节车厢？

wǒ de zuò wèi zài nǎ jié chē xiāng?

Is this seat taken?

这个座位有人吗？

zhè gè zuò wèi yǒu rén ma?

Where is the next stop?

下一站是哪里？

xià yī zhàn shì nǎ lǐ?

How many stops to _____?

到_____有几站？

dào _____ yǒu jǐ zhàn?

What's the train number and where is the destination?

这列火车的车次是什么？目的地是哪里？

zhè liè huǒ chē de chē cì shì shén me? mù dì dì shì nǎ lǐ?

BY BUS

How do I get to the bus station?	我怎样到公共汽车站?
	wǒ zěn yàng dào gōng gòng qì chē zhàn?
Would you take me to the bus station?	可以带我去公共汽车站吗?
	kě yǐ dài wǒ qù gōng gòng qì chē zhàn ma?
May I have a bus schedule?	有公共汽车时刻表吗?
	yǒu gōng gòng qì chē shí kè biǎo ma?
Which bus goes to ____?	哪一班车到_____?
	nǎ yī bān chē dào _____?
Where does it leave from?	这车从哪里驶离?
	zhè chē cóng nǎ lǐ shǐ lí?
How long does the bus take?	这车多长时间到?
	zhè chē duō cháng shí jiān dào?
How much is it?	车票是多少钱?
	chē piào shì duō shǎo qián?
Is there an express bus?	有快速公交吗?
	yǒu kuài sù gōng jiāo ma?
Does it make local stops?	当地有站吗?
	dāng dì yǒu zhàn ma?
Does it run at night?	夜间有车吗?
	yè jiān yǒu chē ma?
When does the next bus leave?	下一班公共汽车什么时间离开?
	xià yī bān gōng gòng qì chē shén me shí jiān lí kāi?

a one-way ticket	单程票
	dān chéng piào
a round-trip ticket	往返票
	wǎng fǎn piào
How long will the bus be stopped?	这班公共汽车将停多长时间?
	zhè bān gōng gòng qì chē jiāng tíng duō cháng shí jiān?
Is there an air conditioned bus?	有空调公共汽车吗?
	yǒu kōng tiáo gōng gòng qì chē ma?
Is this seat taken?	这个座位有人吗?
	zhè gè zuò wèi yǒu rén ma?
Where is the next stop?	下一站是哪里?
	xià yī zhàn shì nǎ lǐ?
Please tell me when we reach ____.	到_____时请告诉我。
	dào _____ shí qǐng gào sù wǒ.
Let me off here.	我就在这下车。
	wǒ jiù zài zhè xià chē.

BY BOAT OR SHIP

Would you take me to the port?	可以带我去港口吗?
	kě yǐ dài wǒ qù gǎng kǒu ma?
When does the ship sail?	轮船什么时间启航?
	lún chuán shén me shí jiān qǐ háng?
How long is the trip?	航行时间有多长?
	háng xíng shí jiān yǒu duō cháng?
Where are the life preservers?	救生用具在哪里?
	jiù shēng yòng jù zài nǎ lǐ?
I would like a private cabin.	我要一个私人舱。
	wǒ yào yī gè sī rén cāng.
Is the trip rough?	此次航行艰险吗?
	cǐ cì háng xíng jiān xiǎn ma?
I feel seasick.	我晕船。
	wǒ yùn chuán.
I need some seasick pills.	我需要一些晕船药。
	wǒ xū yào yī xiē yūn chuán yào.

Where is the bathroom?	浴室在哪里?
	yù shì zài nǎ lǐ?
Does the ship have a casino?	轮船上有赌场吗?
	lún chuán shàng yǒu dǔ chǎng ma?
Will the ship stop at ports along the way?	轮船在沿线各港口都停吗?
	lún chuán zài yán xiàn gè gǎng kǒu dōu tíng ma?

BY SUBWAY

Where's the subway station?	地铁站在哪里?
	dì tiě zhàn zài nǎ lǐ?
Where can I buy a ticket?	我在哪里买票?
	wǒ zài nǎ lǐ mǎi piào?

SUBWAY TICKETS

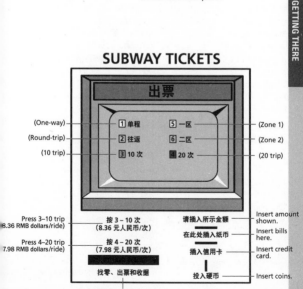

出票

1 单程 (One-way)
2 往返 (Round-trip)
3 10 次 (10 trip)
5 一区 (Zone 1)
6 二区 (Zone 2)
4 20 次 (20 trip)

Press 3–10 trip 8.36 RMB dollars/ride — 按 3 – 10 次 (8.36 元人民币/次)

Press 4–20 trip 7.98 RMB dollars/ride — 按 4 – 20 次 (7.98 元人民币/次)

请插入所示金额 — Insert amount shown.

在此处插入纸币 — Insert bills here.

插入信用卡 — Insert credit card.

投入硬币 — Insert coins.

找零、出票和收据 (Take change, tickets, receipt)

Could I have a map of the subway?	能给我一张地铁路线图吗？ *néng gěi wǒ yī zhāng dì tiě lù xiàn tú ma?*
Which line should I take for ____?	到____应乘几号线？ *dào ____ yīng chéng jǐ hào xiàn?*
Is this the right line for ____?	这是到____的正确路线吗？ *zhè shì dào ____ de zhèng què lù xiàn ma?*
Which stop is it for ____?	到____是哪一站？ *dào ____ shì nǎ yī zhàn?*
How many stops is it to ____?	到____有几站？ *dào ____ yǒu jǐ zhàn?*
Is the next stop ____?	下一站是____吗？ *xià yī zhàn shì ____ ma?*
Where are we?	我们在哪里？ *wǒ mén zài nǎ lǐ?*
Where do I change to ____?	我到____在哪里换乘？ *wǒ dào ____ zài nǎ lǐ huàn chéng?*
What time is the last train to ____?	到____的最后一班火车是什么时间？ *dào ____ de zuì hòu yī bān huǒ chē shì shén me shí jiān?*

CONSIDERATIONS FOR TRAVELERS WITH SPECIAL NEEDS

Do you have wheelchair access?	有轮椅通道吗？ *yǒu lún yǐ tōng dào ma?*
Do you have elevators? Where?	有电梯吗？在哪儿？ *yǒu diàn tī ma? zài nǎ ér?*
Do you have ramps? Where?	有坡道吗？在哪儿？ *yǒu pō dào ma? zài nǎ ér?*

Are the restrooms wheelchair accessible?	轮椅可以进入洗手间吗？ *lún yǐ kě yǐ jìn rù xǐ shǒu jiān ma?*
Do you have audio assistance for the hearing impaired?	可以为听障人士提供声频帮助吗？ *kě yǐ wèi tīng zhàng rén shì tí gōng shēng pín bāng zhù ma?*
I am deaf.	我是听障人士。 *wǒ shì tīng zhàng rén shì.*
May I bring my service dog?	我可以带上我的帮助犬吗？ *wǒ kě yǐ dài shàng wǒ de bāng zhù quǎn ma?*
I am blind.	我是视障人士。 *wǒ shì shì zhàng rén shì.*
I need to charge my power chair.	我需要为我的电动轮椅充电。 *wǒ xū yào wèi wǒ de diàn dòng lún yǐ chōng diàn.*

CHAPTER THREE

LODGING

This chapter will help you find the right accommodations, at the right price, and the amenities you might need during your stay.

ROOM PREFERENCES

Please recommend _____ 请推荐_____
qǐng tuī jiàn_____

a clean hostel. 干净的旅社。
gān jìng de lǚ shè。

a moderately priced hotel. 价格适中的酒店。
jià gé shì zhōng de jiǔ diàn。

a moderately priced B&B. 价格适中的 B&B（床位加早餐）酒店。
jià gé shì zhōng de B&B (chuáng wèi jiā zǎo cān) jiǔ diàn。

a good hotel / motel. 好的酒店 / 汽车旅馆。
hǎo de jiǔ diàn / qì chē lǚ guǎn。

Does the hotel have _____ 酒店有_____
jiǔ diàn yǒu _____

a pool? 游泳池吗？
yóu yǒng chí ma?

suites? 套房吗？
tào fáng ma?

a balcony? 阳台吗？
yáng tái ma?

a fitness center? 健身中心吗？
jiàn shēn zhōng xīn ma?

a spa? 水疗吗？
shuǐ liáo ma?

a private beach? 私人海滩吗？
sī rén hǎi tān ma?

a tennis court?	网球场吗?
	wǎng qiú chǎng ma?
I would like a room for ____.	我要一间房用来_____。
	wǒ yào yī jiān fáng yòng lái _____。

For full coverage of number terms, see p7.

I would like ____	我想要____
	wǒ xiǎng yào ____
a king-sized bed.	一张特大号床。
	yī zhāng tè dà hào chuáng。
a double bed.	一张双人床。
	yī zhāng shuāng rén chuáng。
a twin bed.	一张单人床。
	yī zhāng dān rén chuáng。
adjoining rooms.	毗连的房间。
	pí lián de fáng jiān。
a smoking room.	一间吸烟客房。
	yī jiān xī yān kè fáng。
a non-smoking room.	一间非吸烟客房。
	yī jiān fēi xī yān kè fáng。
a private bathroom.	独立浴室。
	dúlì yù shì。
a shower.	淋浴。
	lín yù。
a bathtub.	浴缸。
	yù gāng。

LODGING

Listen Up: Reservations Lingo

我们没有空房。	We have no vacancies.
wǒ mén méi yǒu kōng fáng。	
您将停留多长时间?	How long will you be staying?
nín jiāng tíng liú duō cháng	
shí jiān?	
吸烟还是不吸烟?	Smoking or non smoking?
xī yān hái shì bù xī yān?	

air conditioning.	空调。
	kōng tiáo。
television.	电视。
	diàn shì。
cable.	有线电视。
	yǒu xiàn diàn shì。
satellite TV.	卫星电视。
	wèi xīng diàn shì。
a telephone.	一部电话。
	yī bù diàn huà。
Internet access.	网络接口。
	wǎng luò jiē kǒu。
high-speed Internet access.	高速网络接口。
	gāo sù wǎng luò jiē kǒu。
a refrigerator.	一台电冰箱。
	yī tái diàn bīng xiāng。
a beach view.	海滩景观。
	hǎi tān jǐng guān。
a city view.	城市景观。
	chéng shì jǐng guān。
a kitchenette.	一间小厨房。
	yī jiān xiǎo chú fáng。
a balcony.	一个阳台。
	yī gè yáng tái。
a suite.	一个套间。
	yī gè tào jiān。
a penthouse.	顶楼房间。
	dǐng lóu fáng jiān。
I would like a room _____	我要一间_____
	wǒ yào yī jiān _____
on the ground floor.	一楼客房。
	yī lóu kè fáng。
near the elevator.	靠近电梯的房间。
	kào jìn diàn tī de fáng jiān。

near the stairs.	靠近楼梯的房间。
	kào jìn lóu tī de fáng jiān。
near the pool.	靠近游泳池的房间。
	kào jìn yóu yǒng chí de fáng jiān。
away from the street.	远离街道的房间。
	yuǎn lí jiē dào de fáng jiān。
I would like a corner room.	我想要一间角房。
	wǒ xiǎng yào yī jiān jiǎo fáng。
Do you have ____	有_____
	yǒu _____
a crib?	婴儿床吗?
	yīng ér chuáng ma?
a foldout bed?	折叠床吗?
	zhé dié chuáng ma?

FOR GUESTS WITH SPECIAL NEEDS

I need a room with ____	我需要一间_____
	wǒ xū yào yī jiān _____
wheelchair access.	有轮椅通道的房间。
	yǒu lún yǐ tōng dào de fáng jiān。
services for the visually impaired.	为视障人士提供服务的房间。
	wéi shì zhàng rén shì tí gōng fú wù de fáng jiān。
services for the hearing impaired.	为听障人士提供服务的房间。
	wéi tīng zhàng rén shì tí gōng fú wù de fáng jiān。
I am traveling with a service dog.	我带着帮助犬旅行。
	wǒ dài zhe bāng zhù quǎn lǚ xíng。

MONEY MATTERS

I would like to make a reservation.	我想预定。
	wǒ xiǎng yù dìng。

LODGING

How much per night?	每晚多少钱?
	měi wǎn duō shǎo qián?
Do you have a ____	您有_____
	nín yǒu _____
weekly / monthly rate?	周 / 月房价吗?
	zhōu / yuè fáng jià ma?
a weekend rate?	有周末价吗?
	yǒu zhōu mò jià ma?
We will be staying for ____ days / weeks.	我们将停留 ____ 天 / 周。
	wǒ mén jiāng tíng liú _____ tiān / zhōu。

For full coverage of number terms, see p7.

When is checkout time?	什么时间退房?
	shén me shí jiān tuì fáng?

For full coverage of time-related terms, see p12.

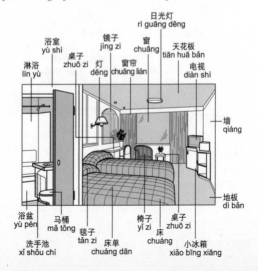

日光灯
rì guāng dēng

浴室
yù shì

镜子
jìng zi

窗
chuāng

天花板
tiān huā bǎn

淋浴
lín yù

桌子
zhuō zi

灯
dēng

窗帘
chuāng lián

电视
diàn shì

墙
qiáng

地板
dì bǎn

浴盆
yù pén

马桶
mǎ tǒng

毯子
tǎn zi

床单
chuáng dān

椅子
yǐ zi

床
chuáng

桌子
zhuō zi

小冰箱
xiǎo bīng xiāng

洗手池
xǐ shǒu chí

Do you accept credit cards / travelers checks?	可以用信用卡 / 旅行支票吗?
	kě yǐ yòng xìn yòng kǎ / lǚ xíng zhī piào ma?
May I see a room?	我可以看一下房间吗?
	wǒ kě yǐ kàn yī xià fáng jiān ma?
How much are taxes?	税是多少?
	shuì shì duō shǎo?
Is there a service charge?	有服务费吗?
	yǒu fú wù fèi ma?
I'd like to speak with the manager.	我想与经理谈谈。
	wǒ xiǎng yǔ jīng lǐ tán tán.

IN-ROOM AMENITIES

I'd like ____	我想_____
	wǒ xiǎng _____
to place an international call.	打一个国际电话。
	dǎ yī gè guó jì diàn huà.
to place a long-distance call.	打一个长途电话。
	dǎ yī gè cháng tú diàn huà.
directory assistance in English.	要英文的目录帮助。
	yào yīng wén de mù lù bāng zhù.
room service.	要客房服务。
	yào kè fáng fú wù.
maid service.	要女仆服务。
	yào nǚ pú fú wù.

LODGING

Instructions for Dialing the Hotel Phone

要呼叫另一个房间，拨打房间号。 *yào hū jiào lìng yī gè fáng jiān, bō dǎ fáng jiān hào.*	To call another room, dial the room number.
要拨打本地电话，先拨 **9**。 *yào bō dǎ běn dì diàn huà, xiān bō 9.*	To make a local call, first dial 9.
要呼叫接线员，拨 **0**。 *yào hū jiào jiē xiàn yuán, bō 0.*	To call the operator, dial 0.

the front desk ATT operator.	找前台 **ATT** 接线员。
	zhǎo qián tái ATT jiē xiàn yuán.
Do you have room service?	有客房服务吗？
	yǒu kè fáng fú wù ma?
When is the kitchen open?	厨房什么时间开放？
	chú fáng shén me shí jiān kāi fàng?
When is breakfast served?	什么时间供应早餐？
	shén me shí jiān gōng yīng zǎo cān?

For full coverage of time-related terms, see p12.

Do you offer massages?	提供按摩服务吗？
	tí gōng àn mó fú wù ma?
Do you have a lounge?	有休息室吗？
	yǒu xiū xī shì ma?
Do you have a business center?	有商务中心吗？
	yǒu shāng wù zhōng xīn ma?
Do you serve breakfast?	提供早餐吗？
	tí gōng zǎo cān ma?
Do you have Wi-Fi?	有无线保真 (**Wi-Fi**) 吗？
	yǒu wú xiàn bǎo zhēn (Wi-Fi) ma?
May I have a newspaper in the morning?	早晨有报纸吗？
	zǎo chén yǒu bào zhǐ ma?
Do you offer a tailor service?	提供裁剪服务吗？
	tí gōng cái jiǎn fú wù ma?
Do you offer laundry service?	提供洗衣服务吗？
	tí gōng xǐ yī fú wù ma?
Do you offer dry cleaning?	提供干洗服务吗？
	tí gōng gān xǐ fú wù ma?
May we have _____	可以_____
	kě yǐ _____
clean sheets today?	给我们换今天的床单吗？
	gěi wǒ mén huàn jīn tiān de chuáng dān ma?
more towels?	多给我们几条毛巾吗？
	duō gěi wǒ mén jǐ tiáo máo jīn ma?

more toilet paper?	多给我们一些卫生纸吗？
	duō gěi wǒ mén yī xiē wèi shēng zhǐ ma?
extra pillows?	多给我们几个枕头吗？
	duō gěi wǒ mén jǐ gè zhěn tóu ma?
Do you have an ice machine?	有制冰机吗？
	yǒu zhì bīng jī ma?
Did I receive any ____	有我的____
	yǒu wǒ de ____
messages?	留言吗？
	liú yán ma?
mail?	邮件吗？
	yóu jiàn ma?
faxes?	传真吗？
	chuán zhēn ma?
A spare key, please.	请给我一份备用钥匙。
	qǐng gěi wǒ yī fèn bèi yòng yào shi.
More hangers please.	请多提供些衣架。
	qǐng duō tí gōng xiē yī jià.
I am allergic to down pillows.	我对羽绒枕过敏。
	wǒ duì yǔ róng zhěn guò mǐn.
I'd like a wake up call.	我想要电话叫醒服务。
	wǒ xiǎng yào diàn huà jiào xǐng fú wù.

For full coverage of how to tell time, see p12.

Do you have alarm clocks?	有闹钟吗？
	yǒu nào zhōng ma?
Is there a safe in the room?	房间有保险箱吗？
	fáng jiān yǒu bǎo xiǎn xiāng ma?
Does the room have a hair dryer?	房间有吹风机吗？
	fáng jiān yǒu chuī fēng jī ma?

LODGING

HOTEL ROOM TROUBLE

May I speak with the manager?	我可以与经理谈谈吗?
	wǒ ké yǐ yǔ jīng lǐ tán tán ma?
The _____ does not work.	_____出问题了。
	_____*chū wèn tí le.*
television	电视
	diàn shì
telephone	电话
	diàn huà
air conditioning	空调
	kōng tiáo
Internet access	网络接口
	wǎng luò jiē kǒu
cable TV	有线电视
	yǒu xiàn diàn shì
There is no hot water.	没有热水。
	méi yǒu rè shuǐ.
The toilet is over-flowing!	马桶溢水了!
	mǎ tǒng yì shuǐ le!
This room is _____	房间_____
	fáng jiān _____
too noisy.	太吵。
	tài chǎo。
too cold.	太冷。
	tài lěng。

too warm.

太热。

tài rè。

This room has _____

房间有_____

fáng jiān yǒu _____

bugs.

虫子。

chóng zi。

mice.

老鼠。

lǎo shǔ。

I'd like a different room.

我想要另一间房。

wǒ xiǎng yào lìng yī jiān fáng。

Do you have a bigger room?

有大一点的房间吗?

yǒu dà yī diǎn de fáng jiān ma?

I locked myself out of my room.

我把自己锁在房间外面了。

wǒ bǎ zì jǐ suǒ zài fáng jiān wài miàn le。

Do you have any fans?

有风扇吗?

yǒu fēng shàn ma?

The sheets are not clean.

床单不干净。

chuáng dān bù gān jìng。

The towels are not clean.

毛巾不干净。

máo jīn bù gān jìng。

The room is not clean.

房间不干净。

fáng jiān bù gān jìng。

The guests next door / above / below are being very loud.

隔壁／楼上／楼下的客人正大声喧哗。

gé bì / lóu shàng / lóu xià de kè rén zhèng dà shēng xuān huá。

CHECKING OUT

I think this charge is a mistake.

我认为这项收费有误。

wǒ rèn wéi zhè xiàng shōu fèi yǒu wù。

Please explain this charge to me.

请向我解释这项收费。

qǐng xiàng wǒ jiě shì zhè xiàng shōu fèi。

Thank you, we enjoyed our stay.	谢谢您，我们在这里住得很愉快。 *xiè xiè nín, wǒ mén zài zhè lǐ zhù dé hěn yú kuài.*
The service was excellent.	服务非常好。 *fú wù fēi cháng hǎo.*
The staff is very professional and courteous.	员工很专业，也很有礼貌。 *yuán gōng hěn zhuān yè, yě hěn yǒu lǐ mào.*
Please call a cab for me.	请为我招一辆出租车。 *qǐng wéi wǒ zhāo yī liàng chū zū chē.*
Would someone please get my bags?	有人愿意帮我拿包吗？ *yǒu rén yuàn yì bāng wǒ ná bāo ma?*

HAPPY CAMPING

I'd like a site for ____	我想找个地方_____ *wǒ xiǎng zhǎo ge dì fāng _____*
a tent.	搭帐篷。 *dā zhàng péng.*
a camper.	露营。 *lù yíng.*
Are there ____	有_____ *yǒu _____*
bathrooms?	浴室吗？ *yù shì ma?*
showers?	淋浴吗？ *lín yù ma?*
Is there running water?	有自来水吗？ *yǒu zì lái shuǐ ma?*
Is the water drinkable?	这水可以喝吗？ *zhè shuǐ kě yǐ hē ma?*
Where is the electrical hookup?	电线板在哪？ *diàn xiàn bǎn zài nǎ?*

CHAPTER FOUR

DINING

This chapter includes a menu reader and the language you need to communicate in a range of dining establishments and food markets.

FINDING A RESTAURANT

| Would you recommend a good ___ restaurant? | 您能否推荐一个好的_____饭店? |
| | *nín néng fǒu tuī jiàn yī gè hǎo de _____ fàn diàn?* |

Cantonese	粤式
	yuè shì
Szechuan	川味
	chuān wèi
Japanese	日本
	rì běn
Thai	泰国
	tài guó
Malaysian	马来
	mǎ lái
Vietnamese	越南
	yuè nán
Italian	意大利
	yì dà lì
French	法国
	fǎ guó
pizza	比萨饼
	bǐ sà bǐng
steakhouse	牛排
	niú pái
family	家庭式
	jiā tíng shì

seafood	海鲜 *hǎi xiān*
vegetarian	素食 *sù shí*
buffet-style	自助式 *zì zhù shì*
budget	经济型 *jīng jì xíng*

Which is the best restaurant in town?
城里哪家饭店最好?
chéng lǐ nǎ jiā fàn diàn zuì hǎo?

Is there a late-night restaurant nearby?
附近有夜宵饭店吗?
fù jìn yǒu yè xiāo fàn diàn ma?

Is there a restaurant that serves breakfast nearby?
附近有提供早饭的饭店吗?
fù jìn yǒu tí gōng zǎo fàn de fàn diàn ma?

Is it very expensive?
很贵吗?
hěn guì ma?

Do I need a reservation?
我需要预定吗?
wǒ xū yào yù dìng ma?

Do I have to dress up?
我需要穿正装吗?
wǒ xū yào chuān zhèng zhuāng ma?

Do they serve lunch?
他们提供午餐吗?
tā mén tí gōng wǔ cān ma?

What time do they open for dinner?
几点开始供应晚餐?
jǐ diǎn kāi shǐ gōng yīng wǎn cān?

For lunch?
午餐?
wǔ cān?

What time do they close?
他们几点钟关门?
tā mén jǐ diǎn zhōng guān mén?

Do you have a take out menu?
你们有没有外卖菜单?
nǐ mén yǒu méi yǒu wài mài cài dān?

Do you have a bar?	你们有酒吧吗？
	nǐ mén yǒu jiǔ bā ma?
Is there a café nearby?	附近有咖啡馆吗？
	fù jìn yǒu kā fēi guǎn ma?

GETTING SEATED

Are you still serving?	你们还提供服务吗？
	nǐ mén hái tí gōng fú wù ma?
How long is the wait?	需要等多长时间？
	xū yào děng duō cháng shí jiān?
Do you have a no-smoking section?	有无烟区吗？
	yǒu wú yān qū ma?
A table for ____, please.	请给我们一张_____人用餐的餐桌。
	qǐng gěi wǒ mén yī zhāng _____
	rén yòng cān de cān zhuō。

For a full list of numbers, see p7.

Do you have a quiet table?	餐馆里有没有安静的地方？
	cān guǎn lǐ yǒu méi yǒu ān jìng de
	dì fāng?
May we sit outside / inside please?	我们能坐在外面 / 里面吗？
	wǒ mén néng zuò zài wài miàn /
	lǐ miàn ma?
May we sit at the counter?	我们能坐在吧台吗？
	wǒ mén néng zuò zài bā tái ma?
A menu please?	请给份菜单。
	qǐng gěi fèn cài dān。

ORDERING

Do you have a special tonight?	你们今晚有什么特色菜？
	nǐ mén jīn wǎn yǒu shén me tè sè cài?
What do you recommend?	您推荐什么？
	nín tuī jiàn shén me?
May I see a wine list?	我可以看一下酒单吗？
	wǒ kě yǐ kàn yī xià jiǔ dān ma?
Do you serve wine by the glass?	您是否卖单杯的酒？
	nín shì fǒu mài dān bēi de jiǔ?

DINING

Listen up: Restaurant Lingo

吸烟区还是无烟区?
xī yān qū hái shì wú yān qū?

Smoking or nonsmoking?

您要穿西装戴领带。
*nín yào chuān xī zhuāng dài
lǐng dài。*

You'll need a tie and jacket.

对不起，饭店内不允许
穿短裤。
*duì bù qǐ, fàn diàn nèi bù yǔn
xǔ chuān duǎn kù。*

I'm sorry, no shorts are allowed.

请问，想喝些什么?
*qǐng wèn, xiǎng hē xiē
shén me?*

May I bring you something to
drink?

您是否要看一下酒单?
*nín shì fǒu yào kàn yī xià
jiǔ dān?*

Would you like to see a wine
list?

您是否想知道我们的特色菜?
*nín shì fǒu xiǎng zhī dào wǒ
mén de tè sè cài?*

Would you like to hear our
specials?

您可以点菜了吗?
nín kě yǐ diǎn cài le ma?

Are you ready to order?

对不起，先生，您的信用卡
被拒收了。
*duì bù qǐ, xiān shēng, nín de
xìn yòng kǎ bèi jù shōu le。*

I'm sorry, sir, your credit card
was declined.

May I see a drink list?	我能否看一下饮料单？
	wǒ néng fǒu kàn yī xià yǐn liào dān?
I would like it cooked ____	请将牛排_____
	qǐng jiāng niú pái _____
rare.	烤得一分熟。
	kǎo dé yī fēn shú。
medium rare.	烤得三分熟。
	kǎo dé sān fēn shú。
medium.	烤得五分熟。
	kǎo dé wǔ fēn shú。
medium well.	烤得七分熟。
	kǎo dé qī fēn shú。
well.	烤得全熟。
	kǎo dé quán shú。
charred.	烤焦。
	kǎo jiāo。
Do you have a ____ menu?	您有_____菜单吗？
	nín yǒu _____ cài dān ma?
diabetic	适合糖尿病人的
	shì hé táng niào bìng rén de
kosher	犹太教徒
	yóu tài jiào tú
vegetarian	素食
	sù shí
children's	儿童
	ér tóng
What is in this dish?	这道菜里都有什么？
	zhè dào cài lǐ dōu yǒu shén me?
How is it prepared?	这道菜是怎么做的？
	zhè dào cài shì zěn me zuò de?
What kind of oil is that cooked in?	这道菜是用什么油炒的？
	zhè dào cài shì yòng shén me yóu chǎo de?
Do you have any low-salt dishes?	你们有低盐菜吗？
	nǐ mén yǒu dī yán cài ma?

On the side, please.	请放在旁边。
	qǐng fàng zài páng biān.
May I make a substitution?	我能换道菜吗？
	wǒ néng huàn dào cài ma?
I'd like to try that.	我想试试那个。
	wǒ xiǎng shì shì nà gè.
Is that fresh?	是新鲜的吗？
	shì xīn xiān de ma?
Waiter!	服务员！
	fú wù yuán!
Extra butter, please.	请多给我一些牛油。
	qǐng duō gěi wǒ yī xiē niú yóu.
No butter, thanks.	不要牛油，谢谢。
	bù yào niú yóu, xiè xiè.
Dressing on the side, please.	请把沙拉酱放在边上。
	qǐng bǎ shā lā jiàng fàng zài biān shàng.
No salt, please.	请不要放盐。
	qǐng bù yào fàng yán.
May I have some oil, please?	请给我加些油。
	qǐng gěi wǒ jiā xiē yóu.
More bread, please.	请再给些面包。
	qǐng zài gěi xiē miàn bāo.
I am lactose intolerant.	我不吃含乳糖的食物。
	wǒ bù chī hán rǔ táng de shí wù.
Would you recommend something without milk?	您能给我推荐不含奶的食品吗？
	nín néng gěi wǒ tuī jiàn bù hán nǎi de shí pǐn ma?
I am allergic to ____	我对____过敏。
	wǒ duì ____ guò mǐn.
seafood.	海鲜
	hǎi xiān
shellfish.	贝类
	bèi lèi

nuts.	坚果 *jiān guǒ*
peanuts.	花生 *huā shēng*
Water ____, please.	请上_____水。 *qǐng shàng _____ shuǐ。*
with ice	加冰 *jiā bīng*
without ice	不加冰 *bù jiā bīng*
I'm sorry, I don't think this is what I ordered.	对不起，我想这不是我点的菜。 *duì bù qǐ, wǒ xiǎng zhè bù shì wǒ diǎn de cài。*
My meat is a little over / under cooked.	这盘肉烧得有点过久 / 火候不够。 *zhè pán ròu shāo dé yǒu diǎn guò jiǔ / huǒ hou bù gòu。*
My vegetables are a little over / under cooked.	这道蔬菜有一点熟过头 / 生。 *zhè dào shū cài yǒu yī diǎn shú guò tóu / shēng。*
There's a bug in my food!	我看见食物里有虫子！ *wǒ kàn jiàn shí wù lǐ yǒu chóng zi!*
May I have a refill?	我可以再加一些吗？ *wǒ kě yǐ zài jiā yī xiē ma?*
A dessert menu, please.	请给我甜点单。 *qǐng gěi wǒ tián diǎn dān。*

DRINKS

alcoholic	含酒精饮料 *hán jiǔ jīng yǐn liào*
neat / straight	不搀水的 / 纯酒的 *bù chān shuǐ de / chún jiǔ de*
on the rocks	加冰 *jiā bīng*
with (seltzer or soda) water	加（矿泉或苏打）水 *jiā (kuàng quán huò sū dǎ) shuǐ*

beer	啤酒
	pí jiǔ
white wine	干白葡萄酒
	gān bái pú tao jiǔ
red wine	红葡萄酒
	hóng pú tao jiǔ
liqueur	利口酒
	lì kǒu jiǔ
brandy	白兰地
	bái lán dì
cognac	干邑酒
	gān yì jiǔ
gin	杜松子酒
	dù sōng zǐ jiǔ
vodka	伏特加
	fú tè jiā
rum	朗姆酒
	lǎng mǔ jiǔ
rice wine	米酒
	mǐ jiǔ
Scotch	苏格兰
	sū gé lán
Whiskey	威士忌
	wēi shì jì
nonalcoholic	非酒精饮料
	fēi jiǔ jīng yǐn liào
hot chocolate	热巧克力
	rè qiǎo kè lì
lemonade	柠檬水
	níng méng shuǐ
milkshake	奶昔
	nǎi xī
milk	牛奶
	niú nǎi

green tea	红茶
	hóngchá
black tea	绿茶
	lùchá
coffee	咖啡
	kā fēi
iced coffee	冰咖啡
	bīng kā fēi
mineral water	矿泉水
	kuàng quán shuǐ
fruit juice	果汁
	guǒ zhī

For a full list of fruits, see p85.

SETTLING UP

I'm stuffed.	我吃饱了。
	wǒ chī bǎo le。
The meal was excellent.	饭菜好极了。
	fàn cài hǎo jí le。
There's a problem with my bill.	我的帐单不太对。
	wǒ de zhàng dān bù tài duì。
Is the tip included?	包括小费吗?
	bāo kuò xiǎo fèi ma?
Check, please.	请给我帐单。
	qǐng gěi wǒ zhàng dān。

MENU READER

Chinese cuisine varies greatly from region to region, but we've tried to make our list of classic dishes as encompassing as possible.

APPETIZERS

barbecued pork	叉烧肉
	chā shāo ròu
braised bamboo shoots	油焖笋
	yóu mèn sǔn
cold platter	冷盘
	lěng pán

dried bean curd	豆腐干 *dòu fǔ gān*
hot pickled cabbage	辣白菜 *là bái cài*
jellyfish	海蜇皮 *hǎi zhē pí*
marinated beef	酱牛肉 *jiàng niú ròu*
pan-fried pork dumplings	锅贴 *guō tiē*
peanuts	花生米 *huā shēng mǐ*
pickled cucumber	腌黄瓜 *yān huáng gua*
pickled vegetables	泡菜 *pào cài*
sesame chicken	芝麻鸡 *zhī ma jī*
smoked chicken	熏鸡 *xūn jī*
spring roll	春卷 *chūn juàn*

SOUPS

egg drop soup	蛋花汤 *dàn huā tāng*
hot and sour soup	酸辣汤 *suān là tāng*
shark's fin soup	鱼翅汤 *yú chì tāng*
wonton soup	馄饨汤 *hún tun tāng*

STARCH DISHES

steamed rice	蒸饭 *zhēng fàn*

fried rice	炒饭
	chǎo fàn
steamed bread	馒头
	mán tóu
pork dumplings	猪肉饺
	zhū ròu jiǎo
vegetarian dumplings	素菜饺
	sù cài jiǎo
noodles	面条
	miàn tiáo
steamed rolls	花卷
	huā juǎn

SEAFOOD DISHES

braised fish	红烧鱼
	hóng shāo yú
clams	蛤蜊
	há li
crabs	螃蟹
	páng xiè
deep-fried shrimp balls	炸虾球
	zhà xiā qiú
jellyfish	海蜇皮
	hǎi zhē pí
lobster	龙虾
	lóng xiā
oysters	蚝
	háo
sautéed prawns	炒明虾
	chǎo míng xiā
scallops	鲜贝
	xiān bèi
sea cucumber (sea slugs)	海参
	hǎi shēn
shrimp with egg white	芙蓉虾仁
	fú róng xiā rén

| steamed whole fish | 清蒸全鱼 |
| | *qīng zhēng quán yú* |

MEAT DISHES

beef	牛肉
	niú ròu
pork	猪肉
	zhū ròu
lamb	羊肉
	yáng ròu
sweet and sour spareribs	糖醋排骨
	táng cù pái gǔ
beef with oyster sauce	蚝油牛肉
	háo yóu niú ròu
Mongolian barbecue	蒙古烤肉
	měng gǔ kǎo ròu
sliced beef with Chinese broccoli	芥兰牛肉
	jiè lán niú ròu
lamb shishkabob	羊肉串
	yáng ròu chuàn

POULTRY DISHES

chicken	鸡
	jī
duck	鸭
	yā
goose	鹅
	é
pigeon	鸽子
	gē zi
diced chicken with cashew nuts	腰果鸡丁
	yāo guǒ jī dīng
lemon chicken	柠檬鸡
	níng méng jī
Peking duck	北京烤鸭
	běi jīng kǎo yā

VEGETARIAN DISHES

braised bean curd in soy
sauce

红烧豆腐

hóng shāo dòu fǔ

family-style bean curd

家常豆腐

jiā cháng dòu fǔ

Chinese cabbage in cream
sauce

奶油白菜

nǎi yóu bái cài

sautéed string beans

干煸四季豆

gān biān sì jì dòu

spicy eggplant with garlic

鱼香茄子

yú xiāng qié zi

DIM SUM

egg tarts

蛋挞

dàn tà

fried pork dumplings

锅贴

guō tiē

shrimp balls

虾丸

xiā wán

shrimp dumplings

虾饺

xiā jiǎo

small steamed pork buns

小笼包

xiǎo lóng bāo

deep fried taro root

炸芋饺

zhà yù jiǎo

stuffed bean curd

酿豆腐

niàng dòu fǔ

stuffed peppers

酿青椒

niàng qīng jiāo

sweet bean buns

豆沙包

dòu shā bāo

radish cake

萝卜糕

luó bo gāo

sweet rice with meat
stuffed in lotus leaves

肉粽

ròu zòng

DESSERTS

almond gelatin	杏仁豆腐
	xìng rén dòu fǔ
sweet bean buns	豆沙包
	dòu shā bāo
cake	蛋糕
	dàn gāo
fresh fruit	新鲜水果
	xīn xiān shuǐ guǒ
ice cream	冰淇淋
	bīng qí lín
red bean soup	红豆汤
	hóng dòu tāng
eight treasures glutinous rice pudding	八宝饭
	bā bǎo fàn

BUYING GROCERIES

In China, groceries can be bought at open-air farmers' markets, neighborhood stores or large supermarkets.

AT THE SUPERMARKET

Which aisle has ____	哪一排卖____
	nǎ yī pái mài ____
spices?	调味料?
	tiáo wèi liào?
soaps and detergents?	肥皂与清洁剂?
	féi zào yǔ qīng jié jì?
canned goods?	罐装食品?
	guàn zhuāng shí pǐn?
snack food?	小吃类食品?
	xiǎo chī lèi shí pǐn?
water?	水?
	shuǐ?
juice?	果汁?
	guǒ zhī?
bread?	面包?
	miàn bāo?

fruit?	水果? *shuǐ guǒ?*
frozen foods?	冷冻食品? *lěng dòng shí pǐn?*

AT THE BUTCHER SHOP

Is the meat fresh?	肉是新鲜的吗? *ròu shì xīn xiān de ma?*
Do you sell fresh ____	你们卖不卖新鲜的_____ *nǐ mén mài bù mài xīn xiān de _____*
beef?	牛肉? *niú ròu?*
pork?	猪肉? *zhū ròu?*
lamb?	羊肉? *yáng ròu?*
I would like a cut of ____	我想买一块_____ *wǒ xiǎng mǎi yī kuài _____*
tenderloin.	里脊肉。 *lǐ jǐ ròu。*
T-bone.	**T**-骨牛排。 *T-gǔ niú pái。*
brisket.	胸肉。 *xiōng ròu。*
rump roast.	大腿肉。 *dà tuǐ ròu。*
chops.	排骨。 *pái gǔ。*
filet.	肉片。 *ròu piàn。*
Thick / Thin cuts please.	请切厚 / 薄片。 *qǐng qiē hòu / báo piàn。*
Please trim the fat.	请割去肥肉。 *qǐng gē qù féi ròu。*
	_____是新鲜的吗?

Is the ____ fresh?	_____ shì xīn xiān de ma?
	鱼
fish	yú
	海鲜
seafood	hǎi xiān
	虾
shrimp	xiā
	章鱼
octopus	zhāng yú
	鱿鱼
squid	yóu yú
	鲈鱼
sea bass	lú yú
	比目鱼
flounder	bǐ mù yú
	蛤肉
clams	há ròu
	牡蛎
oysters	mǔ lì
	鲨鱼肉
shark	shā yú ròu
	海龟肉
turtle	hǎi guī ròu
	我能闻一下吗?
May I smell it?	wǒ néng wén yī xià ma?
	您能_____
Would you please ____	nín néng _____
	切片吗?
filet it?	qiē piàn ma?
	去骨吗?
debone it?	qù gǔ ma?
	去头去尾吗?
remove the head and tail?	qù tóu qù wěi ma?

AT THE PRODUCE STAND / MARKET

Fruits

banana	香蕉 *xiāng jiāo*
apple	苹果 *píng guǒ*
grapes (green, red)	葡萄 *pú tao*
lichee	荔枝 *lì zhī*
orange	桔子 *jú zi*
papaya	木瓜 *mù guā*
peach	桃子 *táo zi*
pear	梨子 *lí zi*
persimmon	柿子 *shì zi*
watermelon	西瓜 *xī guā*

Vegetables

bamboo shoots	竹笋 *zhú sǔn*
beancurd	豆腐 *dòu fǔ*
broccoli	西兰花 *xī lán huā*
cabbage	卷心菜 *juǎn xīn cài*
carrots	胡萝卜 *hú luó bo*
cauliflower	菜花 *cài huā*

corn	玉米
	yù mǐ
lotus root	莲藕
	lián ǒu
straw mushroom	草菇
	cǎo gū
snow pea	雪豆
	xuě dòu
soybean	大豆
	dà dòu
spinach	菠菜
	bō cài
water chestnut	荸荠
	bí qi

Fresh Herbs & Spices

garlic	大蒜
	dà suàn
ginger	姜
	jiāng
hot pepper	辣椒
	là jiāo
mustard	芥末
	jiè mò
pepper	胡椒
	hú jiāo
salt	盐
	yán
sesame oil	香油
	xiāng yóu

CHAPTER FIVE

SOCIALIZING

Whether you're meeting people in a bar or a park, you'll find the language in this chapter to help you make new friends.

GREETINGS

Hello.	您好。
	nín hǎo。
How are you?	您好吗?
	nín hǎo ma?
Fine, thanks.	很好，谢谢。
	hěn hǎo, xiè xiè。
And you?	您呢?
	nín ne?
I'm exhausted from the trip.	我旅行归来很疲惫。
	wǒ lǚ xíng guī lái hěn pí bèi。
I have a headache.	我头痛。
	wǒ tóu tòng。
I'm terrible.	我感觉很槽糕。
	wǒ gǎn jué hěn zāo gāo。
I have a cold.	我感冒了。
	wǒ gǎn mào le。
Good morning.	早晨好。
	zǎo chén hǎo。
Good evening.	晚上好。
	wǎn shàng hǎo。
Good afternoon.	下午好。
	xià wǔ hǎo。
Good night.	晚安。
	wǎn ān。

Listen Up: Common Greetings

很荣幸。 *hěn róng xìng。*	It's a pleasure.
我心欢喜。 *wǒ xīn huān xǐ。*	Delighted.
乐意为您效劳。 / 如您所愿。 *lè yì wéi nín xiào láo。 /* *rú nín suǒ yuàn。*	At your service. / As you wish.
幸会。 *xìng huì。*	Charmed.
一天愉快。 *yī tiān yú kuài。*	Good day.
您好。 *nín hǎo。*	Hello.
最近忙什么? *zuì jìn máng shén me?*	How's it going?
最近怎么样? *zuì jìn zěn me yàng?*	What's up?
拜拜! *bài bài!*	Bye!
再见。 *zài jiàn。*	Goodbye.
回见。 *huí jiàn。*	See you later.

OVERCOMING THE LANGUAGE BARRIER

I don't understand.	我不懂。 *wǒ bù dǒng。*
Please speak more slowly.	请您再说慢点儿。 *qǐng nín zài shuō màn diǎn ér。*
Please speak louder.	请大点声说。 *qǐng dà diǎn shēng shuō。*
Do you speak English?	您说英语吗? *nín shuō yīng yǔ ma?*

I speak ____ better than Chinese.	我的_____语说得比汉语好。
	wǒ de _____ yǔ shuō dé bǐ hàn yǔ hǎo。
Please spell that.	请问它怎么写。
	qǐng wèn tā zěn me xiě。
Please repeat that.	请再说一遍。
	qǐng zài shuō yī biàn。
How do you say ____?	您如何说_____?
	nín rú hé shuō _____?
Would you show me that [word] in this dictionary?	您能在这本字典里把它指给我看吗?
	nín néng zài zhè běn zì diǎn lǐ bǎ tā zhǐ gěi wǒ kàn ma?

Curse Words

Here are some common curse words, used across mainland China.

狗屎	shit
gǒu shǐ	
笨蛋	jerk
bèn dàn	
该死	damn
gāi sǐ	
傻瓜	ass
shǎ guā	
晕	screwed up
yūn	
私生子	bastard
sī shēng zǐ	
靠	fucked up
kào	
他妈的	to fuck
tā mā de	

GETTING PERSONAL

People in China and Taiwan are quite friendly, but more mindful of age and status hierarchies than Americans or Europeans. Remember to use the *nín* form of address for elders and those in higher positions, rather than the informal *ní*.

INTRODUCTIONS

What is your name?	您叫什么名字？ *nín jiào shén me míng zi?*
My name is ____.	我叫_____。 *wǒ jiào _____。*
I'm very pleased to meet you.	很高兴见到您。 *hěn gāo xìng jiàn dào nín。*
May I introduce my ____	我可以介绍我的_____ 吗？ *wǒ kě yǐ jiè shào wǒ de _____ma?*
How is your ____	您的_____好吗？ *nín de _____hǎo ma?*

wife?	妻子 *qī zǐ*
husband?	丈夫 *zhàng fū*
child?	孩子 *hái zi*
friends?	朋友 *péng yǒu*
boyfriend / girlfriend?	男朋友 / 女朋友 *nán péng yǒu / nǚ péng yǒu*
family?	家人 *jiā rén*
mother?	母亲 *mǔ qīn*
father?	父亲 *fù qīn*
brother / sister?	兄弟 / 姐妹 *xiōng dì / jiě mèi*

friend?	朋友 *péng yǒu*
neighbor?	邻居 *lín jū*
boss?	老板 *lǎo bǎn*
cousin?	表哥 / 表弟 / 表姐 / 表妹 *biǎo gē* / biǎo dì* / biǎo jiě* / biǎo mèi**
aunt / uncle?	姑姑 / 阿姨 / 叔叔 / 舅舅 *gū gū / ā yí / shū shū / jiù jiù*
fiancée / fiancé?	未婚妻 / 未婚夫 *wèi hūn qī / wèi hūn fū*

Gender and Age Distinctions

Gender and age hierarchies are clearly distinguished in Chinese terms for relatives. In English, a cousin is just a cousin. Chinese has separate terms, however, for older, younger, female, or male cousins. Similarly, relatives on the mother's side of the family often have the word "wai" — meaning "outside" the paternal family unit — before the actual term for aunt, uncle, grandparents, etc., while those on the father's side of the family will often have the word "zu" (referring to "lineage") preceding such terms.

Cousins

* biǎo gē = older male cousin
* biǎo dì = younger male cousin
* biǎo jiě = older female cousin
* biǎo mèi = younger female cousin

More Gender and Age Distinctions

Gu mu = father's sister (married)
Yi mu = maternal aunt
Yi ma = maternal aunt (married)
Bo mu = wife of father's elder brother
Shu mu = wife of father's younger brother
Bo bo = father's eldest brother
Bo fu = father's elder brother
Shu zu = paternal grandfather's younger brother
Shu zu mu = wife of paternal grandfather's younger brother

partner?	伴侣 *bàn lǚ*
niece / nephew?	侄女 / 侄子 *zhí nǚ / zhí zi*
parents?	父母 *fù mǔ*
grandparents?	祖父母 *zǔ fù mǔ*
Are you married / single?	您结婚了 / 单身吗? *nín jié hūn le / dān shēn ma?*
I'm married.	我结婚了。 *wǒ jié hūn le。*
I'm single.	我单身。 *wǒ dān shēn。*
I'm divorced.	我离婚了。 *wǒ lí hūn le。*
I'm a widow / widower.	我丈夫 / 妻子已经去世了。 *wǒ zhàng fū / qī zǐ yǐ jīng qù shì le。*
We're separated.	我们已分居。 *wǒ mén yǐ fēn jū。*
I live with my boyfriend / girlfriend.	我与我的男朋友 / 女朋友一起生活。 *wǒ yǔ wǒ de nán péng yǒu / nǚ péng yǒu yī qǐ shēng huó。*

How old are you?	您多大了?
	nín duō dà le?
How old are your children?	您的孩子几岁?
	nín de hái zǐ jǐ suì?
Wow! That's very young.	哇！很年轻。
	wa! hěn nián qīng.
No you're not! You're much younger.	怎么会！你看起来一点都不像。
	zěn me huì! nǐ kàn qǐ lái yī diǎn dōu bù xiàng.
Your wife / daughter is beautiful.	您妻子 / 女儿很漂亮。
	nín qī zǐ / nǚ ér hěn piào liang.
Your husband / son is handsome.	您丈夫 / 儿子很英俊。
	nín zhàng fū / ér zǐ hěn yīng jùn.
What a beautiful baby!	多漂亮的宝宝啊！
	duō piào liang de bǎo bǎo ā!
Are you here on business?	您是到这出差吗?
	nín shì dào zhè chū chāi ma?
I am vacationing.	我正在度假。
	wǒ zhèng zài dù jià.
I'm attending a conference.	我在参加一个会议。
	wǒ zài cān jiā yī gè huì yì.
How long are you staying?	您将停留多长时间?
	nín jiāng tíng liú duō cháng shí jiān?
What are you studying?	您在学什么?
	nín zài xué shén me?
I'm a student.	我是一名学生。
	wǒ shì yī míng xué shēng.
Where are you from?	你从哪里来?
	nǐ cóng nǎ lǐ lái?

PERSONAL DESCRIPTIONS

blond(e)	金发的
	jīn fā de
brunette	黑发的
	hēi fā de
redhead	红发的
	hóng fā de

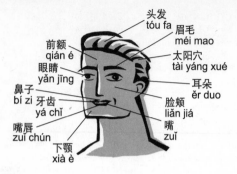

头发
tóu fa

眉毛
méi mao

前额
qián é

太阳穴
tài yáng xué

眼睛
yǎn jīng

鼻子
bí zi

牙齿
yá chǐ

耳朵
ěr duo

脸颊
liǎn jiá

嘴唇
zuǐ chún

嘴
zuǐ

下颚
xià è

straight hair	直发
	zhí fā
curly hair	卷发
	juàn fā
kinky hair	卷缩发
	juàn suō fā
long hair	长发
	cháng fā
short hair	短发
	duǎn fā
tanned	茶色
	chá sè
pale	苍白的
	cāng bái de
mocha-skinned	咖啡色皮肤的
	kā fēi sè pí fū de
black	黑色的
	hēi sè de
white	白色的
	bái sè de
Asian	亚洲人
	yà zhōu rén

African-American	非裔美洲人 *fēi yì měi zhōu rén*
Caucasian	白种人 *bái zhǒng rén*
biracial	混杂种族人 *hùn zá zhǒng zú rén*
tall	高 *gāo*
short	矮 *ǎi*
thin	瘦 *shòu*
fat	胖 *pàng*
blue eyes	蓝眼睛 *lán yǎn jīng*
brown eyes	棕色眼睛 *zōng sè yǎn jīng*
green eyes	绿眼睛 *lǜ yǎn jīng*
hazel eyes	淡褐色眼睛 *dàn hè sè yǎn jīng*
eyebrows	眉毛 *méi mao*
eyelashes	眼睫毛 *yǎn jié máo*
freckles	斑 *bān*
moles	痣 *zhì*
face	脸 *liǎn*

Listen Up: Ethnic Backgrounds

我是中国台湾人。 *wǒ shì zhōng guó tái wān rén。*	I'm Taiwanese.
我是中国西藏人。 *wǒ shì zhōng guó xī cáng rén。*	I'm Tibetan.
我是韩国人。 *wǒ shì hán guó rén。*	I'm Korean.
我是菲律宾人。 *wǒ shì fēi lǜ bīn rén。*	I'm Phillipino.
我是中国人。 *wǒ shì zhōng guó rén。*	I'm Chinese.
我是中国澳门人。 *wǒ shì zhōng guó ào mén rén。*	I'm Macanese.
我是泰国人。 *wǒ shì tài guó rén。*	I'm Thai.
我是马来西亚人。 *wǒ shì mǎ lái xī yà rén。*	I'm Malaysian.
我是越南人。 *wǒ shì yuè nán rén。*	I'm Vietnamese.
我是尼泊尔人。 *wǒ shì ní bó ěr rén。*	I'm Nepalese.
我是老挝人。 *wǒ shì lǎowō rén。*	I'm Laotian.
我是印度人。 *wǒ shì yìn dù rén。*	I'm Indian.
我是缅甸人。 *wǒ shì miǎn diàn rén*	I'm Burmese.
我是俄国人。 *wǒ shì é guó rén。*	I'm Russian
我是日本人。 *wǒ shì rì běn rén。*	I'm Japanese.

For a full list of nationalities, see English / Chinese dictionary.

DISPOSITIONS AND MOODS

sad	伤心
	shāng xīn
happy	高兴
	gāo xìng
angry	生气
	shēng qì
tired	累
	lèi
depressed	沮丧
	jǔ sàng
stressed	有压力的
	yǒu yā lì de
anxious	焦虑的
	jiāo lǜ de
confused	困惑的
	kùn huò de
enthusiastic	热情的
	rè qíng de

PROFESSIONS

What do you do for a living?	您是做什么工作的?
	nín shì zuò shén me gōng zuò de?
Here is my business card.	这是我的名片。
	zhè shì wǒ de míng piàn.
I am _____	我是_____
	wǒ shì _____
a doctor.	医生。
	yī shēng。
an engineer.	工程师。
	gōng chéng shī。
a lawyer.	律师。
	lǜ shī。

a salesperson.	销售。
	xiāo shòu。
a writer.	作家。
	zuò jiā。
an editor.	编辑。
	biān jí。
a designer.	设计师。
	shè jì shī。
an educator.	教育工作者。
	jiào yù gōng zuò zhě。
an artist.	搞艺术的。
	gǎo yì shù de。
a craftsperson.	手艺人。
	shǒu yì rén。
a homemaker.	家庭主妇。
	jiā tíng zhǔ fù。
an accountant.	会计。
	kuài jì。
a nurse.	护士。
	hù shì。
a musician.	搞音乐的。
	gǎo yīnyuè de。
a military professional.	军事专家。
	jūn shì zhuān jiā。
a government employee.	公务员。
	gōng wù yuán。

DOING BUSINESS

I'd like an appointment.	我要安排一次约会。
	wǒ yào ān pái yī cì yuē huì。
I'm here to see ____.	我到这里看_____。
	wǒ dào zhè lǐ kàn _____。
May I photocopy this?	我可以影印这份材料吗?
	wǒ kě yǐ yǐng yìn zhè fèn cái liào ma?

| May I use a computer here? | 我可以使用这里的计算机吗? |
| | *wǒ kě yǐ shǐ yòng zhè lǐ de jì suàn jī ma?* |

| What's the password? | 密码是什么? |
| | *mì mǎ shì shén me?* |

| May I access the Internet? | 我可以上网吗? |
| | *wǒ kě yǐ shàng wǎng ma?* |

| May I send a fax? | 我可以发份传真吗? |
| | *wǒ kě yǐ fā fèn chuán zhēn ma?* |

| May I use the phone? | 我可以使用电话吗? |
| | *wǒ kě yǐ shǐ yòng diàn huà ma?* |

PARTING WAYS

| Keep in touch. | 保持联络。 |
| | *bǎo chí lián luò。* |

| Please write or email. | 请写信或发送电子邮件。 |
| | *qǐng xiě xìn huò fā sòng diàn zǐ yóu jiàn。* |

| Here's my phone number. Call me. | 这是我的电话号码。 打电话给我。 |
| | *zhè shì wǒ de diàn huà hào mǎ。 dǎ diàn huà gěi wǒ。* |

| May I have your phone number / e-mail please? | 请给我您的电话号码 / 电子邮件好吗? |
| | *qǐng gěi wǒ nín de diàn huà hào mǎ / diàn zǐ yóu jiàn hǎo ma?* |

| May I have your card? | 可以给我您的名片吗? |
| | *kě yǐ gěi wǒ nín de míng piàn ma?* |

| Give me your address and I'll write you. | 给我您的地址，我会写信给你。 |
| | *gěi wǒ nín de dì zhǐ, wǒ huì xiě xìn gěi nǐ。* |

TOPICS OF CONVERSATION

As in the United States or Europe, the weather and current affairs are common conversation topics.

THE WEATHER

It's so _____

今天天气_____

jīn tiān tiān qì _____

Is it always so _____ ?

天气总是这样_____?

tiān qì zǒng shì zhè yàng _____?

sunny.	晴朗吗
	qíng lǎng ma
rainy.	多雨吗
	duō yǔ ma
cloudy.	多云吗
	duō yún ma
humid.	潮湿吗
	cháo shī ma
warm.	暖和吗
	nuǎn huó ma
cool.	凉爽吗
	liáng shuǎng ma
windy.	有风吗
	yǒu fēng ma

Do you know the weather forecast for tomorrow?

您知道明天的天气预报吗?

nín zhī dào míng tiān de tiān qì yù bào ma?

THE ISSUES

What do you think about _____

您怎样看待_____

nín zěn yàng kàn dài _____

democracy?	民主主义?
	mín zhǔ zhǔyi?
socialism?	社会主义?
	shè huì zhǔ yì?
American Democrats?	美国民主党?
	měi guó mín zhǔ dǎng?

American Republicans?	美国共和党?
	měi guó gòng hé dǎng?
monarchy?	君主政体?
	jūn zhǔ zhèng tǐ?
the environment?	环境问题?
	huán jìng wèn tí?
climate change?	气候变化?
	qì hòu biàn huà?
the economy?	经济形势?
	jīng jì xíng shì?
What political party do you belong to?	您属于什么党派?
	nín shǔ yú shén me dǎng pài?
What did you think of the election in ____?	你对----的大选怎么看?
	nǐ duì ____ de dà xuǎn zěn me kàn?
What do you think of the war in ____?	您怎样看待_____战争?
	nín zěn yàng kàn dài _____ zhàn zhēng?

RELIGION

Do you go to church / temple / mosque?	您上教堂 / 寺庙 / 清真寺吗?
	nín shàng jiào táng / sì miào / qīng zhēn sì ma?
Are you religious?	您信仰宗教吗?
	nín xìn yǎng zōng jiào ma?
I'm ____ / I was raised ____	我信仰_____ / 我受教于_____
	wǒ xìn yǎng _____ / wǒ shòu jiào yú _____
Protestant.	新教。
	xīn jiào。
Catholic.	天主教。
	tiān zhǔ jiào。
Jewish.	犹太教。
	yóu tài jiào。
Muslim.	穆斯林教 / 伊斯兰教。
	mù sī lín jiào / ī sī lán jiào。

Buddhist.

佛教。
fó jiào。

Greek Orthodox.

希腊正教。
xī là zhèng jiào。

Hindu.

印度教。
yìn dù jiào。

agnostic.

不可知论。
bù kě zhī lùn。

atheist.

无神论。
wú shén lùn。

I'm spiritual but I don't attend services.

我精神上信仰但不参加活动。
wǒ jīng shen shàng xìn yǎng dàn bù cān jiā huó dòng。

I don't believe in that.

我不信仰宗教。
wǒ bù xìn yǎng zōng jiào。

That's against my beliefs.

这违背我的信仰。
zhè wéi bèi wǒ de xìn yǎng。

I'd rather not talk about it.

我不想谈这个问题。
wǒ bù xiǎng tán zhè gè wèn tí。

GETTING TO KNOW SOMEONE

Following are some conversation starters.

MUSICAL TASTES

What kind of music do you like?

您喜欢哪种音乐?
nín xǐ huān nǎ zhǒng yīn yuè?

I like _____

我喜欢_____
wǒ xǐ huān _____

rock 'n' roll.

摇滚乐。
yáo gǔn yuè。

hip hop.

街舞。
jiē wǔ。

techno.

电子音乐。
diàn zǐ yīn yuè。

soul.

灵魂音乐
líng hún yīn yuè

classical.	古典音乐。
	gǔ diǎn yīn yuè。
jazz.	爵士乐。
	jué shì yuè。
country and western.	乡村和西部音乐。
	xiāng cūn hé xī bù yīn yuè。
reggae.	瑞格舞。
	ruì gé wǔ。
opera.	歌剧。
	gē jù。
show-tunes / musicals.	歌剧音乐 / 音乐剧。
	gē jù yīn yuè / yīn yuè jù。
New Age.	新世纪音乐。
	xīn shì jì yīn yuè。
pop.	流行音乐。
	liú xíng yīn yuè。

HOBBIES

What do you like to do in your spare time?	您业余时间喜欢做什么？
	nín yè yú shí jiān xǐ huān zuò shén me?
I like _____	我喜欢_____
	wǒ xǐ huān _____
playing guitar.	弹吉他。
	tán jí tā。
piano.	弹钢琴。
	tán gāng qín。

For other instruments, see the English / Chinese dictionary.

painting / drawing.	画画。
	huà huà。
dancing.	跳舞。
	tiào wǔ。
reading.	阅读。
	yuè dú。
watching TV.	看电视。
	kàn diàn shì。
shopping.	购物。
	gòu wù。

going to the movies.	看电影。
	kàn diàn yǐng。
hiking.	徒步旅行。
	tú bù lǚ xíng。
camping.	露营。
	lù yíng。
hanging out.	闲逛。
	xián guàng。
traveling.	旅行。
	lǚ xíng。
eating out.	到外面吃。
	dào wài miàn chī。
cooking.	烹饪。
	pēng rèn。
sewing.	做缝纫。
	zuò féng rèn。
sports.	做运动。
	zuò yùn dòng。
Do you like to dance?	您喜欢跳舞吗?
	nín xǐ huān tiào wǔ ma?
Would you like to go out?	您喜欢外出吗?
	nín xǐ huān wài chū ma?
May I buy you dinner sometime?	我什么时候能请您吃饭吗?
	wǒ shén me shí hòu néng qǐng nín chī fàn ma?
What kind of food do you like?	您喜欢哪种食物?
	nín xǐ huān nǎ zhǒng shí wù?

For a full list of food types, see Dining in Chapter 4.

Would you like to go _____	您想去_____
	nín xiǎng qù_____
to a movie?	看电影吗?
	kàn diàn yǐng ma?
to a concert?	听音乐会吗?
	tīng yīn yuè huì ma?
to the zoo?	动物园吗?
	dòng wù yuán ma?

to the beach?	海滩吗？
	hǎi tān ma?
to a museum?	博物馆吗？
	bó wù guǎn ma?
for a walk in the park?	公园散步吗？
	gōng yuán sàn bù ma?
dancing?	跳舞吗？
	tiào wǔ ma?
Would you like to ____	您想_____
	nín xiǎng _____
have lunch?	吃午餐吗？
	chī wǔ cān ma?
have coffee?	喝咖啡吗？
	hē kā fēi ma?
have dinner?	吃晚餐吗？
	chī wǎn cān ma?
What kind of books do you like to read?	您喜欢读哪种类型的书？
	nín xǐ huān dú nǎ zhǒng lèi xíng de shū?
I like ____	我喜欢_____
	wǒ xǐ huān _____
mysteries.	神话故事。
	shén huà gù shì。
Westerns.	西部题材。
	xī bù tí cái。
dramas.	戏剧。
	xì jù。
novels.	小说。
	xiǎo shuō。
biographies.	传记。
	zhuàn jì。
auto-biographies.	自传。
	zì zhuàn。
romance.	浪漫爱情故事。
	làng màn ài qíng gù shì。
history.	历史。
	lì shǐ。

For dating terms, see Nightlife in Chapter 10.

CHAPTER SIX

MONEY & COMMUNICATIONS

This chapter covers money, the mail, phone, Internet service, and other tools you need to connect with the outside world.

MONEY

Do you accept _____	可以_____
	kě yǐ _____

Visa / MasterCard /
Discover / American
Express / Diners' Club?
credit cards?

用 **Visa** 卡 / **MasterCard** 卡 /
Discover 卡 / **American**
Express 卡 / **Diners' Club** 卡吗?
用信用卡吗?
yòng Visa kǎ / MasterCard kǎ /
Discover kǎ / American
Express kǎ / Diners' Club kǎ ma?
yòng xìn yòng kǎ ma?

bills?

用纸币吗?
yòng zhǐ bì ma?

coins?

用硬币吗?
yòng yìng bì ma?

checks?

用支票吗?
yòng zhī piào ma?

travelers checks?

用旅行支票吗?
yòng lǚ xíng zhī piào ma?

money transfer?

转帐吗?
zhuǎn zhàng ma?

May I wire transfer funds
here?

可以在这里办电汇吗?
kě yǐ zài zhè lǐ bàn diàn huì ma?

Would you please tell me
where to find _____

您能告诉我哪里有_____吗?
nín néng gào sù wǒ nǎ lǐ yǒu
_____ma?

a bank?

银行
yín háng

a credit bureau?	信用局
	xìn yòng jú
an ATM?	自动取款机
	zì dòng qǔ kuǎn jī
a currency exchange?	货币兑换处
	huò bì duì huàn chù

A receipt, please.
请给我一份收据。
qǐng gěi wǒ yī fèn shōu jù.

Would you tell me ____
您能告诉我_____
nín néng gào sù wǒ _____

the exchange rate for
dollars to ____?
美元对____的汇率吗?
měi yuán duì ____ de huì lǜ ma?

the exchange rate for
pounds to ____?
英镑对____的汇率吗?
yīng bàng duì ____de huìlǜ ma?

Is there a service charge?
有服务费吗?
yǒu fú wù fèi ma?

May I have a cash advance
on my credit card?
我可以在我的信用卡上预提现金吗?
*wǒ kě yǐ zài wǒ de xìn yòng kǎ
shàng yù tí xiàn jīn ma?*

Will you accept a
credit card?
可以用信用卡吗?
kě yǐ yòng xìn yòng kǎ ma?

Listen Up: Bank Lingo

请在这里签字。	Please sign here.
qǐng zài zhè lǐ qiān zì.	
这是您的收据。	Here is your receipt.
zhè shì nín de shōu jù.	
请出示一下您的身份证，好吗?	May I see your ID, please?
qǐng chū shì yī xià nín de shēn fèn zhèng, hǎo ma?	
我们接受旅行支票。	We accept travelers checks.
wǒ mén jiē shòu lǚ xíng zhī piào.	
只收现金。	Cash only.
zhǐ jǐn shōu xiàn jīn.	

May I have smaller bills, please.	我能要些面额小点的钞票吗？
	wǒ néng yào xiē miàn é xiǎo diǎn de chāo piào ma?
Can you make change?	可以换零钱吗？
	kě yǐ huàn líng qián ma?
I only have bills.	我只有纸币。
	wǒ zhǐ yǒu zhǐ bì.
Some coins, please.	请给我一些硬币。
	qǐng gěi wǒ yī xiē yìng bì.

ATM Machine

账户余额
Account balance

请输入个人识别码
Enter personal identification number

明细
Statement

输入
Enter

清除
Clear

取款（从支票帐户和储蓄帐户）
Withdraw (from checking & savings)

取消
Cancel

退出交易
Exit transaction

请插入您的银行卡
Please insert your card

收据
Receipt

接受的信用卡
Credit cards accepted

PHONE SERVICE

Where can I buy or rent a cell phone?	在哪里可以买到或租到移动电话？
	zài nǎ lǐ kě yǐ mǎi dào huò zū dào yí dòng diàn huà?
What rate plans do you have?	请问是怎么收费的？
	qǐng wèn shì zěn me shōu fèi de?
Is this good throughout the country?	这在全国通用吗？
	zhè zài quán guó tōng yòng ma?

May I have a prepaid phone?	给我一部预付费电话好吗？ *gěi wǒ yī bù yù fù fèi diàn huà hǎo ma?*
Where can I buy a phone card?	在哪里能买到电话卡？ *zài nǎ lǐ néng mǎi dào diàn huà kǎ?*
May I add more minutes to my phone card?	电话卡里还能添加更多分钟吗？ *diàn huà kǎ lǐ hái néng tiān jiā gèng duō fēn zhōng ma?*

MAKING A CALL

May I dial direct?	可以直接拨号吗？ *kě yǐ zhí jiē bō hào ma?*
Operator please.	请找接线员。 *qǐng zhǎo jiē xiàn yuán。*
I'd like to make an international call.	我想打一个国际电话。 *wǒ xiǎng dǎ yī gè guó jì diàn huà。*

Listen Up: Telephone Lingo

您好？ *Nín hǎo?*	Hello?
号码是多少？ *Hào mǎ shì duō shǎo?*	What number?
对不起，您拨的电话正忙。 *duì bù qǐ, nín bō de diàn huà zhèng máng。*	I'm sorry, the line is busy.
请挂掉再重拨。 *qǐng guà diào zài chóng bō。*	Please, hang up and redial.
对不起，您拨的电话无人接听。 *duì bù qǐ, nín bō de diàn huà wú rén jiē tīng。*	I'm sorry, nobody is answering.
您的电话卡还可用十分钟。 *nín de diàn huà kǎ hái kě yòng shí fēn zhōng。*	Your card has ten minutes left.

I'd like to make a collect call.	我想打一个对方付费电话。
	wǒ xiǎng dǎ yī gè duì fāng fù fèi diàn huà.
I'd like to use a calling card.	我想用电话卡。
	wǒ xiǎng yòng diàn huà kǎ.
Bill my credit card.	用我的信用卡付款。
	yòng wǒ de xìn yòng kǎ fù kuǎn.
May I bill the charges to my room?	可以把费用转到我的房费上吗?
	kě yǐ bǎ fèi yòng zhuǎn dào wǒ de fáng fèi shàng ma?
May I bill the charges to my home phone?	可以把费用转到我的家庭电话上吗?
	kě yǐ bǎ fèi yòng zhuǎn dào wǒ de jiā tíng diàn huà shàng ma?
Information desk, may I help you?	请讲。
	qǐng jiǎng.
I'd like the number for ___.	我想要_____号码。
	wǒ xiǎng yào _____ hào mǎ.
I just got disconnected.	我的电话刚刚断了。
	wǒ de diàn huà gāng gāng duàn le.
The line is busy.	线路正忙。
	xiàn lù zhèng máng.
I lost the connection.	我断线了。
	wǒ duàn xiàn le.

INTERNET ACCESS

Where is an Internet café?
哪里有网吧？
nǎ lǐ yǒu wǎng bā?

Is there a wireless hub nearby?
附近有无线通讯中枢吗？
fù jìn yǒu wú xiàn tōng xùn zhōng shū ma?

How much do you charge per minute / hour?
每分钟 / 小时收费是多少？
měi fēn zhōng / xiǎo shí shōu fèi shì duō shǎo?

Can I print here?
这里能打印吗？
zhè lǐ néng dǎ yìn ma?

Can I burn a CD?
我能刻张 CD 吗？
wǒ néng kè zhāng CD ma?

Would you please help me change the language preference to English?
请帮我把首选语言改成英语好吗？
qǐng bāng wǒ bǎ shǒu xuǎn yǔ yán gǎi chéng yīng yǔ hǎo ma?

May I scan something?
我能扫描一些资料吗？
wǒ néng sǎo miáo yì xiē zī liào ma?

Can I upload photos?
我能上传照片吗？
wǒ néng shàng chuán zhào piàn ma?

Do you have a USB port so I can download music?
有 USB 接口吗？我想下载音乐。
yǒu USB jiē kǒu ma? wǒ xiǎng xià zǎi yīn yuè。

Do you have a machine compatible with iTunes?	有能兼容 **iTunes** 的机器吗？
	yǒu néng jiān róng iTunes de jī qì ma?
Do you have a Mac?	有苹果机吗？
	yǒu píng guǒ jī ma?
Do you have a PC?	有个人计算机吗？
	yǒu gè rén jì suàn jī ma?
Do you have a newer version of this software?	这个软件有更新的版本吗？
	zhè gè ruǎn jiàn yǒu gēng xīn de bǎn běn ma?
Do you have broadband?	有宽带吗？
	yǒu kuān dài ma?
How fast is your connection speed here?	这里的连接速度有多快？
	zhè lǐ de lián jiē sù dù yǒu duō kuài?

GETTING MAIL

Where is the post office?	邮局在哪里？
	yóu jú zài nǎ lǐ?
May I send an international package?	我可以寄一个国际包裹吗？
	wǒ ké yǐ jì yī gè guó jì bāo guǒ ma?
Do I need a customs form?	我需要填写海关表格吗？
	wǒ xū yào tián xiě hǎi guān biǎo gé ma?
Do you sell insurance for packages?	可以为包裹购买保险吗？
	ké yǐ wéi bāo guǒ gòu mǎi bǎo xiǎn ma?
Please, mark it fragile.	请标明易碎物品。
	qǐng biāo míng yì suì wù pǐn。
Please, handle with care.	请小心轻放。
	qǐng xiǎo xīn qīng fàng。
Do you have twine?	有细绳吗？
	yǒu xì shéng ma?

Listen Up: Postal Lingo

下一个！ *xià yī gè!*	Next!
请放在这里。 *qǐng fàng zài zhè lǐ。*	Please, set it here.
哪一类？ *nǎ yī lèi?*	Which class?
您想要哪种服务？ *nín xiǎng yào nǎ zhǒng fú wù?*	What kind of service would you like?
可以为您做些什么？ *kě yǐ wéi nín zuò xiē shén me?*	How can I help you?
邮件投入窗口 *yóu jiàn tóu rù chuāng kǒu*	dropoff window
领取窗口 *lǐng qǔ chuāng kǒu*	pickup window

COMMUNICATIONS

Where is a DHL office?	哪里有 DHL 营业所？ *nǎ lǐ yǒu DHL yíng yè suǒ?*
Do you sell stamps?	卖邮票吗？ *mài yóu piào ma?*
Do you sell postcards?	卖明信片吗？ *mài míng xìn piàn ma?*
May I send that first class?	我可以按第一类邮件邮寄吗？ *wǒ kě yǐ àn dì yī lèi yóu jiàn yóu jì ma?*
How much to send that express / air mail?	特快专递 / 空邮要多少钱？ *tè kuài zhuān dì / kōng yóu yào duō shǎo qián?*
Do you offer overnight delivery?	提供隔夜交付服务吗？ *tí gōng gé yè jiāo fù fú wù ma?*

How long will it take to reach the United States?	寄到美国需要多长时间?
	jì dào měi guó xū yào duō cháng shí jiān?
I'd like to buy an envelope.	我想买一张信封。
	wǒ xiǎng mǎi yī zhāng xìn fēng。
May I send it airmail?	我可以寄航空邮件吗?
	wǒ kě yǐ jì háng kōng yóu jiàn ma?
I'd like to send it certified / registered mail.	我想寄挂号邮件。
	wǒ xiǎng jì guà hào yóu jiàn。

CHAPTER SEVEN

CULTURE

CINEMA

Is there a movie theater nearby?
附近有电影院吗?
fù jìn yǒu diàn yǐng yuàn ma?

What's playing tonight?
今晚放什么片子?
jīn wǎn fàng shén me piān zi?

Is that in English or Chinese?
是英语的还是汉语的?
shì yīng yǔ de hái shì hàn yǔ de?

Are there English subtitles?
有英文字幕吗?
yǒu yīng wén zì mù ma?

Is the theater air conditioned?
电影院有空调吗?
diàn yǐng yuàn yǒu kōng tiáo ma?

How much is a ticket?
一张票多少钱?
yī zhāng piào duō shǎo qián?

Do you have a ____ discount?
有_____折扣吗?
yǒu _____ zhé kòu ma?

  senior
老年人
lǎo nián rén

  student
学生
xué shēng

  children's
儿童
ér tóng

What time is the movie showing?
电影几点放映?
diàn yǐng jǐ diǎn fàng yìng?

How long is the movie?
电影片长是多久?
diàn yǐng piàn cháng shì duō jiǔ?

May I buy tickets in advance?
我可以提前买票吗?
wǒ kě yǐ tí qián mǎi piào ma?

Is it sold out?
票售完了吗?
piào shòu wán le ma?

When does it begin?
什么时候开始?
shén me shí hòu kāi shǐ?

PERFORMANCES

Do you have ballroom dancing?	有交际舞吗？
	yǒu jiāo jì wǔ ma?
Are there any plays showing right now?	现在有什么片子正在放映吗？
	xiàn zài yǒu shén me piān zi zhèng zài fàng yìng ma?
Is there a dinner theater?	有晚餐剧场吗？
	yǒu wǎn cān jù chǎng ma?
Where can I buy tickets?	在哪里能买到票？
	zài nǎ lǐ néng mǎi dào piào?
Are there student discounts?	有学生折扣吗？
	yǒu xué shēng zhé kòu ma?
I need ____ seats.	我需要_____座位。
	wǒ xū yào _____ zuò wèi.

For a full list of numbers, see p7.

An aisle seat.	靠过道的座位。
	kào guò dào de zuò wèi.
Orchestra seat, please.	请给我前排座位。
	qǐng gěi wǒ qián pái zuò wèi.

Listen Up: Box Office Lingo

您想看什么片子？	What would you like to see?
nín xiǎng kàn shén me piān zi?	
几张？	How many?
jǐ zhāng?	
两个成年人吗？	For two adults?
liǎng gè chéng nián rén ma?	
要爆米花吗？	Would you like some popcorn?
yào bào mǐ huā ma?	
还需要其他的吗？	Would you like anything else?
hái xū yào qí tā de ma?	

What time does the play start?

演出什么时候开始？

yǎn chū shén me shí hòu kāi shǐ?

Is there an intermission?

有幕间休息吗？

yǒu mù jiān xiū xi ma?

Do you have an opera house?

有歌剧院吗？

yǒu gē jù yuàn ma?

Is there a local symphony?

有本地交响乐团吗？

yǒu běn dì jiāo xiǎng yuè tuán ma?

May I purchase tickets over the phone?

可以电话购票吗？

kě yǐ diàn huà gòu piào ma?

What time is the box office open?

售票处什么时候开始售票？

shòu piào chù shén me shí hòu kāi shǐ shòu piào?

I need space for a wheelchair, please.

麻烦您，我需要方便坐轮椅的人观看的位置。

má fan nín, wǒ xū yào fāng biàn zuò lún yǐ de rén guān kàn de wèi zhì。

Do you have private boxes available?

有独立包厢吗？

yǒu dú lì bāo xiāng ma?

Is there a church concert?

有教堂音乐会吗？

yǒu jiào táng yīn yuè huì ma?

A program, please.

请给我一张节目单。

qǐng gěi wǒ yī zhāng jié mù dān。

Please show us to our seats.

请帮我们带位。

qǐng bāng wǒ mén dài wèi。

MUSEUMS, GALLERIES & SIGHTS

Do you have a museum guide?

有博物馆指南吗?

yǒu bó wù guǎn zhǐ nán ma?

Do you have guided tours?

有配导游的旅游吗?

yǒu pèi dǎo yóu de lǚ yóu ma?

What are the museum hours?

博物馆什么时间开放?

bó wù guǎn shén me shí jiān kāi fàng?

Do I need an appointment?

我需要预约吗?

wǒ xū yào yù yuē ma?

What is the admission fee?

门票是多少钱?

mén piào shì duō shǎo qián?

Do you have ____

您有_____吗?

nín yǒu _____ ma?

student discounts?

学生折扣

xué sheng zhé kòu

senior discounts?

老年人折扣

lǎo nián rén zhé kòu

Do you have services for the hearing impaired?

有为听障人士提供的服务吗?

yǒu wèi tīng zhàng rén shì tí gōng de fú wù ma?

Do you have audio tours in English?

有用英文解说的语音导览设备吗?

yǒu yòng yīng wén jiě shuō de yǔ yīn dǎo lǎn shè bèi ma?

CHAPTER EIGHT

SHOPPING

This chapter covers the phrases you'll need to shop in a variety of settings, from the mall to the town square artisan market. We also threw in the terminology you'll need to visit the barber or hairdresser.

For coverage of food and grocery shopping, see p82.

GENERAL SHOPPING TERMS

Please tell me _____	请告诉我_____
	qǐng gào sù wǒ _____
how to get to a mall?	如何到购物中心？
	rú hé dào gòu wù zhōng xīn?
the best place for shopping?	最好的购物场所？
	zuì hǎo de gòu wù chǎng suǒ?
how to get downtown?	如何到市区？
	rú hé dào shì qū?
Where can I find a _____	哪里有_____？
	nǎ lǐ yǒu _____？
shoe store?	鞋店
	xié diàn
men's / women's / children's clothing store?	男式／女式／儿童服装店
	Nán shì / nǚ shì / ér tóng fú zhuāng diàn
designer fashion shop?	时装设计店
	shí zhuāng shè jì diàn
vintage clothing store?	古董服装店
	gǔ dǒng fú zhuāng diàn
jewelry store?	珠宝店
	zhū bǎo diàn
bookstore?	书店
	shū diàn

toy store?	玩具店
	wán jù diàn
stationery store?	文具店
	wén jù diàn
antique shop?	古董店
	gǔ dǒng diàn
cigar shop?	烟草商店
	yān cǎo shāng diàn
souvenir shop?	纪念品店
	jì niàn pǐn diàn
flea market?	跳蚤市场?
	tiào zǎo shì chǎng?

CLOTHES SHOPPING

I'd like to buy ____	我想买_____。
	wǒ xiǎng mǎi _____。
men's shirts.	男式衬衫
	nán shì chèn shān
women's shoes.	女式鞋
	nǚ shì xié
children's clothes.	儿童服装
	ér tóng fú zhuāng
toys.	玩具
	wán jù

For a full list of numbers, see p7.

I'm looking for a size ____	我要_____号。
	wǒ yào _____ hào。
small.	小
	xiǎo
medium.	中
	zhōng
large.	大
	dà
extra-large.	超大
	chāo dà

耳环
ěr huán

手表
ǒu biǎo

衣服
yī fu

衬衣
chèn yī

领带
lǐng dài

上衣
shàng yī

皮带
pí dài

裤子
kù zi

鞋
xié

I'm looking for ____	我要____
	wǒ yào ____
a silk blouse.	丝质宽松上衣。
	sī zhì kuān sōng shàng yī。
cotton pants.	棉质裤子。
	mián zhì kù zǐ。
a hat.	帽子。
	mào zǐ。
sunglasses.	太阳镜。
	tài yáng jìng。
underwear.	内衣。
	nèi yī。
cashmere.	羊绒衫。
	yáng róng shān。
socks.	短袜。
	duǎn wà。
sweaters.	毛衣。
	máo yī。

SHOPPING

眼镜
yǎn jìng

T 恤
T xù

牛仔裤
niú zǎi kù

运动鞋
yùn dòng xié

a coat.	外套。 *wài tào。*
a swimsuit.	泳衣。 *yǒng yī。*
May I try it on?	我可以试穿吗？ *wǒ kě yǐ shì chuān ma?*
Do you have fitting rooms?	有试衣间吗？ *yǒu shì yī jiān ma?*
This is _____	这件_____ *zhè jiàn _____*
too tight.	太紧。 *tài jǐn。*
too loose.	太松。 *tài sōng。*
too long.	太长。 *tài cháng。*
too short.	太短。 *tài duǎn。*
This fits great!	这件很合身！ *zhè jiàn hěn hé shēn!*

Thanks, I'll take it.	谢谢，就买这件了。
	xiè xiè, jiù mǎi zhè jiàn le。
Do you have that in ____	那件衣服有_____
	nà jiàn yī fu yǒu _____
a smaller / larger size?	更小 / 更大的号吗？
	gèng xiǎo / gèng dà de hào ma?
a different color?	别的颜色吗？
	bié de yán sè ma?
How much is it?	这个多少钱？
	zhè gè duō shǎo qián?

ARTISAN MARKET SHOPPING

Is there a craft / artisan market?	有工艺品市场吗？
	yǒu gōng yì pǐn shì chǎng ma?
That's beautiful. May I look at it?	那个很漂亮。
	我可以看一下吗？
	nà gè hěn piào liang。
	wǒ kě yǐ kàn yī xià ma?
When is the farmers' market open?	农贸市场什么时间开放？
	nóng mào shì chǎng shén me shí jiān kāi fàng?
Is that open every day of the week?	一周的每一天都开放吗？
	yī zhōu de měi yī tiān dōu kāi fàng ma?
How much does that cost?	那需要多少钱？
	nà xū yào duō shǎo qián?
That's too expensive.	太贵了。
	tài guì le。
How much for two?	两个多少钱？
	liǎng gè duō shǎo qián?
Do I get a discount if I buy two or more?	如果我买两个或两个以上可以打折吗？
	rú guǒ wǒ mǎi liǎng gè huò liǎng gè yǐ shàng kě yǐ dǎ zhé ma?
Do I get a discount if I pay in cash?	如果我付现金可以打折吗？
	rú guǒ wǒ fù xiàn jīn kě yǐ dǎ zhé ma?

Listen Up: Market Lingo

要想细瞧商品，请先打个招呼。
yào xiǎng xì qiáo shāng pǐn,
qǐng xiān dǎ gè zhāo hū.

Please ask for help before handling goods.

这是找您的零钱。
zhè shì zhǎo nín de líng qián.

Here is your change.

两个共四十，先生。
liǎng gè gòng sì shí, xiān sheng.

Two for forty, sir.

No thanks, maybe I'll come back.	不，谢谢，可能我会回来的。 *bù, xiè xiè, kě néng wǒ huì huí lái de.*
Would you take $____?	____ 美元怎么样？ *____ měi yuán zěn me yàng?*

For a full list of numbers, see p7.

That's a deal!	就这么定了！ *jiù zhè me dìng le!*
Do you have a less expensive one?	有便宜点的吗？ *yǒu pián yi diǎn de ma?*
Is there tax?	有税吗？ *yǒu shuì ma?*

BOOKSTORE / NEWSSTAND SHOPPING

Is there a ____ nearby?	附近有_____吗？ *fù jìn yǒu _____ ma?*
a bookstore	书店 *shū diàn*
a newsstand	报亭 *bào tíng*
Do you have ____ in English?	您有英文的_____吗？ *nín yǒu yīng wén de _____ ma?*
books	书 *shū*

newspapers	报纸
	bào zhǐ
magazines	杂志
	zá zhì
books about local history	地方历史书籍
	dì fāng lì shǐ shū jí
picture books	图画书
	tú huà shū

SHOPPING FOR ELECTRONICS

Electricity used in China is 220 volts, so most devices from North America cannot be used without a transformer. Most outlets take the North American two-flat-pin plug, or the two-round-pin plugs common in Europe.

Can I play this in the United States?	在美国能玩这个吗?
	zài měi guó néng wán zhè gè ma?
Will this game work on my game console in the United States?	这款游戏可以在我的美国游戏机上运行吗?
	zhè kuǎn yóu xì kě yǐ zài wǒ de měi guó yóu xì jī shàng yùn xíng ma?
Do you have this in a U.S. market format?	您有这个产品的美国市场版本吗?
	nín yǒu zhè gè chǎn pǐn de měi guó shì chǎng bǎn běn ma?
Can you convert this to a U.S. market format?	您能把这个转换成美国市场版本吗?
	nín néng bǎ zhè gè zhuǎn huàn chéng měi guó shì chǎng bǎn běn ma?
Will this work with a 110 VAC adapter?	这个能使用 110 伏交流电适配器吗?
	zhè gè néng shǐ yòng 110 fú jiāo liú diàn shì pèi qì ma?
Do you have an adapter plug for 110 to 220?	您有用于 110 转 220 伏的适配器插头吗?
	nín yǒu yòng yú 110 zhuǎn 220 fú de shì pèi qì chā tóu ma?

Do you sell electronics adapters here?	这里卖电子适配器吗?
	zhè lǐ mài diàn zǐ shì pèi qì ma?
Is it safe to use my laptop with this adapter?	我的笔记本电脑使用这个适配器安全吗?
	wǒ de bǐ jì běn diàn nǎo shǐ yòng zhè gè shì pèi qì ān quán ma?
If it doesn't work, may I return it?	如果不能用, 我可以退货吗?
	rú guǒ bù néng yòng, wǒ kě yǐ tuì huò ma?
May I try it here in the store?	可以在店里试一下吗?
	kě yǐ zài diàn lǐ shì yī xià ma?

AT THE BARBER / HAIRDRESSER

Do you have a style guide?	有发型样式介绍吗?
	yǒu fà xíng yàng shì jiè shào ma?
A trim, please.	剪发。
	jiǎn fà。
I'd like it bleached.	我想把头发漂白。
	wǒ xiǎng bǎ tóu fà piǎo bái。
Would you change the color ____	您能把颜色变得_____
	nín néng bǎ yán sè biàn dé _____
darker?	更深吗?
	gèng shēn ma?
lighter?	更浅吗?
	gèng qiǎn ma?
Would you just touch it up a little?	稍稍剪高一点好吗?
	shāo shāo jiǎn gāo yī diǎn hǎo ma?
I'd like it curled.	我想把头发弄卷。
	wǒ xiǎng bǎ tóu fà nòng juàn。
Do I need an appointment?	我需要预约吗?
	wǒ xū yào yù yuē ma?

Wash, dry, and set.	清洗、吹干并做个发型。
	qīng xǐ、chuī gān bìng zuò gè fà xíng。
Do you do permanents?	您做烫发吗？
	nín zuò tàng fà ma?
May I make an appointment?	我可以预约吗？
	wǒ kě yǐ yù yuē ma?
Please use low heat.	请使用低热。
	qǐng shǐ yòng dī rè。
Please don't blow dry it.	请不要吹干。
	qǐng bù yào chuī gān。
Please dry it curly / straight.	请弄卷 / 拉直后吹干。
	qǐng nòng juàn / lā zhí hòu chuī gàn。
Would you fix my braids?	您能修我的发辫吗？
	nín néng xiū wǒ de fà biàn ma?
Would you fix my highlights?	您能修我的挑染部分吗？
	nín néng xiū wǒ de tiāo rǎn bù fēn ma?
Do you wax?	您会去毛吗？
	nín huì qù máo ma?
Please wax my ____	请_____
	qǐng _____
legs.	帮我去腿毛。
	bāng wǒ qù tuǐ máo。
bikini line.	去除我比基尼泳装所遮盖的三点部位线条的毛。
	qù chú wǒ bǐ jī ní yǒng zhuāng suǒ zhē gài de sān diǎn bù wèi xiàn tiáo de máo。
eyebrows.	帮我去眉毛。
	bāng wǒ qù méi máo。
under my nose.	去除我上唇上的毛。
	qù chú wǒ shàng chún shàng de máo。

Please trim my beard.	请修剪我的胡子。
	qǐng xiū jiǎn wǒ de hú zǐ.
A shave, please.	请帮我刮面。
	qǐng bāng wǒ guā miàn.
Use a fresh blade please.	请用新的刀片。
	qǐng yòng xīn de dāo piàn.
Sure, cut it all off.	当然，全剪掉。
	dāng rán, quán jiǎn diào.

CHAPTER NINE
SPORTS & FITNESS

GETTING FIT

Is there a gym nearby?
附近有体育馆吗?
fù jìn yǒu tǐ yù guǎn ma?

Do you have free weights?
有自由重量训练吗?
yǒu zì yóu zhòng liàng xùn liàn ma?

I'd like to go for a swim.
我想去游泳。
wǒ xiǎng qù yóu yǒng。

Do I have to be a member?
我必须是会员吗?
wǒ bì xū shì huì yuán ma?

May I come here for one day?
我可以来这里一天吗?
wǒ kě yǐ lái zhè lǐ yī tiān ma?

How much does a membership cost?
成为会员得花多少钱?
chéng wéi huì yuán děi huā duō shǎo qián?

I need to get a locker please.
麻烦您, 我需要一个存物柜。
má fan nín, wǒ xū yào yī gè cún wù guì。

Do you have a lock?
有锁吗?
yǒu suǒ ma?

Do you have a treadmill?
有跑步机吗?
yǒu pǎo bù jī ma?

Do you have a stationary bike?	有健身车吗？ *yǒu jiàn shēn chē ma?*
Do you have handball / squash courts?	有手球 / 壁球场吗？ *yǒu shǒu qiú / bì qiú chǎng ma?*
Are they indoors?	是在室内吗？ *shì zài shì nèi ma?*
I'd like to play tennis.	我想打网球。 *wǒ xiǎng dǎ wǎng qiú。*
Would you like to play?	您想玩吗？ *nín xiǎng wán ma?*
I'd like to rent a racquet.	我想租一副球拍。 *wǒ xiǎng zū yī fù qiú pāi。*
I need to buy some ____	我需要买一些_____ *wǒ xū yào mǎi yī xiē _____*
new balls.	新球。 *xīn qiú。*
safety glasses.	防护镜。 *fáng hù jìng。*
May I rent a court for tomorrow?	我可以租一个场地明天用吗？ *wǒ kě yǐ zū yī gè chǎng dì míng tiān yòng ma?*
May I have clean towels?	可以给我干净的毛巾吗？ *kě yǐ gěi wǒ gān jìng de máo jīn ma?*
Where are the showers / locker-rooms?	淋浴室 / 存物室在哪里？ *lín yù shì / cún wù shì zài nǎ lǐ?*
Do you have a workout room for women only?	有女性专用的健身房吗？ *yǒu nǚ xìng zhuān yòng de jiàn shēn fáng ma?*
Do you have aerobics classes?	有有氧运动课吗？ *yǒu yǒu yǎng yùn dòng kè ma?*

Do you have a women's pool?	有女士游泳池吗？ *yǒu nǚ shì yóu yǒng chí ma?*
Let's go for a jog.	我们去跑步吧。 *wǒ mén qù pǎo bù bā.*
That was a great workout.	这是很好的体育锻炼。 *zhè shì hěn hǎo de tǐ yù duàn liàn.*

CATCHING A GAME

Where is the stadium?	体育场在哪里？ *tǐ yù chǎng zài nǎ lǐ?*
Who is the best goalie?	最好的守门员是谁？ *zuì hǎo de shǒu mén yuán shì shéí?*
Are there any women's teams?	有女子队吗？ *yǒu nǚ zǐ duì ma?*
Do you have any amateur / professional teams?	有业余 / 专业队吗？ *yǒu yè yú / zhuān yè duì ma?*
Is there a game I could play in?	有我能参加的比赛吗？ *yǒu wǒ néng cān jiā de bǐ sài ma?*
Which is the best team?	哪一队是最好的？ *nǎ yī duì shì zuì hǎo de?*
Will the game be on television?	这比赛会上电视吗？ *zhè bǐ sài huì shàng diàn shì ma?*

Where can I buy tickets?	在哪里能买到票？
	zài nǎ lǐ néng mǎi dào piào?
The best seats, please.	请给我最好的座位。
	qǐng gěi wǒ zuì hǎo de zuò wèi.
The cheapest seats, please.	请给我最便宜的座位。
	qǐng gěi wǒ zuì pián yi de zuò wèi.
How close are these seats?	这些座位离赛场有多远？
	zhè xiē zuò wèi lí sài chǎng yóu duō yuǎn?
May I have box seats?	可以给我包厢座位吗？
	kě yǐ gěi wǒ bāo xiāng zuò wèi ma?
Wow! What a game!	哇！多精彩的比赛啊！
	wa! duō jīng cǎi de bǐ sài ā!
Go Go Go!	加油加油加油！
	jiā yóu jiā yóu jiā yóu!
Oh No!	噢，不！
	ō, bù!
Give it to them!	传给他们！
	chuán gěi tā mén!
Go for it!	全力以赴！
	quán lì yǐ fù!
Score!	得分！
	dé fēn!
What's the score?	得分是多少？
	dé fēn shì duō shǎo?
Who's winning?	谁赢了？
	shéi yíng le?

HIKING

Where can I find a guide to hiking trails?	哪里能找到徒步游向导？
	nǎ lǐ néng zhǎo dào tú bù yóu xiàng dǎo?
Do we need to hire a guide?	我们需要雇一位导游吗？
	wǒ mén xū yào gù yī wèi dǎo yóu ma?

Where can I rent equipment?
在哪里能租到装备?
zài nǎ lǐ néng zū dào zhuāng bèi?

Do they have rock climbing there?
那里有攀岩吗?
nà lǐ yǒu pān yán ma?

We need more ropes and carabiners.
我们需要更多的绳子和铁锁。
wǒ mén xū yào gèng duō de shéng zǐ hé tiě suǒ。

Where can we go mountain climbing?
我们在哪里能爬山?
wǒ mén zài nǎ lǐ néng pá shān?

Are the routes ____
路线_____
lù xiàn _____

   well marked?
   标志明确吗?
   biāo zhì míng què ma?

   in good condition?
   情形良好吗?
   qíng xíng liáng hǎo ma?

What is the altitude there?
那里海拔多高?
nà lǐ hǎi bá duō gāo?

How long will it take?
将用多长时间?
jiāng yòng duō cháng shí jiān?

Is it very difficult?

很困难吗？

hěn kùn nán ma?

I'd like a challenging climb, but I don't want to take oxygen.

我喜欢富有挑战性的爬山，但我不想带氧气。

wǒ xǐ huān fù yǒu tiǎo zhàn xìng de pá shān, dàn wǒ bù xiǎng dài yǎng qì.

I want to hire someone to carry my excess gear.

我想雇人携带我过多的装备。

wǒ xiǎng gù rén xié dài wǒ guò duō de zhuāng bèi.

We don't have time for a long route.

我们没时间走长线路。

wǒ mén méi shí jiān zǒu cháng xiàn lù.

I don't think it's safe to proceed.

我认为继续前进不安全。

wǒ rèn wéi jì xù qián jìn bù ān quán.

Do we have a backup plan?

我们有备用计划吗？

wǒ mén yǒu bèi yòng jì huà ma?

If we're not back by tomorrow, send a search party.

如果我们明天没有返回，请派出搜寻队。

rú guǒ wǒ mén míng tiān méi yǒu fǎn huí, qǐng pài chū sōu xún duì.

Are the campsites marked?

露营地做标志了吗？

lù yíng dì zuò biāo zhì le ma?

Can we camp off the trail?

我们能在线路外露营吗？

wǒ mén néng zài xiàn lù wài lù yíng ma?

Is it okay to build fires here?

在这里点火没有问题吧？

zài zhè lǐ diǎn huǒ méi yǒu wèn tí bā?

Do we need permits?

我们需要许可吗？

wǒ mén xū yào xǔ kě ma?

For more camping terms, see p68.

BOATING OR FISHING

When do we sail?

我们什么时候启航？

wǒ mén shén me shí hou qǐ háng?

Where are the life preservers?

救生用具在哪里？

jiù shēng yòng jù zài nǎ lǐ?

Can I purchase bait?

我能买些饵吗？

wǒ néng mǎi xiē ěr ma?

Can I rent a pole?

我能租一根杆吗？

wǒ néng zū yī gēn gǎn ma?

How long is the voyage?

航程有多长？

háng chéng yǒu duō cháng?

Are we going up river or down?

我们在沿河上行还是下行？

wǒ mén zài yán hé shàng xíng hái shì xià xíng?

How far are we going?

我们走多远了？

wǒ mén zǒu duō yuǎn le?

How fast are we going?

我们走多快？

wǒ mén zǒu duō kuài?

How deep is the water here?

这里的水有多深？

zhè lǐ de shuǐ yǒu duō shēn?

I got one!

我钓到了！

wǒ diào dào le!

I can't swim.

我不会游泳。

wǒ bù huì yóu yǒng。

Can we go ashore?

我们能去岸上吗？

wǒ mén néng qù àn shàng ma?

For more boating terms, see p54.

DIVING

I'd like to go snorkeling.

我想去浮潜。

wǒ xiǎng qù fú qián.

I'd like to go scuba diving.

我想去深潜。

wǒ xiǎng qù shēn qián.

I have a NAUI / PADI certification.

我有 **NAUI / PADI** 证书。

wǒ yǒu NAUI / PADI zhèng shū.

I need to rent gear.

我需要租装备。

wǒ xū yào zū zhuāng bèi.

We'd like to see some shipwrecks if we can.

如果可以，我们希望能看到失事船只残骸。

rú guǒ kě yǐ, wǒ mén xī wàng néng kàn dào shī shì chuán zhǐ cán hái.

Are there any good reef dives?

有好的跳水帆船吗？

yǒu hǎo de tiào shuǐ fān chuán ma?

I'd like to see a lot of sea-life.

我想看许多海洋生物。

wǒ xiǎng kàn xǔ duō hǎi yáng shēng wù.

Are the currents strong?

水流强吗？

shuǐ liú qiáng ma?

How clear is the water?

水有多清澈？

shuǐ yǒu duō qīng chè?

I want / don't want to go with a group.

我想 / 不想跟团去。

wǒ xiǎng / bù xiǎng gēn tuán qù.

Can we charter our own boat?

我们能自己包艘小船吗？

wǒ mén néng zì jǐ bāo sōu xiǎo chuán ma?

SURFING

I'd like to go surfing.

我想去冲浪。

wǒ xiǎng qù chōng làng.

Are there any good beaches?

有好的海滩吗？

yǒu hǎo de hǎi tān ma?

Can I rent a board?

我能租一艘船吗？

wǒ néng zū yī sōu chuán ma?

How are the currents?

水流怎么样？

shuǐ liú zěn me yàng?

How high are the waves?

波浪有多高？

bō làng yǒu duō gāo?

Is it usually crowded?

经常那么拥挤吗？

jīng cháng nà me yōng jǐ ma?

Are there facilities on that beach?

那个海滩上有设施吗？

nà gè hǎi tān shàng yǒu shè shī ma?

Is there wind surfing there also?

那里也有滑浪风帆吗？

nà lǐ yě yǒu huá làng fēng fān ma?

GOLFING

I'd like to reserve a tee-time, please.

麻烦您，我想预定开球时间。

má fan nín, wǒ xiǎng yù dìng kāi qiú shí jiān。

Do we need to be members to play?

我们需要是会员才能玩吗？

wǒ mén xū yào shì huì yuán cái néng wán ma?

How many holes is your course?

您的球场有多少洞？

nín de qiú chǎng yǒu duō shǎo dòng?

What is par for the course?

球场的标准杆数是多少？

qiú chǎng de biāo zhǔn gǎn shù shì duō shǎo?

I need to rent clubs.

我需要租球棒。

wǒ xū yào zū qiú bàng。

I need to purchase a sleeve of balls.	我需要买一筒球。
	wǒ xū yào mǎi yī tǒng qiú.
I need a glove.	我需要一副手套。
	wǒ xū yào yī fù shǒu tào.
I need a new hat.	我需要一顶新帽子
	wǒ xū yào yī dǐng xīn mào zǐ.
Do you require soft spikes?	您需要软道钉吗？
	nín xū yào ruǎn dào dìng ma?
Do you have carts?	您有高尔夫车吗？
	nín yǒu gāo ěr fū chē ma?
I'd like to hire a caddy.	我想雇一名球童。
	wǒ xiǎng gù yī míng qiú tóng.
Do you have a driving range?	有练习场吗？
	yǒu liàn xí chǎng ma?
How much are the greens fees?	果岭费是多少钱？
	guǒ lǐng fèi shì duō shǎo qián?
Can I book a lesson with the pro?	我能与职业高球手预订一节课吗？
	wǒ néng yǔ zhí yè gāo qiú shǒu yù dìng yī jié kè ma?
I need to have a club repaired.	我有一副球棒要修理。
	wǒ yǒu yī fù qiú bàng yào xiū lǐ.
Is the course dry?	球场干吗？
	qiú chǎng gān ma?
Are there any wildlife hazards?	有野生物危险吗？
	yǒu yě shēng wù wēi xiǎn ma?
How many meters is the course?	球场有多少米？
	qiú chǎng yǒu duō shǎo mǐ?
Is it very hilly?	很陡吗？
	hěn dǒu ma?

CHAPTER TEN

NIGHTLIFE

For coverage of movies and cultural events, see p115, Chapter Seven, "Culture."

CLUB HOPPING

Where can I find ____	在哪里能找到_____ *zài nǎ lǐ néng zhǎo dào _____*
a good nightclub?	好的夜总会? *hǎo de yè zǒng huì?*
a club with a live band?	有现场乐队演奏的俱乐部? *yǒu xiàn chǎng yuè duì yǎn zòu de jù lè bù?*
a reggae club?	瑞格舞俱乐部? *ruì gé wǔ jù lè bù?*
a hip hop club?	街舞俱乐部? *jiē wǔ jù lè bù?*
a techno club?	电子音乐俱乐部? *diàn zǐ yīn yuè jù lè bù?*
a jazz club?	爵士乐俱乐部? *jué shì yuè jù lè bù?*
a country-western club?	乡村音乐俱乐部? *xiāng cūn yīn yuè jù lè bù?*
a gay / lesbian club?	男同性恋 / 女同性恋俱乐部? *nán tóng xìng liàn / nǚ tóng xìng liàn jù lè bù?*
a club where I can dance?	可以跳舞的俱乐部? *kě yǐ tiào wǔ de jù lè bù?*
a club with Spanish / Mexican music?	有西班牙 / 墨西哥音乐的俱乐部? *yǒu xī bān yá / mò xī gē yīn yuè de jù lè bù?*
the most popular club in town?	本市最热门的俱乐部? *běn shì zuì rè mén de jù lè bù?*

a singles bar?

单身酒吧?

dān shēn jiǔ bā?

a piano bar?

钢琴酒吧?

gāng qín jiǔ bā?

the most upscale club?

最高级的俱乐部?

zuì gāo jí de jù lè bù?

What's the hottest bar these days?

这些天最热闹的酒吧是哪个?

zhè xiē tiān zuì rè nào de jiǔ bā shì nǎ gè?

What's the cover charge?

入场费是多少?

rù chǎng fèi shì duō shǎo?

Do they have a dress code?

有着装规则吗?

yǒu zhuó zhuāng guī zé ma?

Is it expensive?

贵吗?

guì ma?

What's the best time to go?

什么时间去最好?

shén me shí jiān qù zuì hǎo?

What kind of music do they play there?

那里放什么音乐?

nà lǐ fàng shén me yīn yuè?

Is smoking allowed?

允许吸烟吗?

yǔn xǔ xī yān ma?

Is it nonsmoking?

禁止吸烟吗?

jìn zhǐ xī yān ma?

I'm looking for ____

我在找_____

wǒ zài zhǎo _____

a good cigar shop.

好的雪茄店。

hǎo de xuě jiā diàn。

a pack of cigarettes.

一包香烟。

yī bāo xiāng yān。

I'd like ____

我想要_____

wǒ xiǎng yào _____

a drink please.

一杯饮料。

yī bēi yǐn liào。

a bottle of beer please.

一瓶啤酒。

yī píng pí jiǔ。

Do You Mind If I Smoke?

您有香烟吗？
nín yǒu xiāng yān ma?

您有打火机吗？
nín yǒu dǎ huǒ jī ma?

我能帮您点火吗？
wǒ néng bāng nín diǎn huǒ ma?

禁止吸烟。
jìn zhǐ xī yān。

Do you have a cigarette?

Do you have a light?

May I offer you a light?

Smoking not permitted.

NIGHTLIFE

A beer on tap please.

请给我一杯扎啤。
qǐng géi wǒ yī bēi zhā pí。

A shot of ____ please.

请给我一口杯_____。
qǐng géi wǒ yī kǒu bēi _____。

For a full list of drinks, see p75.

Make it a double please!

请烈酒量加倍！
qǐng liè jiǔ liàng jiā bèi!

With ice, please.

请加冰。
qǐng jiā bīng。

And one for the lady / the gentleman!

给这位女士 / 先生一份！
géi zhè wèi nǚ shì / xiān sheng yī fèn!

How much for a bottle / glass of beer?

一瓶 / 杯啤酒多少钱？
yī píng / bēi pí jiǔ duō shǎo qián?

I'd like to buy a drink for that woman / man over there.

我想为那边那位女士/先生买份饮料。
wǒ xiǎng wéi nà biān nà wèi nǚ shì / xiān sheng mǎi fèn yǐn liào。

A pack of cigarettes, please.

请给我一包香烟。
qǐng géi wǒ yī bāo xiāng yān。

Do you have a lighter or matches?

有打火机或火柴吗？
yǒu dǎ huǒ jī huò huǒ chái ma?

Do you smoke?	您吸烟吗？
	nín xī yān ma?
Would you like a cigarette?	您想来支香烟吗？
	nín xiǎng lái zhī xiāng yān ma?
May I run a tab?	可以记帐最后总付吗？
	kě yǐ jì zhàng zuì hòu zǒng fù ma?
What's the cover?	入场费是多少？
	rù chǎng fèi shì duō shǎo?

ACROSS A CROWDED ROOM

Excuse me; may I buy you a drink?	对不起；可以请您喝杯饮料吗？
	duì bù qǐ; kě yǐ qǐng nín hē bēi yǐn liào ma?
You look amazing.	您看上去棒极了。
	nín kàn shàng qù bàng jí le。
You look like the most interesting person in the room.	您看上去是这房间里最有趣的人。
	nín kàn shàng qù shì zhè fáng jiān lǐ zuì yǒu qù de rén。
Would you like to dance?	您想跳舞吗？
	nín xiǎng tiào wǔ ma?
Do you like to dance fast or slow?	您喜欢跳快舞还是慢舞？
	nín xǐ huān tiào kuài wǔ hái shì màn wǔ?

Give me your hand.	把你的手给我。
	bǎ nǐ de shǒu gěi wǒ.
What would you like to drink?	您想喝点什么？
	nín xiǎng hē diǎn shén me?
You're a great dancer.	您舞跳得真棒。
	nín wǔ tiào dé zhēn bàng.
I don't know that dance!	我不会跳那种舞！
	wǒ bú huì tiào nà zhǒng wǔ!
Do you like this song?	你喜欢这首歌吗？
	nǐ xǐ huān zhè shǒu gē ma?
You have nice eyes!	你的眼睛真漂亮！
	nǐ de yǎn jīng zhēn piào liàng!

For a full list of features, see p93.

May I have your phone number?	可以把你的电话号码给我吗？
	kě yǐ bǎ nǐ de diàn huà hào mǎ gěi wǒ ma?

NIGHTLIFE

GETTING CLOSER

You're very attractive.	你很迷人。
	nǐ hěn mí rén.
I like being with you.	我喜欢和你在一起。
	wǒ xǐ huān hé nǐ zài yī qǐ.
I like you.	我喜欢你。
	wǒ xǐ huān nǐ.
I want to hold you.	我想抱抱你。
	wǒ xiǎng bào bào nǐ.

Kiss me.	吻我。
	wěn wǒ。
May I give you ____	我可以给你_____
	wǒ kě yǐ gěi nǐ _____
a hug?	一个拥抱吗？
	yī gè yōng bào ma?
a kiss?	一个吻吧？
	yī gè wěn ba?
Would you like ____	您想要_____
	nín xiǎng yào _____
a back rub?	揉背吗？
	róu bèi ma?
a massage?	按摩吗？
	àn mó ma?

GETTING INTIMATE

Would you like to come inside?	你想进来吗？
	nǐ xiǎng jìn lái ma?
May I come inside?	我可以进来吗？
	wǒ kě yǐ jìn lái ma?
Let me help you out of that.	让我帮你。
	ràng wǒ bāng nǐ。
Would you help me out of this?	你能帮我吗？
	nǐ néng bāng wǒ ma?
You smell so good.	你闻起来好香。
	nǐ wén qǐ lái hǎo xiāng。
You're beautiful / handsome.	你真漂亮 / 英俊。
	nǐ zhēn piào liàng / yīng jùn。
May I?	我可以吗？
	wǒ kě yǐ ma?
OK?	好了吗？
	hǎo le ma?
Like this?	象这样吗？
	xiàng zhè yàng ma?
How?	应该怎么做？
	yīng gāi zěn me zuò?

HOLD ON A SECOND

Please don't do that.	请不要那样做。
	qǐng bù yào nà yàng zuò。
Stop, please.	请停下来。
	qǐng tíng xià lái。
Do you want me to stop?	您要我停下来吗？
	nín yào wǒ tíng xià lái ma？
Let's just be friends.	让我们仅仅做个朋友。
	ràng wǒ mén jǐn jǐn zuò gè péng you。
Do you have a condom?	您有避孕套吗？
	nín yǒu bì yùn tào ma？
Are you on birth control?	您在避孕吗？
	nín zài bì yùn ma？
I have a condom.	我有避孕套。
	wǒ yǒu bì yùn tào。
Do you have anything you should tell me first?	有什么要先告诉我的吗？
	yǒu shén me yào xiān gào sù wǒ de ma？

NIGHTLIFE

BACK TO IT

That's it.	就这样。
	jiù zhè yàng。
That's not it.	不是这样。
	bú shì zhè yàng。
Here.	这里。
	zhè lǐ。
There.	那里。
	nà lǐ。

For a full list of features, see p93.
For a full list of body parts, see p152.

More.	更多。
	gèng duō。
Harder.	再猛烈些。
	zài měng liè xiē。
Faster.	再快些。
	zài kuài xiē。

Deeper.	再深些。
	zài shēn xiē。
Slower.	再慢些。
	zài màn xiē。
Easier.	再温和些。
	zài wēn he xiē。

COOLDOWN

You're great.	您真棒。
	nín zhēn bàng。
That was great.	太好了。
	tài hǎo le。
Would you like ____	您想要_____
	nín xiǎng yào _____
a drink?	一杯饮料吗?
	yī bēi yǐn liào ma?
a snack?	一份小吃吗?
	yī fèn xiǎo chī ma?
a shower?	淋浴吗?
	lín yù ma?
May I stay here?	我可以待在这里吗?
	wǒ kě yǐ dāi zài zhè lǐ ma?
Would you like to stay here?	您想待在这里吗?
	nín xiǎng dāi zài zhè lǐ ma?
I'm sorry. I have to go now.	我很抱歉。我现在必须走。
	wǒ hěn bào qiàn。wǒ xiàn zài bì xū zǒu。
Where are you going?	你去哪里?
	nǐ qù nǎ lǐ?
I have to work early.	我必须早上班。
	wǒ bì xū zǎo shàng bān。
I'm flying home in the morning.	我将在上午乘飞机回家。
	wǒ jiāng zài shàng wǔ chéng fēi jī huí jiā。
I have an early flight.	我得赶早班飞机。
	wǒ déi gǎn zǎo bān fēi jī。

I think this was a mistake.	我认为这是一个错误。
	wǒ rèn wéi zhè shì yí gè cuò wù.
Will you make me breakfast too?	您也会为我做早餐吗？
	nín yě huì wéi wǒ zuò zǎo cān ma?
Stay. I'll make you breakfast.	留下来吧。我为您做早餐。
	liú xià lái ba. wǒ wéi nín zuò zǎo cān.

IN THE CASINO

How much is this table?	这张桌子赌注多少钱？
	zhè zhāng zhuō zǐ dǔ zhù duō shǎo qián?
Deal me in.	让我参加。
	ràng wǒ cān jiā.
Put it on red!	放在红色上！
	fàng zài hóng sè shàng!
Put it on black!	放在黑色上！
	fàng zài hēi sè shàng!
Let it ride!	让它转！
	ràng tā zhuàn!
21!	**21!**
	èr shí yī!
Snake-eyes!	蛇眼！
	shé yǎn!
Seven.	七点。
	qī diǎn.

For a full list of numbers, see p7.

Damn, eleven.	该死，十一点。
	gāi sǐ, shí yī diǎn.
I'll pass.	我不投赌注。
	wǒ bù tóu dǔ zhù.
Hit me!	快转到我这儿！
	kuài zhuàn dào wǒ zhè lǐ!
Split.	分牌。
	fēn pái.

Are the drinks complimentary?	饮料是免费赠送吗?
	yǐn liào shì miǎn fèi zèng sòng ma?
May I bill it to my room?	可以把费用转到我的房费上吗?
	kě yǐ bǎ fèi yòng zhuǎn dào wǒ de fáng fèi shàng ma?
I'd like to cash out.	我想兑现。
	wǒ xiǎng duì xiàn。
I'll hold.	我等一下好了。
	wǒ děng yī xià hǎo le。
I'll see your bet.	我看你赌。
	wǒ kàn nǐ dǔ。
I call.	我指挥。
	wǒ zhǐ huī。
Full house!	满堂彩!
	mǎn táng cǎi!
Royal flush.	同花大顺。
	tóng huā dà shùn。
Straight.	顺子。
	shùn zǐ。

CHAPTER ELEVEN

HEALTH & SAFETY

This chapter covers the terms you'll need to maintain your health and safety—including the most useful phrases for the pharmacy, the doctor's office, and the police station.

AT THE PHARMACY

Please fill this prescription.
请填写这张处方。
qǐng tián xiě zhè zhāng chǔ fāng.

Do you have something for _____
有什么药治_____
yǒu shén me yào zhì _____

  a cold?
  感冒?
  gǎn mào?

  a cough?
  咳嗽?
  ké sou?

I need something _____
我需要一些_____
wǒ xū yào yī xiē _____

  to help me sleep.
  有助于睡眠的药。
  yǒu zhù yú shuì mián de yào.

  to help me relax.
  有助于放松的药。
  yǒu zhù yú fàng sōng de yào.

I want to buy _____
我想买_____
wǒ xiǎng mǎi _____

  condoms.
  避孕套。
  bì yùn tào.

  an antihistamine.
  抗组胺剂。
  kàng zǔ àn jì.

  antibiotic cream.
  抗生素膏。
  kàng shēng sù gāo.

  aspirin.
  阿司匹林。
  ā sī pǐ lín.

  non-aspirin pain reliever.
  非阿司匹林止疼药。
  fēi ā sī pǐ lín zhǐ téng yào.

medicine with codeine.	含可待因的药。
	hán kě dài yīn de yào。
insect repellant.	杀虫剂。
	shā chóng jì。
I need something for ____	我需要一些药治____
	wǒ xū yào yī xiē yào zhì ____
corns.	鸡眼。
	jī yǎn。
congestion.	充血。
	chōng xuè。
warts.	疣。
	yóu。
constipation.	便秘。
	biàn mì。
diarrhea.	腹泻。
	fù xiè。
indigestion.	消化不良。
	xiāo huà bù liáng。
nausea.	反胃。
	fǎn wèi。
motion sickness.	运动病。
	yùn dòng bìng。
seasickness.	晕船。
	yùn chuán。
acne.	痤疮。
	cuó chuāng。

AT THE DOCTOR'S OFFICE

I would like to see ____	我想看____
	wǒ xiǎng kàn ____
a doctor.	医生。
	yī shēng。
a chiropractor.	脊椎指压治疗医生。
	jǐ zhuī zhǐ yā zhì liáo yī shēng。
a gynecologist.	妇科医生。
	fù kē yī shēng。

an eye / ears / nose / throat specialist.	眼 / 耳 / 鼻 / 喉专家。 yǎn / ěr / bí / hóu zhuān jiā。
a dentist.	牙医。 yá yī。
an optometrist.	验光师。 yàn guāng shī。
Do I need an appointment?	我需要预约吗? wǒ xū yào yù yuē ma?
I have an emergency.	我有急诊。 wǒ yǒu jí zhěn。
I need an emergency prescription refill.	我需要一份续急诊处方。 wǒ xū yào yī fèn xù jí zhěn chǔ fāng。
Please call a doctor.	请叫医生。 qǐng jiào yī shēng。
I need an ambulance.	我需要救护车。 wǒ xū yào jiù hù chē。

SYMPTOMS

For a full list of body parts, see p152.

My ____ hurts.	我的_____受伤了。 wǒ de _____ shòu shāng le。
My ____ is stiff.	我的_____僵硬。 wǒ de _____ jiāng yìng。
I think I'm having a heart attack.	我认为我心脏病发作了。 wǒ rèn wéi wǒ xīn zàng bìng fā zuò le。
I can't move.	我不能动。 wǒ bù néng dòng。
I fell.	我跌倒了。 wǒ diē dǎo le。
I fainted.	我晕倒了。 wǒ yūn dǎo le。
I have a cut on my ____.	我的_____上有伤口。 wǒ de _____ shàng yǒu shāng kǒu。

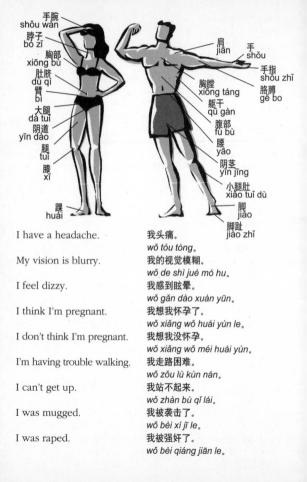

手腕
shǒu wàn

脖子
bó zi

胸部
xiōng bù

肚脐
dù qi

臂
bì

大腿
dà tuǐ

阴道
yīn dào

腿
tuǐ

膝
xī

踝
huái

肩
jiān

手
shǒu

手指
shǒu zhǐ

胳膊
gē bo

胸膛
xiōng táng

躯干
qū gàn

腹部
fù bù

腰
yāo

阴茎
yīn jīng

小腿肚
xiǎo tuǐ dù

脚
jiǎo

脚趾
jiǎo zhǐ

I have a headache.	我头痛。 *wǒ tóu tòng。*
My vision is blurry.	我的视觉模糊。 *wǒ de shì jué mó hu。*
I feel dizzy.	我感到眩晕。 *wǒ gǎn dào xuàn yūn。*
I think I'm pregnant.	我想我怀孕了。 *wǒ xiǎng wǒ huái yùn le。*
I don't think I'm pregnant.	我想我没怀孕。 *wǒ xiǎng wǒ méi huái yùn。*
I'm having trouble walking.	我走路困难。 *wǒ zǒu lù kùn nán。*
I can't get up.	我站不起来。 *wǒ zhàn bù qǐ lái。*
I was mugged.	我被袭击了。 *wǒ bèi xí jī le。*
I was raped.	我被强奸了。 *wǒ bèi qiáng jiān le。*

A dog attacked me.

我被狗咬了。

wǒ bèi gǒu yǎo le。

A snake bit me.

我被蛇咬了。

wǒ bèi shé yǎo le。

I can't move my _____ without pain.

我移动_____时会疼痛。

wǒ yí dòng _____ shí huì téng tòng。

MEDICATIONS

Please fill this prescription.

请按这个处方抓药。

qǐng àn zhè gè chǔ fāng zhuā yào。

I need a prescription for _____

我需要开一剂 _____ 药。

wǒ xū yào kāi yī jì _____ yào。

I need morning-after pills.

我需要一些房事后避孕药。

wǒ xū yào yī xiē fáng shì hòu bì yùn yào。

I need birth control pills.

我需要一些避孕丸。

wǒ xū yào yī xiē bì yùn wán。

I lost my eyeglasses and need new ones.

我弄丢了眼镜，需要配副新的。

wǒ nòng diū le yǎn jìng, xū yào pèi fù xīn de。

I need new contact lenses.

我需要新的隐形眼镜。

wǒ xū yào xīn de yǐn xíng yǎn jìng。

I need erectile dysfunction pills.

我需要一些治疗勃起功能障碍的药。

wǒ xū yào yī xiē zhì liáo bó qǐ gōng néng zhàng ài de yào。

It's cold in here!

这里很冷！

zhè lǐ hěn lěng!

I am allergic to _____

我对_____过敏。

wǒ duì _____ guò mǐn。

penicillin.

青霉素

qīng méi sù

antibiotics.

抗生素

kàng shēng sù

sulfa drugs.

磺胺药

huáng ān yào

steroids.

类固醇

lèi gù chún

I have asthma.	我有哮喘。
	wǒ yǒu xiào chuǎn。

DENTAL PROBLEMS

I have a toothache.	我牙痛。
	wǒ yá téng。
I chipped a tooth.	我一颗牙齿有缺口。
	wǒ yī kuài yá chǐ yǒu quē kǒu。
My bridge came loose.	我的齿桥松了。
	wǒ de chǐ qiáo sōng le。
I lost a crown.	我掉了一个齿冠。
	wǒ diào le yī gè chǐ guàn。
I lost a denture plate.	我掉了一个托牙板。
	wǒ diào le yī gè tuō yá bǎn。

AT THE POLICE STATION

I'm sorry, did I do something wrong?	很抱歉，我做错了什么事吗？
	hěn bào qiàn, wǒ zuò cuò le shén me shì ma?
I am _____	我是_____
	wǒ shì _____
an American.	美国人。
	měi guó rén。
British.	英国人。
	yīng guó rén。
a Canadian.	加拿大人。
	jiā ná dà rén。
Irish.	爱尔兰人。
	ài ěr lán rén。
an Australian.	澳大利亚人。
	ào dà lì yà rén。
a New Zealander.	新西兰人。
	xīn xī lán rén。
The car is a rental.	这车是租来的。
	zhè chē shì zū lái de。

Listen Up: Police Lingo

请出示您的执照、登记文件和保单。 *qǐng chū shì nín de zhí zhào、dēng jì wén jiàn hé bǎo dān。*	Your license, registration and insurance, please.
罚款是 100 人民币。 *fá kuǎn shì yī bǎi rén mín bì。*	The fine is 100 ¥.
请出示您的护照。 *qǐng chū shì nín de hù zhào。*	Your passport please?
您去哪里? *nín qù nǎ lǐ?*	Where are you going?
您为何那么着急? *nín wèi hé nà me zháo jí?*	Why are you in such a hurry?

Do I pay the fine to you?	我付罚款给您吗? *wǒ fù fá kuǎn gěi nín ma?*
Do I have to go to court?	我必须上法庭吗? *wǒ bì xū shàng fǎ tíng ma?*
When?	什么时候? *shén me shí hou?*
I'm sorry, my Chinese isn't very good.	很抱歉,我的汉语不太好。 *hěn bào qiàn, wǒ de hàn yǔ bù tài hǎo。*
I need an interpreter.	我需要一位翻译。 *wǒ xū yào yī wèi fān yì。*
I'm sorry, I don't understand the ticket.	很抱歉,我看不懂这张罚单。 *hěn bào qiàn, wǒ kàn bù dǒng zhè fá dān。*
May I call my embassy?	我可以打电话给我的大使馆吗? *wǒ kě yǐ dǎ diàn huà gěi wǒ de dà shǐ guǎn ma?*
I was robbed.	我被抢劫了。 *wǒ bèi qiǎng jié le。*

I was mugged.	我被袭击了。
	wǒ bèi xí jī le.
I was raped.	我被强奸了。
	wǒ bèi qiáng jiān le.
Do I need to make a report?	我需要做份报告吗?
	wǒ xū yào zuò fèn bào gào ma?
Somebody broke into my room.	有人闯入了我的房间。
	yǒu rén chuǎng rù le wǒ de fáng jiān.
Someone stole my purse / wallet.	有人偷了我的钱包 / 钱夹。
	yǒu rén tōu le wǒ de qián bāo / qián jiā.

DICTIONARY KEY

n	名词 *míng cí*	v	动词 *dòng cí*
adj	形容词 *xíng róng cí*	prep	介词 *jiè cí*
adv	副词 *fù cí*	pron	代词 *dài cí*

Chinese verbs are not conjugated. Here, they are listed in their most basic form. To form tenses, see p26.

For food terms, see the Menu Reader (p77) and Grocery section (p82) in Chapter 4, Dining.

A

able, to be able to (can) v 能够 *néng gòu*

above *adj* 上面的 *shàng miàn de*

accept, to accept v 接受 *jiē shòu*

Do you accept credit cards? 可以用信用卡吗? *kě yǐ yòng xìn yòng kǎ ma?*

accident n 交通事故 *jiāo tōng shì gù*

I've had an accident. 我出了事故。 *wǒ chū le shì gù.*

account n 账户 *zhàng hù*

I'd like to transfer to / from my checking / savings account. 我想转帐到我的支票账户 / 储蓄账户。/ 我想从我的支票账户 / 储蓄账户转帐。 *wǒ xiǎng zhuǎn zhàng dào wǒ de zhī piào zhàng hù / chǔ xù zhàng hù。 / wǒ xiǎng cóng wǒ de zhī piào zhàng hù / chǔ xù zhàng hù zhuān zhàng。*

acne n 痤疮 *cuó chuāng*

across prep 在...对面 *zài ...duì miàn*

across the street 在街道对面 *zài jiē dào duì miàn*

actual *adj* 实际的 *shí jì de*

adapter plug n 适配器插头 *shì pèi qì chā tóu*

address n 地址 *dì zhǐ*

What's the address? 地址是什么? *dì zhǐ shì shén me?*

admission fee n 门票 *mén piào*

in advance 提前 *tí qián*

African-American *adj* 非裔美国人 *fēi yì měi guó rén*

afternoon n 下午 *xià wǔ*

in the afternoon 在下午 *zài xià wǔ*

age n 年龄 *nián líng*

What's your age? 您多大了？
nín duō dà le?

agency n 代理处 *dài lǐ chù*

car rental agency 汽车租赁公
司 *qì chē zū lìn gōng sī*

agnostic adj 不可知论 *bù kě
zhī lùn*

air conditioning n 空调 *kōng
tiáo*

**Would you lower / raise the
air conditioning?** 您能调低 /
调高空调温度吗？ *nín néng
tiáo dī / tiáogāo kōng tiáo
wēn dù ma?*

airport n 机场 *jī chǎng*

I need a ride to the airport.
我需要乘车到机场。 *wǒ xū
yào chéng chē dào jī chǎng。*

**How far is it from the
airport?** 离机场有多远？ *lí jī
chǎng yǒu duō yuǎn?*

airsickness bag n 晕机呕吐袋
yūn jī ǒu tù dài

aisle (in store) n 过道（商店里）
guò dào (shāng diàn lǐ)

Which aisle is it in? 它在哪一
过道？ *tā zài nǎ yī guò dào?*

alarm clock n 闹钟 *nào zhōng*

alcohol n 酒精饮料 *jiǔ jīng yǐn
liào*

Do you serve alcohol? 您提
供酒精饮料吗？ *nín tí gōng jiǔ
jīng yǐn liào ma?*

I'd like nonalcoholic beer. 我
想要不含酒精的啤酒。 *wǒ
xiǎng yào bù hán jiǔ jīng de
pí jiǔ。*

all n 全部 *quán bù*

all adj 所有的 *suǒ yǒu de*

all of the time 一直 *yī zhí*

That's all, thank you. 就那些，
谢谢您。 *jiù nà xiē, xiè xiè nín。*

allergic adj 过敏的 *guò mǐn de*

I'm allergic to ____. 我对____
____过敏。 *wǒ duì ____ guò
mǐn。 See p74 and 153 for
common allergens.*

altitude n 海拔 *hǎi bá*

aluminum n 铝 *lǚ*

ambulance n 救护车 *jiù hù chē*

American adj 美国的 *měi guó de*

amount n 数量 *shù liàng*

angry adj 生气的 *shēng qì de*

animal n 动物 *dòng wù*

another adj 另外的 *lìng wài de*

answer n 答案 *dá àn*

**answer, to answer (phone call,
question)** v 回答 *huí dá p26*

Answer me, please. 请回答
我。 *qǐng huí dá wǒ。*

antibiotic n 抗生素 *kàng
shēng sù*

I need an antibiotic. 我需要抗生素。 wǒ xū yào kàng shēng sù。

antihistamine n 抗组胺剂 kàng zǔ àn jì

anxious adj 焦虑的 jiāo lù de

any adj 任何的 rèn hé de

anything n 任何事 rèn hé shì

anywhere adv 任何地方 rèn hé dì fāng

April n 四月 sì yuè

appointment n 约定 yuē dìng

Do I need an appointment? 我需要预约吗? wǒ xū yào yù yuē ma?

are v See be, to be.

Argentinian adj 阿根廷的 ā gēn tíng de

arm n 胳膊 gē bo

arrive, to arrive v 到达 dào dá

arrival(s) n 到达 dào dá

art n 艺术品 yì shù pǐn

exhibit of art 艺术品展览 yì shù pǐn zhǎn lǎn **See for art types.**

art adj 艺术的 yì shù de

art museum 艺术博物馆 yì shù bó wù guǎn

artist n 艺术家 yì shù jiā

Asian adj 亚洲的 yà zhōu de

ask for (request) v 请求 qǐng qiú

ask a question v 问一个问题 wèn yī gè wèn tí

aspirin n 阿司匹林 ā sī pǐ lín

assist v 援助 yuán zhù

assistance n 援助 yuán zhù

asthma n 哮喘 xiāo chuǎn

I have asthma. 我有哮喘。 wǒ yǒu xiāo chuǎn。

atheist adj 无神论的 wú shén-lùn de

ATM n 自动取款机 zì dòng qǔ kuǎn jǐ

I'm looking for an ATM. 我在找自动取款机。 wǒ zài zhǎo zì dòng qǔ kuǎn jǐ。

attend v 参加 cān jiā

audio adj 音频的 yīn pín de

August n 八月 bā yuè

aunt n 姑妈 gū mā

Australia n 澳大利亚 ào dà lì yà

Australian adj 澳大利亚的 ào dà lì yà de

autumn n 秋天 qiū tiān

available adj 可得的 kě dé de

B

baby n 婴儿 yīng ér

baby adj 婴儿的 yīng ér de

Do you sell baby food? 卖婴儿食品吗? mài yīng ér shí pǐn ma?

babysitter n 临时照看幼儿者 *lín shí zhào kàn yòu ér zhě*

Do you have babysitters who speak English? 有会说英语的临时照看幼儿者吗? *yǒu huì shuō yīng yǔ de lín shí zhào kàn yòu ér zhě ma?*

back n 背部 *bèi bù*

My back hurts. 我的背部受伤了。 *wǒ de bèi bù shòu shāng le。*

back rub n 揉背 *róu bèi*

backed up (toilet) adj 堵着的（马桶）*dǔ zhe de (mǎ tǒng)*

The toilet is backed up. 马桶堵上了。 *mǎ tǒng dǔ shàng le。*

bag n 袋子 *dài zǐ*

airsickness bag 晕机呕吐袋 *yūn jǐ ǒu tù dài*

My bag was stolen. 我的袋子被偷了。 *wǒ de dài zǐ bèi tōu le。*

I lost my bag. 我的袋子丢了。 *wǒ de dài zǐ diū le。*

bag v 袋子 *dài zǐ*

baggage n 行李 *xíng li*

baggage adj 行李的 *xíng li de*

baggage claim 行李领取处 *xíng li lǐng qǔ chǔ*

bait n 饵 *ěr*

balance (on bank account) n （银行账户上的）余额 *(yín háng zhàng hù shàng de) yú é*

balance v 平衡 *píng héng*

balcony n 阳台 *yáng tái*

ball (sport) n 球（运动）*qiú (yùn dòng)*

ballroom dancing n 交际舞 *jiāo jì wǔ*

band (musical ensemble) n 乐队（音乐团体）*yuè duì (yīn yuè tuán tǐ)*

band-aid n 创可贴 *chuàng kě tiē*

bank n 银行 *yín háng*

Can you help me find a bank? 您能帮我找家银行吗? *nín néng bāng wǒ zhǎo jiā yín háng ma?*

bar n 酒吧 *jiǔ bā*

barber n 理发师 *lǐ fā shī*

bass (instrument) n 贝司（乐器）*bèi sī (yuè qì)*

bath n 洗澡 *xǐ zǎo*

bathroom (restroom) n 卫生间 *wèi shēng jiān*

Where is the nearest public bathroom? 最近的公共卫生间在哪里? *zuì jìn de gōng gòng wèi shēng jiān zài nǎ lǐ?*

bathtub n 浴缸 *yù gāng*

bathe, to bathe oneself v 沐浴 *mù yù*

battery (for flashlight) n 电池（手电筒使用的）*diàn chí (shǒu diàn tǒng shǐ yòng de)*

battery (for car) n 蓄电池（汽车使用的）xù diàn chí (qì chē shǐ yòng de)

bee n 蜜蜂 mì fēng

I was stung by a bee. 我被蜜蜂蛰了。wǒ bèi mì fēng zhé le。

be, to be (temporary state, condition, mood) v 处于 chǔ yú

be, to be (permanent quality) v 是 shì

beach n 海滩 hǎi tān

beach v 拖上岸 tuō shàng àn

beard n 胡子 hú zǐ

beautiful adj 漂亮的 piào liang de

bed n 床 chuáng

beer n 啤酒 pí jiǔ

beer on tap 扎啤 zhā pí

begin v 开始 kāi shǐ

behave v 举动 jǔ dòng

behind adv 在...后面 zài...hòu miàn

below adv 在...下面 zài...xià miàn

belt n 带 dài

conveyor belt 传送带 chuán sòng dài

berth n 停泊处 tíng bó chù

best 最好的 zuì hǎo de

bet, to bet v 打赌 dǎ dǔ

better 更好 gèng hǎo

big adj 大的 dà de

bilingual adj 双语的 shuāng yǔ de

bill (currency) n 票据 piào jù

bill v 纸币 zhǐ bì

biography n 传记 zhuàn jì

biracial adj 混杂种族人 hùn zá zhǒng zú rén

bird n 小鸟 xiǎo niǎo

birth control n 避孕 bì yùn

birth control adj 避孕的 bì yùn de

I'm out of birth control pills. 我没有避孕药丸了。wǒ méi yǒu bì yùn yào wán le。

I need more birth control pills. 我需要更多的避孕药丸。wǒ xū yào gèng duō de bì yùn yào wán。

bit (small amount) n 少量 shǎo liàng

black adj 黑色的 hēi sè de

blanket n 毛毯 máo tǎn

bleach n 漂白剂 piǎo bái jì

blind adj 盲的 máng de

block v 阻塞 zǔ sè

blond(e) adj 金发的 jīn fà de

blouse n 宽松上衣 kuān sōng shàng yī

blue adj 蓝色的 lán sè de

blurry adj 模糊的 mó hu de

board *n* 舱内 *cāng nèi*

on board 在飞机上 *zài fēi jǐ shàng*

board *v* 上飞机 *shàng fēi jǐ*

boarding pass *n* 登机牌 *dēng jǐ pái*

boat *n* 小船 *xiǎo chuán*

Bolivian *adj* 玻利维亚的 *bō lì wéi yà de*

bomb *n* 炸弹 *zhà dàn*

book *n* 书 *shū*

bookstore *n* 书店 *shū diàn*

boss *n* 老板 *lǎo bǎn*

bottle *n* 瓶子 *píng zǐ*

May I heat this (baby) bottle someplace? 有地方可以给奶瓶加热吗? *yǒu dì fāng kě yǐ gěi nǎi píng jiā rè ma?*

box (seat) *n* 包厢 *bāo xiāng*

box office *n* 售票处 *shòu piào chù*

boy *n* 男孩 *nán hái*

boyfriend *n* 男朋友 *nán péng yǒu*

braid *n* 发辫 *fà biàn*

braille, American *n* 美国盲人 *měi guó máng rén*

brake *n* 刹车 *shā chē*

emergency brake 紧急刹车 *jǐn jí shā chē*

brake *v* 刹车 *shā chē*

brandy *n* 白兰地 *bái lán dì*

bread *n* 面包 *miàn bāo*

break *v* 打断 *dǎ duàn*

breakfast *n* 早餐 *zǎo cān*

What time is breakfast? 早餐时间是几点? *zǎo cān shí jiān shì jǐ diǎn?*

bridge (across a river, dental) *n* 桥（横跨河两岸, 牙齿结构） *qiáo (héng kuà hé liǎng àn, yá chǐ jié gòu)*

briefcase *n* 公文包 *gōng wén bāo*

bright *adj* 明亮的 *míng liàng de*

broadband *n* 宽带 *kuān dài*

bronze *adj* 青铜色的 *qīng tóng sè de*

brother *n* 兄弟 *xiōng di*

brown *adj* 棕色的 *zōng sè de*

brunette *n* 黑发女孩 *hēi fà nǚ hái*

Buddhist *n* 佛教徒 *fó jiào tú*

budget *n* 预算 *yù suàn*

buffet *n* 自助餐 *zì zhù cān*

bug *n* 虫子 *chóng zǐ*

bull *n* 公牛 *gōng niú*

bullfight *n* 斗牛 *dòu niú*

bullfighter *n* 斗牛士 *dòu niú shì*

burn *v* 刻录 *kè lù*

Can I burn a CD here? 我能在这里刻张 CD 吗? *wǒ néng zài zhè lǐ kè zhāng CD ma?*

bus *n* 公共汽车 *gōng gòng qì chē*

Where is the bus stop? 公共汽车站在哪里？ gōng gòng qì chē zhàn zài nǎ lǐ?

Which bus goes to ____? 哪班公共汽车到_____？ nǎ bān gōng gòng qì chē dào _____?

business n 商业 shāng yè

business adj 商业的 shāng yè de

business center 商业中心 shāng yè zhōng xīn

busy adj 忙碌的 máng lù de （饭店）(fàn diàn) 占线的 zhàn xiàn de（电话）(diàn huà)

butter n 黄油 huáng yóu

buy, to buy v 买 mǎi

C

café n 咖啡馆？ kā fēi guǎn?

Internet café 网吧 wǎng bā

call, to call v 呼叫 hū jiào（喊）(hǎn) 打电话 dǎ diàn huà（电话）(diàn huà)

camp, to camp v 露营 lù yíng

camper n 露营者 lù yíng zhě

camping adj 露营的 lù yíng de

Do we need a camping permit? 我们需要露营许可吗？ wǒ mén xū yào lù yíng xǔ kě ma?

campsite n 露营地 lù yíng dì

can n 罐头 guàn tóu

can (able to) v 能 néng

Canada n 加拿大 jiā ná dà

Canadian adj 加拿大的 jiā ná dà de

cancel, to cancel v 取消 qǔ xiāo

My flight was canceled. 我的航班被取消了。 wǒ de háng bān bèi qǔ xiāo le。

canvas n 画布 huà bù（用于画画）(yòngyú huàhuà)，帆布 fān bù（布）(bù liào)

cappuccino n 卡普契诺咖啡 kǎ pǔ qì nuò kā fēi

car n 小汽车 xiǎo qì chē

car rental agency 汽车租赁公司 qì chē zū lìn gōng sī

I need a rental car. 我需要租一辆小汽车。 wǒ xū yào zū yī liàng xiǎo qì chē。

card n 卡 kǎ

Do you accept credit cards? 可以用信用卡吗？ kě yǐ yòng xìn yòng kǎ ma?

May I have your business card? 可以给我您的名片吗？ kě yǐ gěi wǒ nín de míng piàn ma?

car seat (child's safety seat) n 汽车座位（儿童的安全座位） qì chē zuò wèi (ér tóng de ān quán zuò wèi)

Do you rent car seats for children? 您租童用汽车座位吗? nín zū tóng yòng qì chē zuò wèi ma?

carsickness n 晕车 yùn chē

cash n 现金 xiàn jīn

cash only 只收现金 zhǐ shōu xiàn jīn

cash, to cash v 兑现 duì xiàn

to cash out (gambling) 兑现 (赌博) duì xiàn (dǔ bó)

cashmere n 羊绒衫 yáng róng shān

casino n 赌场 dǔ chǎng

cat n 猫 māo

Catholic adj 天主教的 tiān zhǔ jiào de

cavity (tooth cavity) n 蛀洞 (牙洞) zhù dòng (yá dòng)

I think I have a cavity. 我想我的牙齿有蛀洞了。wǒ xiǎng wǒ de yá chǐ yǒu zhù dòng le.

CD n CD

CD player n CD 播放器 CD bō fàng qì

celebrate, to celebrate v 庆祝 qìng zhù

cell phone n 移动电话 yí dòng diàn huà

centimeter n 厘米 lí mǐ

chamber music n 室内乐 shì nèi yuè

change (money) n 零钱 líng qián

I'd like change, please. 请给我找零钱。qǐng gěi wǒ zhǎo líng qián.

This isn't the correct change. 找的零钱不对。zhǎo de líng qián bù duì.

change (to change money, clothes) v 换 (换钱、衣服) huàn (huàn qián, yī fu)

changing room n 更衣室 gèng yī shì

charge, to charge (money) v 收钱 shōu qián

charge, to charge (a battery) v 充电 chōng diàn

charmed adj 幸会 xìng huì

charred (meat) adj 烤焦的 (肉) kǎo jiāo de (ròu)

charter, to charter v 包 (船) bāo (chuán)

cheap adj 便宜的 pián yi de

check n 支票 zhī piào

May I use traveler's check? 可以用旅行支票吗? kě yǐ yòng lǚ xíng zhī piào ma?

check, to check v 托运 tuō yùn

checked (pattern) adj 选中的 (样式) xuǎn zhōng de (yàng shì)

check-in n 办登机手续 bàn dēng jī shǒu xù

What time is check-in? 什么时间办登记手续? shén me shí jiān bàn dēng jì shǒu xù?

check-out n 退房 tuì fáng

check-out time 退房时间 tuì fáng shí jiān

What time is check-out? 什么时间退房? shén me shí jiān tuì fáng?

check out, to check out v 退房 tuì fáng

cheese n 奶酪 nǎi lào

chicken n 鸡肉 jī ròu

child n 儿童 ér tóng

children n 儿童 ér tóng

Are children allowed? 小孩可以吗? xiǎo hái kě yǐ ma?

Do you have children's programs? 有小孩的节目吗? yǒu xiǎo hái de jié mù ma?

Do you have a children's menu? 有小孩的菜单吗? yǒu xiǎo hái de cài dān ma?

Chinese adj 中国的 zhōng guó de

chiropractor n 脊椎指压治疗者 jī zhuī zhǐ yā zhì liáo zhě

church n 教堂 jiào táng

cigar n 雪茄 xuě jiā

cigarette n 香烟 xiāng yān

a pack of cigarettes 一包香烟 yī bāo xiāng yān

cinema n 电影院 diàn yǐng yuàn

city n 城市 chéng shì

claim n 索赔 suǒ péi

I'd like to file a claim. 我想提出索赔。 wǒ xiǎng tí chū suǒ péi.

clarinet n 竖笛 shù dí

class n 等级 děng jí

business class 商务舱 shāng wù cāng

economy class 经济舱 jīng jì cāng

first class 头等舱 tóu děng cāng

classical (music) adj 古典的（音乐）gǔ diǎn de (yīn yuè)

clean adj 干净的 gàn jing de

clean, to clean v 打扫 dǎ sǎo

Please clean the room today. 今天请打扫房间。 jīn tiān qíng dǎ sǎo fáng jiān。

clear v 清晰的 qīng xī de

clear adj 清澈的 qīng chè de

climbing n 攀登 pān dēng

climb, to climb v 爬 pá

to climb a mountain 爬山 pá shān

to climb stairs 爬楼梯 pá lóu tī

close, to close v 关闭 guān bì

close (near) 靠近的 kào jìn de

closed adj 靠近的 kào jìn de

cloudy adj 多云的 duō yún de

clover n 三叶草 sān yè cǎo

go clubbing, to go clubbing v 露营 lù yíng

coat n 外套 wài tào

cockfight n 斗鸡 dòu jī

coffee n 咖啡 kā fēi

iced coffee 冰咖啡 bīng kā fēi

cognac n 法国白兰地酒 fǎ guó bái lán dì jiǔ

coin n 硬币 yìng bì

cold n 冷 lěng

I have a cold. 我感冒了。 wǒ gǎn mào le.

cold adj 冷的 lěng de

I'm cold. 我很冷。 wǒ hěn lěng.

It's cold out. 外边很冷。 wài biān hěn lěng.

coliseum n 音乐厅 yīn yuè tīng

collect adj 由对方付费的 yóu duì fāng fù fèi de

I'd like to place a collect call. 我想打一个对方付费电话。 wǒ xiǎng dǎ yī gè duì fāng fù fèi diàn huà.

collect, to collect v 收集 shōu jí

college n 大学 dà xué

Colombian adj 哥伦比亚的 gē lún bǐ yà de

color n 颜色 yán sè

color v 变色 biàn sè

computer n 计算机 jì suàn jī

concert n 音乐会 yīn yuè huì

condition n 条件 tiáo jiàn

in good / bad condition 情形 很好 / 差 qíng xíng hěn hǎo / chà

condom n 避孕套 bì yùn tào

Do you have a condom? 您有 避孕套吗? nín yǒu bì yùn tào ma?

not without a condom 没有 避孕套不行 méi yǒu bì yùn tào bù xíng

condor n 秃鹰 tū yīng

confirm, to confirm v 确认 què rèn

I'd like to confirm my reservation. 我想确认我的预 定。 wǒ xiǎng què rèn wǒ de yù dìng.

confused adj 困惑的 kùn huò de

congested adj 拥挤的 yōng jǐ de

connection speed n 连接速度 lián jiē sù dù

constipated adj 患便秘的 huàn biàn mì de

I'm constipated. 我便秘了。 wǒ biàn mì le.

contact lens n 隐形眼镜 yǐn xíng yǎn jìng

I lost my contact lens. 我的隐 形眼镜丢了。 wǒ de yǐn xíng yǎn jìng diū le.

continue, to continue v 继续 jì xù

convertible *n* 兑换 duì huàn

cook, to cook *v* 烹饪 pēng rèn

> **I'd like a room where I can cook.** 我要一间能做饭的房间。 wǒ yào yī jiān néng zuò fàn de fáng jiān。

cookie *n* 小甜饼 xiǎo tián bǐng

copper *adj* 铜的 tóng de

corner *n* 角落 jiǎo luò

> **on the corner** 在角落 zài jiǎo luò

correct *v* 纠正 jiū zhèng

correct *adj* 正确的 zhèng què de

> **Am I on the correct train?** 我乘的火车对吗? wǒ chéng de huǒ chē duì ma?

cost, to cost *v* 花费 huā fèi

> **How much does it cost?** 那得花多少钱? nà dé huā duō shǎo qián?

Costa Rican *adj* 哥斯达黎加 gē sī dá lí jiā

costume *n* 装束 zhuāng shù

cotton *n* 棉线 mián xiàn

cough *n* 咳嗽 ké sou

cough *v* 咳嗽 ké sou

counter (in bar) *n* 吧台 bā tái

country-and-western *n* 乡村音乐 xiāng cūn yīn yuè

court (legal) *n* 法院 fǎ yuàn

court (sport) *n* 球场（运动）qiú chǎng (yùn dòng)

courteous *adj* 有礼貌的 yǒu lǐ mào de

cousin *n* 姑妈 gū mā

cover charge (in bar) *n* 入场最低消费（酒吧）rù chǎng zuì dī xiāo fèi (jiǔ bā)

cow *n* 母牛 mǔ niú

crack (in glass object) *n* 裂缝（玻璃品上）liè féng (bō li pǐn shàng)

craftsperson *n* 手艺人 shǒu yì rén

cream *n* 奶油 nǎi yóu

credit card *n* 信用卡 xìn yòng kǎ

> **Do you accept credit cards?** 可以用信用卡吗? kě yǐ yòng xìn yòng kǎ ma?

crib *n* 婴儿床 yīng ér chuáng

crown (dental) *n* 齿冠（牙科）chǐ guàn (yá kē)

curb *n* 围栏 wéi lán

curl *n* 卷发 juǎn fà

curly *adj* 卷发的 juǎn fà de

currency exchange *n* 货币兑换处 huò bì duì huàn chù

> **Where is the nearest currency exchange?** 最近的货币兑换处在哪儿? zuì jìn de huò bì duì huàn chù zài nǎ er?

current (water) *n* 流（水）liú (shuǐ)

customs n 海关 hǎi guān

cut (wound) n 伤口 shāng kǒu

> **I have a bad cut.** 我有一个很严重的伤口。wǒ yǒu yī gè hěn yán zhòng de shāng kǒu。

cut, to cut v 切 qiē

cybercafé n 网吧 wǎng bā

> **Where can I find a cybercafé?** 哪里有网吧? nǎ lǐ yǒu wǎng bā?

D

damaged adj 损坏的 sǔn huài de

Damn! expletive 该死! gāi sǐ!

dance v 跳舞 tiào wǔ

danger n 危险 wēi xiǎn

dark n 黑暗 hēi àn

dark adj 黑色的 hēi sè de

daughter n 女儿 nǚ ér

day n 天 tiān

> **the day before yesterday** 前天 qián tiān

> **these last few days** 最后这些日子 zuì hòu zhè xiē rì zǐ

dawn n 黎明 lí míng

> **at dawn** 在黎明 zài lí míng

deaf adj 聋的 lóng de

deal (bargain) n 交易 jiāo yì

> **What a great deal!** 这笔交易真划算! zhè bǐ jiāo yì zhēn huá suàn!

deal (cards) v 发牌 fā pái

> **Deal me in.** 让我参加进来。ràng wǒ cān jiā jìn lái。

December n 十二月 shí èr yuè

declined adj 拒付的 jù fù de

> **Was my credit card declined?** 我的信用卡被拒付了吗? wǒ de xìn yòng kǎ bèi jù fù le ma?

behave v 申报 shēn bào

> **I have nothing to declare.** 我没有要申报的东西。wǒ méi yǒu yào shēn bào de dōng xi。

deep adj 深的 shēn de

delay n 延误 yán wù

> **How long is the delay?** 延误时间有多长? yán wù shí jiān yǒu duō cháng?

delighted adj 高兴的 gāo xīng de

democracy n 民主主义 mín zhǔ zhǔ yì

dent v 凹进 āo jìn

> **He / She dented the car.** 他/她把车撞凹了。tā/tā bǎ chē zhuàng āo le。

dentist n 牙医 yá yī

denture n 假牙 jiǎ yá

> **denture plate** 托牙板 tuō yá bǎn

departure n 离开 lí kāi

designer n 设计师 shè jì shī

dessert n 餐后甜点 cān hòu tián diǎn

ENGLISH—CHINESE

dessert menu 餐后甜点菜单 *cān hòu tián diǎn cài dān*

destination *n* 目的地 *mù dì dì*

diabetic *adj* 糖尿病的 *táng niào bìng de*

dial (a phone) *v* 拨（电话）*bō (diàn huà)*

dial direct 直拨 *zhí bō*

diaper *n* 尿布 *niào bù*

Where can I change a diaper? 在哪里可以换尿布? *zài nǎ lǐ kě yǐ huàn niào bù?*

diarrhea *n* 痢疾 *lì jí*

dictionary *n* 词典 *cí diǎn*

different (other) *adj* 不同的（其它的）*bù tóng de (qí tā de)*

difficult *adj* 困难的 *kùn nán de*

dinner *n* 晚餐 *wǎn cān*

directory assistance (phone) *n* 查号服务（电话）*chá hào fú wù (diàn huà)*

disability *n* 残疾 *cán ji*

disappear *v* 消失 *xiāo shī*

disco *n* 迪士高 *dí shì gāo*

disconnected *adj* 断线 *duàn xiàn*

Operator, I was disconnected. 接线员，我的电话断了。*jiē xiàn yuán, wǒ de diàn huà duàn le.*

discount *n* 折扣 *zhé kòu*

Do I qualify for a discount? 我有资格获得折扣吗? *wǒ yǒu zī gé huò dé zhé kòu ma?*

dish *n* 盘子 *pán zi*

dive *v* 潜水 *qián shuǐ*

scuba dive 水肺潜水 *shuǐ fèi qián shuǐ*

divorced *adj* 离异的 *lí yì de*

dizzy *adj* 晕眩的 *yūn xuàn de*

do, to do *v* 做 *zuò*

doctor *n* 医生 *yī shēng*

doctor's office *n* 医生办公室 *yī shēng bàn gōng shì*

dog *n* 狗 *gǒu*

service dog 帮助犬 *bāng zhù quǎn*

dollar *n* 美元 *měi yuán*

door *n* 门 *mén*

double *adj* 双倍的 *shuāng bèi de*

double bed 双人床 *shuāng rén chuáng*

double vision 双瞳 *shuāng tóng*

down *adj* 下面的 *xià miàn de*

download *v* 下载 *xià zǎi*

downtown *n* 市区 *shì qū*

dozen *n* 一打 *yī dá*

drain *n* 消耗 *xiāo hào*

drama *n* 戏剧 *xì jù*

drawing (work of art) *n* 图画（艺术品）*tú huà (yì shù pǐn)*

dress (garment) *n* 服装 *fú zhuāng*

dress (general attire) *n* 礼服 *lǐ fú*

What's the dress code? 有什么着装规则? yǒu shén me zhuó zhuāng guī zé?

dress v 穿衣 chuān yī

Should I dress up for that affair. 这次活动, 我需要穿正装吗? zhè cì huó dòng, wǒ xū yào chuān zhèng zhuāng ma?

dressing (salad) n 调味品 (沙拉) tiáo wèi pǐn (shā lā)

dried adj 干的 gān de

drink n 饮料 yǐn liào

I'd like a drink. 我想要杯饮料。 wǒ xiǎng yào bēi yǐn liào.

drink, to drink v 喝 hē

drip v 滴下 dī xià

drive v 驾驶 jià shǐ

driver n 司机 sī jī

driving range n 高尔夫球练习场 gāo ěr fū qiú liàn xí chǎng

drum n 鼓 gǔ

dry adj 干的 gān de

This towel isn't dry. 这条毛巾不干。 zhè tiáo máo jīn bù gān.

dry, to dry v 使干燥 shǐ gān zào

I need to dry my clothes. 我需要烘干我的衣服。 wǒ xū yào hōng gān wǒ de yī fu.

dry cleaner n 干洗店 gān xǐ diàn

dry cleaning n 干洗 gān xǐ

duck n 鸭子 yā zǐ

duty-free adj 免税 miǎn shuì

duty-free shop n 免税商店 miǎn shuì shāng diàn

DVD n DVD

Do the rooms have DVD players? 房间有 DVD 播放器吗? fáng jiān yǒu DVD bō fàng qì ma?

Where can I rent DVDs or videos? 哪里可以租到 DVD 或录像带? nǎ lǐ kě yǐ zū dào DVD huò lù xiàng dài?

E

early adj 早的 zǎo de

It's early. 时间还早。 shí jiān hái zǎo.

eat v 吃 chī

to eat out 去馆子吃饭 qù guǎn zǐ chī fàn

economy n 经济 jīng jì

Ecuadorian adj 厄瓜多尔的 è guā duō ěr de

editor n 编辑 biān jí

educator n 教育工作者 jiào yù gōng zuò zhě

eight n 八 bā

eighteen n 十八 shí bā

eighth n 第八 dì bā

eighty n 八十 bā shí

election n 选举 xuǎn jǔ

electrical hookup *n* 电线板 *diàn xiàn bǎn*

elevator *n* 电梯 *diàn tī*

eleven *n* 十一 *shí yī*

e-mail *n* 电子邮件 *diàn zǐ yóu jiàn*

May I have your e-mail address? 可以给我您的电子邮件地址吗? *kě yǐ gěi wǒ nín de diàn zǐ yóu jiàn dì zhǐ ma?*

e-mail message 电子邮件消息 *diàn zǐ yóu jiàn xiāo xi*

e-mail, to send e-mail *v* 发送电子邮件 *fā sòng diàn zǐ yóu jiàn*

embarrassed *adj* 尴尬的 *gān gà de*

embassy *n* 大使馆 *dà shǐ guǎn*

emergency *n* 紧急情况 *jǐn jí qíng kuàng*

emergency brake *n* 紧急刹车 *jǐn jí shā chē*

emergency exit *n* 紧急出口 *jǐn jí chū kǒu*

employee *n* 雇员 *gù yuán*

employer *n* 雇主 *gù zhǔ*

engine *n* 引擎 *yǐn qíng*

engineer *n* 工程师 *gōng chéng shī*

England *n* 英格兰 *yīng gé lán*

English *n, adj* 英国的 *yīng guó de*

Do you speak English? 您说英语吗? *nín shuō yīng yǔ ma?*

enjoy, to enjoy *v* 享受 *xiǎng shòu*

enter, to enter *v* 进入 *jìn rù*

Do not enter. 不准进入。 *bù zhǔn jìn rù.*

enthusiastic *adj* 热情的 *rè qíng de*

entrance *n* 入口 *rù kǒu*

envelope *n* 信封 *xìn fēng*

environment *n* 环境 *huán jìng*

escalator *n* 电动扶梯 *diàn dòng fú tī*

espresso *n* 浓咖啡 *nóng kā fēi*

exchange rate *n* 汇率 *huì lǜ*

What is the exchange rate for US / Canadian dollars? 美国 / 加拿大元的兑换率是多少? *měi guó / jiā ná dà yuán de duì huàn lǜ shì duō shǎo?*

excuse (pardon) *v* 原谅 *yuán liàng*

Excuse me. 对不起。 *duì bù qǐ.*

exhausted *adj* 疲惫的 *pí bèi de*

exhibit *n* 展览 *zhǎn lǎn*

exit *n* 出口 *chū kǒu*

not an exit 非出口 *fēi chū kǒu*

exit *v* 退出 *tuì chū*

expensive *adj* 昂贵的 *áng guì de*

explain *v* 解释 *jiě shì*

express *adj* 急速的 *jí sù de*

express check-in 快办登机手续 *kuài bàn dēng jǐ shǒu xù*

extra (additional) *adj* 额外的 *é wài de*

extra-large *adj* 超大的 *chāo dà de*

eye *n* 眼睛 *yǎn jīng*

eyebrow *n* 眉毛 *méi mao*

eyeglasses *n* 眼镜 *yǎn jìng*

eyelash *n* 睫毛 *jié máo*

F

fabric *n* 纤维 *xiān wéi*

face *n* 脸 *liǎn*

faint *v* 晕倒 *yūn dǎo*

fall (season) *n* 秋季 *qiū jì*

fall *v* 倒下 *dǎo xià*

family *n* 家人 *jiā rén*

fan *n* 扇子 *shàn zi*

far 远的 *yuǎn de*

How far is it to _____? 到_____有多远? *dào _____ yǒu duō yuǎn?*

fare *n* 费用 *fèi yòng*

fast *adj* 快的 *kuài de*

fat *adj* 胖的 *pàng de*

father *n* 父亲 *fù qīn*

faucet *n* 龙头 *lóng tóu*

fault *n* 过错 *guò cuò*

I'm at fault. 我是过错方。 *wǒ shì guò cuò fāng。*

It was his fault. 是他的过错。 *shì tā de guò cuò。*

fax *n* 传真 *chuán zhēn*

February *n* 二月 *èr yuè*

fee *n* 费 *fèi*

female *adj* 女性的 *nǚ xìng de*

fiancé(e) *n* 新娘 *xīn niáng*

fifteen *adj* 十五 *shí wǔ*

fifth *adj* 第五 *dì wǔ*

fifty *adj* 五十 *wǔ shí*

find *v* 发现 *fā xiàn*

fine (for traffic violation) *n* 罚款（交通违规）*fá kuǎn (jiāo tōng wéi guī)*

fine 好的 *hǎo de*

I'm fine. 我很好。 *wǒ hěn hǎo。*

fire! *n* 火 *huǒ*

first *adj* 第一的 *dì yī de*

fishing pole *n* 鱼竿 *yú gān*

fitness center *n* 健身中心 *jiàn shēn zhōng xīn*

fit (clothes) *v* 合身（衣服）*hé shēn (yī fu)*

Does this look like it fits? 这件看上去合身吗? *zhè jiàn kàn shàng qù hé shēn ma?*

fitting room *n* 试衣间 *shì yī jiān*

five *adj* 五 *wǔ*

flight *n* 航班 *háng bān*

Where do domestic flights arrive / depart? 国内航班在哪里到达 / 离开? guó nèi háng bān zài nǎ lǐ dào dá / lí kāi?

Where do international flights arrive / depart? 国际航班在哪里到达 / 离开? guó jì háng bān zài nǎ lǐ dào dá / lí kāi?

What time does this flight leave? 这架航班什么时候起飞? zhè jià háng bān shén me shí hou qǐ fēi?

flight attendant 航班服务员 háng bān fú wù yuán

floor n 层 céng

ground floor 底层 dǐ céng
second floor 二楼 èr lóu

flower n 花 huā

flush (gambling) n 顺子（赌博）shùn zǐ (dǔ bó)

flush, to flush v 冲刷 chōng shuā

This toilet won't flush. 马桶无法冲水。mǎ tǒng wú fǎ chōng shuǐ。

flute n 长笛 cháng dí

food n 食物 shí wù

foot (body part, measurement) n 脚、尺 jiǎo、chǐ

forehead n 前额 qián é

formula n 配方 pèi fāng

Do you sell infants' formula? 卖婴儿配方奶粉吗? mài yīng ér pèi fāng nǎi fēn ma?

forty adj 四十 sì shí

forward adj 向前 xiàng qián

four adj 四 sì

fourteen adj 十四 shí sì

fourth adj 第四 dì sì

one-fourth 四分之一 sì fēn zhī yī

fragile adj 易碎的 yì suì de

freckle n 雀斑 què bān

French adj 法国的 fǎ guó de

fresh adj 新鲜的 xīn xiān de

Friday n 星期五 xīng qī wǔ

friend n 朋友 péng you

front adj 前面的 qián miàn de

front desk 前台 qián tái
front door 前门 qián mén

fruit n 水果 shuǐ guǒ

fruit juice n 果汁 guǒ zhī

full, to be full (after a meal) adj 饱的 bǎo de

Full house! n 满堂彩 mǎn táng cǎi

fuse n 保险丝 bǎo xiǎn sī

G

gallon n 加仑 jiā lún

garlic n 大蒜 dà suàn

gas n 汽油 qì yóu

gas gauge 油表 *yóu biǎos*

out of gas 没油了 *méi yóu le*

gate (at airport) *n* 登机口（在机场）*dēng jī kǒu (zài jī chǎng)*

German *adj* 德国的 *dé guó de*

gift *n* 礼物 *lǐ wù*

gin *n* 杜松子酒 *dù sōng zǐ jiǔ*

girl *n* 女孩 *nǚ hái*

girlfriend *n* 女朋友 *nǚ péng yōu*

give, to give *v* 给 *gěi*

glass *n* 玻璃杯 *bō li bēi*

Do you have it by the glass? 是用玻璃杯喝吗? *shì yòng bō li bēi hē ma?*

I'd like a glass please. 请给我来一杯。*qǐng gěi wǒ lái yī bēi.*

glasses (eye) *n* 眼镜 *yǎnjing*

I need new glasses. 我需要配副新眼镜。*wǒ xū yào pèi fù xīn yǎn jing.*

glove *n* 手套 *shǒu tào*

go, to go *v* 去 *qù*

goal (sport) *n* 得分（运动）*dé fēn (yùn dòng)*

goalie *n* 守门员 *shǒu mén yuán*

gold *adj* 金色的 *jīn sè de*

golf *n* 高尔夫球 *gāo ěr fū qiú*

golf, to go golfing *v* 打高尔夫球 *dǎ gāo ěr fū qiú*

good *adj* 好的 *hǎo de*

goodbye *n* 再见 *zài jiàn*

grade (school) *n* 年级（学校）*nián jí (xué xiào)*

gram *n* 克 *kè*

grandfather *n* 祖父 *zǔ fù*

grandmother *n* 祖母 *zǔ mǔ*

grandparent *n* 祖父母 *zǔ fù mǔ*

grape *n* 葡萄 *pú tao*

gray *adj* 灰色的 *huī sè de*

great *adj* 美妙的 *měi miào de*

Greek *adj* 希腊的 *xī là de*

Greek Orthodox *adj* 希腊正教的 *xī là zhèng jiào de*

green *adj* 绿色的 *lǜ sè de*

groceries *n* 杂货 *zá huò*

group *n* 团体 *tuán tǐ*

grow, to grow (get larger) *v* 增长 *zēng cháng*

Where did you grow up? 您在哪里长大? *nín zài nǎ lǐ cháng dà?*

guard *n* 保安 *bǎo ān*

security guard 保安 *bǎo ān*

Guatemalan *adj* 危地马拉的 *wēi dì mǎ lā de*

guest *n* 客人 *kè rén*

guide (of tours) *n* 导游 *dǎo yóu*

guide (publication) *n* 指南（出版物）*zhǐ nán (chū bǎn wù)*

guide, to guide *v* 指导 *zhǐ dǎo*

guided tour *n* 配导游的旅游 *pèi dǎo yóu de lǚ yóu*

ENGLISH—CHINESE

guitar n 吉他 jí tā

gym n 体育馆 tǐ yù guǎn

gynecologist n 妇科医生 fù kē yī shēng

H

hair n 头发 tóu fa

haircut n 理发 lǐ fà

I need a haircut. 我需要理发。wǒ xū yào lǐ fà。

How much is a haircut? 理发多少钱? lǐ fà duō shǎo qián?

hairdresser n 美容师 měi róng shī

hair dryer n 吹风机 chuī fēng jī

half n 半个 bàn gè

one-half 二分之一 èr fēn zhī yī

hallway n 走廊 zǒu láng

hand n 手 shǒu

handicapped-accessible adj 残疾人可用的 cán jí rén kě yòng de

handle, to handle v 处理 chǔ lǐ

handsome adj 英俊的 yīng jùn de

hangout (hot spot) n 逛街（热闹的市区）guàng jiē (rè nào de shì qū)

hang out (to relax) v 逛街（休息）guàng jiē (xiū xi)

hang up (to end a phone call) v 挂断电话（结束通话）guà duàn diàn huà (jié shù tōng huà)

hanger n 衣架 yī jià

happy adj 快乐的 kuài lè de

hard adj 艰难的牢固的 jiān nán de láo gù de

hat n 帽子 mào zi

have v 有 yǒu

hazel adj 淡褐色的 dàn hè sè de

headache n 头痛 tóu tòng

headlight n 前灯 qián dēng

headphones n 耳机 ěr jī

hear v 听见 tīng jiàn

hearing-impaired adj 听障的 tīng zhàng de

heart n 心脏 xīn zàng

heart attack n 心脏病 xīn zàng bìng

hectare n 公顷 gōng qǐng

hello n 您好 nín hǎo

Help! n 帮帮我！bāng bāng wǒ!

help, to help v 帮助 bāng zhù

hen n 母鸡 mǔ jī

her adj 她的 tā de

herb n 药草 yào cǎo

here n 这里 zhè lǐ

high adj 高的 gāo de

highlights (hair) n挑染（头发）tiáo rǎn (tóu fa)

highway n高速公路 gāo sù gōng lù

hike, to hike v远足 yuǎn zú

him pron他 tā

Hindu adj印度教的 yìn dù jiào de

hip-hop n街舞 jiē wǔ

his adj他的 tā de

historical adj历史性的 lì shǐ xìng de

history n历史 lì shǐ

hobby n爱好 ài hǎo

hold, to hold v握着 wò zhe

to hold hands牵手 qiān shǒu

Would you hold this for me? 能帮我拿着这个吗? néng bāng wǒ ná zhe zhè gè ma?

hold, to hold (to pause) v暂停 zàn tíng

Hold on a minute! 稍等！shāo děng!

I'll hold. 我等一下好了。wǒ děng yī xià hǎo le。

hold, to hold (gambling) v握着（赌博）wò zhe (dǔ bó)

holiday n假期 jià qī

home n家 jiā

homemaker n家庭主妇 jiā tíng zhǔ fù

Honduran adj洪都拉斯的 hóng dōu lā sī de

horn n角 jiǎo

horse n马 mǎ

hostel n旅社 lǚ shè

hot adj热的 rè de

hot chocolate n热巧克力 rè qiǎo kè lì

hotel n酒店 jiǔ diàn

Do you have a list of local hotels? 您有当地酒店的名单吗? nín yǒu dāng dì jiǔ diàn de míng dān ma?

hour n时间 shí jiān

hours (at museum) n开放时间（博物馆）kāi fàng shí jiān (bó wù guǎn)

how adv多少 duō shǎo

humid adj潮湿的 cháo shī de

hundred n百 bǎi

hurry v赶紧 gǎn jǐn

I'm in a hurry. 我很着急。wǒ hěn zháo jí。

Hurry, please! 请快点！qǐng kuài diǎn!

hurt, to hurt v伤害 shāng hài

Ouch! That hurts! 哎哟！很痛！āi yō! hěn tòng!

husband n丈夫 zhàng fū

I

I pron我 wǒ

ice n冰 bīng

identification n证明 zhèng míng

inch n 英寸 yīng cùn

indigestion n 消化不良 xiāo huà bùl iáng

inexpensive adj 便宜的 pián yi de

infant n 幼儿 yòu ér

Are infants allowed? 幼儿可以吗? yòu ér kěyǐ ma ?

information n 信息 xìn xī

information booth n 信息亭 xìn xī tíng

injury n 伤害 shāng hài

insect repellent n 杀虫剂 shā chóng jì

inside 里边的 lǐ biān de

insult v 侮辱 wǔ rǔ

insurance n 保险 bǎo xiǎn

intercourse (sexual) n 性交 xìng jiāo

interest rate n 利率 lì lǜ

intermission n 兑换 duì huàn

Internet n 网络 wǎng luò

High-speed Internet 高速网络 gāo sù wǎng luò

Do you have Internet access? 可以上网吗? kě yǐ shàng wǎng ma?

Where can I find an Internet café? 哪里有网吧? nǎ lǐ yǒu wǎng bā?

interpreter n 口译人员 kǒu yì rén yuán

I need an interpreter. 我需要一位口译人员。 wǒ xū yào yī wèi kǒu yì rén yuán 。

introduce, to introduce v 介绍 jiè shào

I'd like to introduce you to ____. 我想把你介绍给——。 wǒ xiǎng bǎ nǐ jiè shào gěi____。

Ireland n 爱尔兰 ài ěr lán

Irish adj 爱尔兰的 ài ěr lán de

is v See be (to be)

Italian adj 意大利的 yì dà lì de

J

jacket n 夹克衫 jiā kè shān

January n 一月 yī yuè

Japanese adj 日本的 rì běn de

jazz n 爵士乐 jué shì yuè

Jewish adj 犹太教的 yóu tài jiào de

jog, to run v 慢跑 màn pǎo

juice n 汁 zhī

June n 六月 liù yuè

July n 七月 qī yuè

K

keep, to keep v 保持 bǎo chí

kid n 小孩 xiǎo hái

Are kids allowed? 小孩可以吗? xiǎo hái kě yǐ ma?

Do you have children's programs? 有小孩的节目吗? *yǒu xiǎo hái de jiémù ma?*

Do you have a kids' menu? 有小孩的菜单吗? *yǒu xiǎo hái de cài dān ma?*

kilo *n* 千 *qiān*

kilometer *n* 千米 *qiān mǐ*

kind *n* 种类 *zhǒng lèi*

What kind is it? 这是哪一种? *zhè shì nǎ yī zhǒng?*

kiss *n* 吻 *wěn*

kitchen *n* 厨房 *chú fáng*

know, to know (something) *v* 知道（某事）*zhī dao (mǒu shì)*

know, to know (someone) *v* 认识（某人）*rèn shí (mǒurén)*

kosher *adj* 犹太教的 *yóu tài jiào de*

L

lactose-intolerant *adj* 忌乳糖的 *jì rǔ táng de*

land, to land *v* 着陆 *zhuó lù*

landscape *n* 风景 *fēng jǐng*

language *n* 语言 *yǔ yán*

laptop *n* 笔记本电脑 *bǐ jì běn diàn nǎo*

large *adj* 大的 *dà de*

last, to last *v* 持续 *chí xù*

last *adv* 最后 *zuì hòu*

late *adj* 晚的 *wǎn de*

Please don't be late. 请不要晚了。*qǐng bù yào wǎn le。*

later *adv* 后来 *hòu lái*

See you later. 回头见。*huí tóu jiàn。*

laundry *n* 洗衣店 *xǐ yī diàn*

lavender *adj* 淡紫色的 *dàn zǐ sè de*

law *n* 法律 *fǎ lǜ*

lawyer *n* 律师 *lǜ shī*

least *n* 至少 *zhì shǎo*

least *adj* 最少的 *zuì shǎo de*

leather *n* 皮革 *pí gé*

leave, to leave (depart) *v* 离开 *lí kāi*

left *adj* 左边的 *zuǒ biān de*

on the left 在左边 *zài zuǒ biān*

leg *n* 腿 *tuǐ*

lemonade *n* 柠檬水 *níng méng shuǐ*

less *adj* 少的 *shǎo de*

lesson *n* 课程 *kè chéng*

license *n* 执照 *zhí zhào*

driver's license 驾驶执照 *jià shǐ zhí zhào*

life preserver *n* 救生用具 *jiù shēng yòng jù*

light *n* (lamp) 灯 *d ng*

light (for cigarette) *n* 打火机 *dǎ huǒ jī*

May I offer you a light? *n* 借个火好吗? *jiè gè huǒ hǎo ma?*

like, desire *v* 渴望 *kě wàng*

I would like _____. 我想要——。 *wǒ xiǎng yào _____。*

like, to like *v* 喜欢 *xǐ huān*

I like this place. 我喜欢这个地方。 *wǒ xǐ huān zhè gè dì fāng。*

limo *n* 豪华大巴 *háo huá dà bā*

liquor *n* 白酒 *bái jiǔ*

liter *n* 升 *shēng*

little *adj* 小的（尺寸）少的（数量）*xiǎo de (chǐ cùn) shǎo de (shù liàng)*

live, to live *v* 居住 *jū zhù* p23

Where do you live? 您住在哪里? *nín zhù zài nǎ lǐ?*

living *n* 生活 *shēng huó*

What do you do for a living? 您是做什么工作的? *nín shì zuò shén me gōng zuò de?*

local *adj* 本地 *běn dì*

lock *n* 锁 *suǒ*

lock, to lock *v* 锁上 *suǒ shàng*

I can't lock the door. 我锁不上门。 *wǒ suǒ bù shàng mén。*

I'm locked out. 我被锁在门外了。 *wǒ bèi suǒ zài mén wài le。*

locker *n* 存物柜 *cún wù guì*

storage locker 储藏柜 *chǔ cáng guì*

locker room 存物室 *cún wù shì*

long *adv* 长期地 *cháng qī dì*

For how long? 多长时间? *duō cháng shí jiān?*

long *adj* 长期的 *cháng qī de*

look, to look *v* (to observe) 观看 *guān kàn*

I'm just looking. 我只是看看。 *wǒ zhǐ shì kàn kàn。*

Look here! 看这里！ *kàn zhè lǐ！*

look, to look *v* (to appear) 显得 *xiǎn dé*

How does this look? 这看起来怎么样? *zhè kàn qǐ lái zěn me yàng?*

look for, to look for (to search) *v* 寻找 *xún zhǎo*

I'm looking for a porter. 我在找搬运工。 *wǒ zài zhǎo bān yùn gōng。*

loose *adj* 松的 *sōng de*

lose, to lose *v* 遗失 *yí shī*

I lost my passport. 我的护照丢了。 *wǒ de hùzhào diū le。*

I lost my wallet. 我的钱夹丢了。 *wǒ de qián jiā diū le。*

I'm lost. 我迷路了。 *wǒ mí lù le。*

loud *adj* 大声的

loudly adv 大声地 dà shēng de

lounge n 休息室 xiū xī shì

lounge, to lounge v 闲荡 xián dàng

love n 爱 ài

love, to love v 爱 ài

to love (family) 爱家庭 ài jiā tíng

to love (a friend) 爱朋友 ài péng you

to love (a lover) 爱情人 ài qíng rén

to make love 做爱 zuò ài

low adj 低的 dī de

lunch n 午餐 wǔ cān

luggage n 行李 xíng li

Where do I report lost luggage? 我到哪里报告丢失了行李? wǒ dào nǎ lǐ bào gào diū shī le xíng li?

Where is the lost luggage claim? 丢失行李领取处在哪里? diū shī xíng li lǐng qǔ chǔzài nǎ lǐ?

M

machine n 机器 jī qì

made of adj 组成的 zǔ chéng de

magazine n 杂志 zá zhì

maid (hotel) n 女仆（酒店）nǚ pú (jiǔ diàn)

maiden adj 未婚的 wèi hūn de

That's my maiden name. 那是我的娘家姓。nà shì wǒ de niáng jia xìng。

mail n 邮件 yóu jiàn

air mail 航空邮件 háng kōng yóu jiàn

registered mail 挂号邮件 guà hào yóu jiàn

mail v 邮寄 yóu jì

make, to make v 制造 zhì zào

makeup n 组成 zǔ chéng

make up, to make up (apologize) v 和解（抱歉）hé jiě (bàoqiàn)

make up, to make up (apply cosmetics) v 化妆（用化妆品）huà zhuāng (yòng huà zhuāng pǐn)

male n 男性 nán xìng

male adj 男性的 nán xìng de

mall n 购物中心 gòu wù zhōng xīn

man n 男人 nán rén

manager n 经理 jīng lǐ

manual (instruction booklet) n 手册 shǒu cè

many adj 许多的 xǔ duō de

map n 地图 dì tú

March (month) n 三月 sān yuè

market n 市场 shì chǎng

flea market 跳蚤市场 tiào zǎo shì chǎng

open-air market 露天市场 *lù tiān shì chǎng*

married *adj* 已婚的 *yǐ hūn de*

marry, to marry *v* 结婚 *jié hūn*

massage, to massage *v* 按摩 *àn mó*

match (sport) *n* 比赛（运动）*bǐ sài (yùndòng)*

match *n* 比赛 *bǐ sài*

book of matches 一包火柴 *yī bāo huǒ chái*

match, to match *v* 匹配 *pǐ pèi*

Does this ____ match my outfit? ____和我的衣服搭配吗? ____ *hé wǒ de yīfu dā pèi ma?*

May (month) *n* 五月 *wǔ yuè*

may *v aux* 可能 *kě néng*

May I ____? 我可以____吗? *wǒ kě yǐ ____ ma?*

meal *n* 膳食 *shàn shí*

meat *n* 肉 *ròu*

meatball *n* 肉丸子 *ròu wán zī*

medication *n* 药物 *yào wù*

medium (size) *adj* 中（号）*zhōng (hào)*

medium rare (meat) *adj* 四分熟的（肉）*sì fēn shú de (ròu)*

medium well (meat) *adj* 七分熟的（肉）*qī fēn shú de (ròu)*

member *n* 成员 *chéng yuán*

menu *n* 菜单 *cài dān*

May I see a menu? 我可以看一下菜单吗? *wǒ kě yǐ kàn yī xià cài dān ma?*

children's menu 儿童菜单 *ér tóng cài dān*

diabetic menu 糖尿病人菜单 *táng niào bìng rén cài dān*

kosher menu 犹太教徒菜单 *yóu tài jiào tú cài dān*

metal detector *n* 金属探测器 *jīn shǔ tàn cè qì*

meter *n* 米 *mǐ*

Mexican *adj* 墨西哥的 *mò xī gē de*

middle *adj* 中间的 *zhōng jiān de*

midnight *n* 午夜 *wǔ yè*

mile *n* 英里 *yīng lǐ*

military *n* 军事 *jūn shì*

milk *n* 牛奶 *niú nǎi*

milk shake 奶昔 *nǎi xī*

milliliter *n* 毫升 *háo shēng*

millimeter *n* 毫米 *háo mǐ*

minute *n* 分钟 *fēn zhōng*

in a minute 马上 *mǎ shàng*

miss, to miss (a flight) *v* 错过（航班）*cuò guò (háng bān)*

missing *adj* 丢失的 *diū shī de*

mistake *n* 错误 *cuò wù*

moderately priced *adj* 价格适中的 *jià gé shì zhōng de*

mole (facial feature) *n* 痣（脸部特征）zhì (liǎn bù tè zhēng)

Monday *n* 星期一 xīng qī yī

money *n* 金钱 jīn qián

money transfer 转帐 zhuǎn zhàng

month *n* 月 yuè

morning *n* 早晨 zǎo chén

in the morning 在早晨 zài zǎo chén

mosque *n* 清真寺 qīng zhēn sì

mother *n* 母亲 mǔ qīn

mother, to mother *v* 生育 shēng yù

motorcycle *n* 摩托车 mó tuō chē

mountain *n* 山 shān

mountain climbing 爬山 pá shān

mouse *n* 老鼠 lǎo shǔ

mouth *n* 嘴 zuǐ

move, to move *v* 移动 yí dòng

movie *n* 电影 diàn yǐng

much *n* 许多 xǔ duō

mug, to mug (someone) *v* 袭击 xí jī

mugged *adj* 受袭击的 shòu xí jī de

museum *n* 博物馆 bó wù guǎn

music *n* 音乐 yīn yuè

live music 现场音乐 xiàn chǎng yīn yuè

musician *n* 音乐家 yīn yuè jiā

muslim *adj* 穆斯林的 mù sī lín de

mustache *n* 胡子 hú zǐ

mystery (novel) *n* 神秘故事 shén mì gù shì

N

name *n* 名字 míng zi

My name is ___. 我叫_____。 wǒ jiào _____。

What's your name? 您叫什么名字? nín jiào shén me míng zi?

napkin *n* 纸巾 zhǐ jīn

narrow *adj* 狭窄的 xiá zhǎi de

nationality *n* 民族 mín zú

nausea *n* 晕船 yùn chuán

near *adj* 靠近的 kào jìn de

nearby *adj* 靠近的 kào jìn de

neat (tidy) *adj* 干净的 gànjìng de

need, to need *v* 需要 xū yào

neighbor *n* 邻居 lín jū

nephew *n* 侄子 zhí zǐ

network *n* 网络 wǎng luò

new *adj* 新的 xīn de

newspaper *n* 报纸 bào zhǐ

newsstand *n* 报亭 bào tíng

New Zealand n 新西兰 xīn xī lán

New Zealander adj 新西兰的 xīn xī lán de

next prep 紧邻地 jǐn lín de

next to 靠近 kào jìn

the next station 下一站 xià yī zhàn

Nicaraguan adj 尼加拉瓜的 ní jiā lā guā de

nice adj 美好的 měi hǎo de

niece n 侄女 zhí nǚ

night n 夜晚 yè wǎn

at night 在夜晚 zài yè wǎn

per night 每夜 měi yè

nightclub n 夜总会 yè zǒng huì

nine adj 九 jiǔ

nineteen adj 十九 shí jiǔ

ninety adj 九十 jiǔ shí

ninth adj 第九 dì jiǔ

no adv 不 bù

noisy adj 噪杂的 zào zá de

none n 没人 méi rén

nonsmoking adj 禁止吸烟的 jìn zhǐ xī yān de

nonsmoking area 禁烟区 jìn yān qū

nonsmoking room 禁烟房间 jìn yān fáng jiān

noon n 中午 zhōng wǔ

nose n 鼻子 bí zǐ

novel n 小说 xiǎo shuō

November n 十一月 shí yī yuè

now adv 现在 xiàn zài

number n 数字 shù zì

Which room number? 哪一房间号? nǎ yī fáng jiān hào?

May I have your phone number? 可以给我您的电话号码吗? kě yǐ gěi wǒ nín de diàn huà hào mǎ ma?

nurse n 护士 hù shì

nurse v 看护 kān hù

Do you have a place where I can nurse? 有地方我可以喂奶吗? yǒu dì fāng wǒ kě yǐ wèi nǎi ma?

nursery n 托儿所 tuō ér suǒ

Do you have a nursery? 您这儿有托儿所吗? nín zhè ér yǒu tuō ér suǒ ma?

nut n 坚果 jiān guǒ

O

o'clock adv 点钟 diǎn zhōng

two o'clock 两点钟 liǎng diǎn zhōng

October n 十月 shí yuè

offer, to offer v 提供 tí gōng

officer n 军官 jūn guān

oil n 油 yóu

okay adv 好 hǎo

old adj 老的 lǎo de

olive n 橄榄色 gǎn lǎn sè

one *adj* 一个的 *yī gè de*

one way (traffic sign) *adj* 单行线（交通标志）*dān xíng xiàn (jiāo tōng biāo zhì)*

open (business) *adj* 营业中 *yíng yè zhōng*

Are you open? 在营业吗? *zài yíng yè ma ?*

opera *n* 歌剧 *gē jù*

operator (phone) *n* 接线员 *jiē xiàn yuán*

optometrist *n* 验光师 *yàn guāng shī*

orange (color) *adj* 橙色 *chéng sè*

orange juice *n* 橙汁 *chéng zhī*

order, to order (demand) *v* 命令 *mìng lìng*

order, to order (request) *v* 要求 *yāo qiú*

organic *adj* 有机的 *yǒu jī de*

Ouch! *interj* 哎唷！*āi yō!*

outside *n* 外面 *wài miàn*

overcooked *adj* 煮得过久的 *zhǔ dé guò jiǔ de*

overheat, to overheat *v* 过热 *guò rè*

The car overheated. 车变得过热了。*chē biàn dé guò rè le.*

overflowing *adv* 溢出 *yì chū*

oxygen tank *n* 氧气罐 *yǎng qì guàn*

P

package *n* 包裹 *bāo guǒ*

pacifier *n* 抚慰者 *fǔ wèi zhě*

page, to page (someone) *v* 呼叫（某人）*hū jiào (mǒu rén)*

paint, to paint *v* 绘画 *huì huà*

painting *n* 油画 *yóu huà*

pale *adj* 苍白的 *cāng bái de*

Panamanian *adj* 巴拿马的 *bā ná mǎ de*

paper *n* 纸 *zhǐ*

parade *n* 游行 *yóu xíng*

Paraguayan *adj* 巴拉圭的 *bā lā guī de*

parent *n* 父母 *fù mǔ*

park *n* 公园 *gōng yuán*

park, to park *v* 停放 *tíng fàng*

no parking 禁止停车 *jìn zhǐ tíng chē*

parking fee 停车费 *tíng chē fèi*

parking garage 停车场 *tíng chē chǎng*

partner *n* 伙伴 *huǒ bàn*

party *n* 政党 *zhèng dǎng*

party *n* 党派 *dǎng pai*

political party 政党 *zhèng dǎng*

pass, to pass *v* 通过 *tōng guò*

I'll pass. 我会过关的。*wǒ huì guòguān de.*

passenger *n* 乘客 *chéng kè*

passport n 护照 hù zhào

I've lost my passport. 我的护照丢了。wǒ de hù zhào diū le.

pay, to pay v 支付 zhī fù

peanut n 花生 huā shēng

pedestrian adj 徒步的 tú bù de

pediatrician n 儿科医师 ér kē yī shī

Can you recommend a pediatrician? 您能推荐一位儿科医师吗? nín néng tuī jiàn yī wèi ér kē yī shī ma?

permit n 许可证 xǔ kě zhèng

Do we need a permit? 我们需要许可证吗? wǒmén xū yào xǔkě zhèng ma?

permit, to permit v 允许 yǔn xǔ

Peruvian adj 秘鲁的 mì lǔ de

phone n 电话机 diàn huà jī

May I have your phone number? 可以给我您的电话号码吗? kěyǐ gěi wǒ nín de diàn huà hào mǎ ma?

Where can I find a public phone? 哪里有公用电话? nǎ lǐ yǒu gōng yòng diàn huà?

phone operator 电话接线员 diàn huà jiē xiàn yuán

Do you sell prepaid phones? 卖预付费电话吗? mài yù fù fèi diàn huà ma?

phone adj 电话 diàn huà

Do you have a phone directory? 您有电话号码黄页吗? nín yǒu diàn huà hào mǎ huáng yè ma?

phone call n 电话 diàn huà

I need to make a collect phone call. 我需要打一个对方付费电话。wǒ xū yào dǎ yī gè duì fāng fù fèi diàn huà.

an international phone call 一个国际电话 yī gè guó jì diàn huà

photocopy, to photocopy v 影印 yǐng yìn

piano n 钢琴 gāng qín

pillow n 枕头 zhěn tóu

down pillow 羽绒枕 yǔ róng zhěn

pink adj 粉红色的 fěn hóng sè de

pint n 品脱 pǐn tuō

pizza n 比萨 bǐ sà

place, to place v 放置 fàng zhì

plastic n 塑料 sù liào

play n 游戏 yóu xì

play, to play (a game) v 进行比赛 jìn xíng bǐ sài

play, to play (an instrument) v 演奏 yǎn zòu

playground n 运动场 yùn dòng chǎng

Do you have a playground? 有运动场吗? yǒu yùn dòng chǎng ma?

please (polite entreaty) *adv* 请
（礼貌的请求）qǐng (lǐ mào
de qǐng qiú)

please, to be pleasing to *v* 使
愉快 shǐ yú kuài

pleasure *n* 愉快 yú kuài

It's a pleasure. 见到您很高兴。
jiàn dào nín hěn gāo xīng.

plug *n* 插头 chā tóu

plug, to plug *v* 插上 chā shàng

point, to point *v* 指出 zhǐ chū

Would you point me in the
direction of____? 您能为我
指出＿＿＿＿的方向吗? nín
néng wéi wǒ zhǐ chū ＿＿＿＿
de fāng xiàng ma?

police *n* 警察 jǐng chá

police station *n* 警察局 jǐng chá
jú

pool *n* 台球 tái qiú

pool (the game) *n* 台球（游戏）
tái qiú (yóu xi)

pop music *n* 流行音乐 liú xíng
yīn yuè

popular *adj* 受欢迎的 shòu
huān yíng de

port (beverage) *n* 波尔图葡萄
酒 bō ěr tú pú táo jiǔ

port (for ship) *n* 港口 gǎng kǒu

porter *n* 搬运工人 bān yùn
gōng rén

portion *n* 一部分 yī bù fēn

portrait *n* 肖像 xiāo xiàng

postcard *n* 明信片 míng xìn
piàn

post office *n* 邮局 yóu jú

Where is the post office? 哪
里有邮局? nǎ lǐ yǒu yóu jú?

poultry *n* 家禽 jiā qín

pound *n* 磅 páng

prefer, to prefer *v* 更喜欢 gèng
xǐ huān

pregnant *adj* 怀孕的 huái yùn
de

prepared *adj* 准备好的 zhǔn bèi
hǎo de

prescription *n* 处方 chǔ fāng

price *n* 价格 jià gé

print, to print *v* 打印 dǎ yìn

private berth / cabin *n* 私人泊
位 / 舱 sī rén bó wèi / cāng

problem *n* 难题 nán tí

process, to process *v* 处理
chǔ lǐ

product *n* 产品 chǎn pǐn

professional *adj* 专业的 zhuān
yè de

program *n* 节目单 jié mù dān

May I have a program? 可以
给我一份节目单吗? kě yǐ gěi
wǒ yī fèn jié mù dān ma?

Protestant *n* 新教徒 xīn jiào tú

publisher *n* 发行人 fā xíng rén

Puerto Rican *adj* 波多黎各的 bō
duō lí gè de

ENGLISH—CHINESE

pull, to pull v 拉 lā

pump n 泵 bèng

purple adj 紫色的 zǐ sè de

purse n 钱包 qián bāo

push, to push v 推 tuī

put, to put v 放 fàng

Q

quarter adj 四分之一的 sì fēn zhī yī de

one-quarter 四分之一 sì fēn zhī yī

quiet adj 安静的 ān jìng de

R

rabbit n 兔子 tù zǐ

radio n 无线电广播 wú xiàn diàn guǎng bō

satellite radio 卫星广播 wèi xīng guǎng bō

rain, to rain v 下雨 xià yǔ

Is it supposed to rain? 天会下雨吗? tiān huì xià yǔ ma?

rainy adj 多雨的 duō yǔ de

It's rainy. 天在下雨。 tiān zài xià yǔ。

ramp, wheelchair n 坡道 pō dào

rare (meat) adj 三分熟的 (肉) sān fēn shú de (ròu)

rate (for car rental, hotel) n 费用 fèi yòng

What's the rate per day? 每天的费用是多少? měi tiān de fèi yòng shì duō shǎo?

What's the rate per week? 每周的费用是多少? měi zhōu de fèi yòng shì duō shǎo?

rate plan (cell phone) n 收费计划（移动电话）shōu fèi jì huà (yí dòng diàn huà)

rather adv 相当 xiāng dāng

read, to read v 读 dú

really adv 真正地 zhēn zhèng dì

receipt n 收据 shōu jù

receive, to receive v 收到 shōu dào

recommend, to recommend v 推荐 tuī jiàn

red adj 红色的 hóng sè de

redhead n 红头发 hóng tóu fa

reef n 帆 fān

refill (of beverage) n 再斟满 zài zhēn mǎn

refill (of prescription) n 续处方 xù chǔ fāng

reggae adj 瑞格舞的 ruì gé wǔ de

relative (family) n 亲属 qīn shǔ

remove, to remove v 移动 yí dòng

rent, to rent v 租用 zū yòng

I'd like to rent a car. 我想租一辆车。 wǒ xiǎng zū yī liàng chē。

repeat, to repeat v 重复
chóng fù

Would you please repeat that? 请您再重复一遍好吗?
qǐng nín zài chóng fù yī biàn hǎo ma?

reservation n 预定 *yù dìng*

I'd like to make a reservation for ____. 我想预定____。
wǒ xiǎng yù dìng ____.
See p7 for numbers.

restaurant n 饭店 *fàn diàn*

Where can I find a good restaurant? 哪里有好的饭店? *nǎ lǐ yǒu hǎo de fàn diàn?*

restroom n 洗手间 *xǐ shǒu jiān*

Do you have a public restroom? 有公共洗手间吗?
yǒu gōng gòng xǐ shǒu jiān ma?

return, to return (to a place) v 返回 *fǎn huí*

return, to return (something to a store) v 退货 *tuì huò*

ride, to ride v 乘 *chéng*

right adj 右边的 *yòu biān de*

It is on the right. 在右边。*zài yòu biān.*

Turn right at the corner. 在拐角处右转。*zài guǎi jiǎo chù yòu zhuǎn.*

rights n pl 权利 *quán lì*

civil rights 民权 *mín quán*

river n 河 *hé*

road n 道路 *dào lù*

road closed sign n 道路封闭标志 *dào lù fēng bì biāo zhì*

rob, to rob v 抢夺 *qiǎng duó*

I've been robbed. 我被抢了。
wǒ bèi qiǎng le.

rock and roll n 摇滚 *yáo gǔn*

rock climbing n 攀岩 *pān yán*

rocks (ice) n 冰块 *bīng kuài*

I'd like it on the rocks. 我想加上冰块。*wǒ xiǎng jiā shàng bīng kuài.*

romance (novel) n 爱情小说 *ài qíng xiǎo shuō*

romantic adj 浪漫的 *làng màn de*

room (hotel) n 客房（酒店）*kè fáng (jiǔ diàn)*

room for one / two 单人／双人间。*dān rén / shuāng rén jiān.*

room service 客房服务 *kè fáng fú wù*

rope n 绳子 *shéng zǐ*

rose n 玫瑰 *méi gui*

royal flush n 同花大顺 *tóng huā dà shùn*

rum n 朗姆酒 *lǎng mǔ jiǔ*

run, to run v 运行 *yùn xíng*

ENGLISH—CHINESE

S

sad *adj* 伤心的 *shāng xīn de*

safe (for storing valuables) *n*
保险箱（存储贵重物品）*bǎo
xiǎn xiāng (cún chǔ guì zhòng
wù pǐn)*

> **Do the rooms have safes?** 房
> 间有保险箱吗？*fáng jiān yǒu
> bǎo xiǎn xiāng ma?*

safe (secure) *adj* 安全的 *ān
quán de*

> **Is this area safe?** 该地区安
> 全吗？*gāi dì qū ān quán ma?*

sail *n* 航行 *háng xíng*

sail, to sail *v* 启航 *qǐ háng*

> **When do we sail?** 我们什么时
> 候启航？*wǒmen shén me shí
> hou qǐ háng?*

salad *n* 沙拉 *shā lā*

salesperson *n* 销售人员 *xiāo
shòu rén yuán*

salt *n* 盐 *yán*

> **Is that low-salt?** 那是低盐的
> 吗？*nà shì dī yán de ma?*

Salvadorian *adj* 萨尔瓦多的 *sà
ěr wǎ duō de*

satellite *n* 卫星 *wèi xīng*

> **satellite radio** 卫星广播 *wèi
> xīng guǎng bō*
>
> **satellite tracking** 卫星跟踪
> *wèi xīng gēn zōng*

Saturday *n* el 星期六 *xīng qī liù*

sauce *n* 沙司 *shā sī*

say, to say *v* 说 *shuō*

scan, to scan *v* **(document)** 扫
描（文档）*sǎo miáo (wén
dàng)*

schedule *n* 时间表 *shí jiān biǎo*

school *n* 学校 *xué xiào*

scooter *n* 踏板 *tà bǎn*

score *n* 得分 *dé fēn*

Scottish *adj* 苏格兰的 *sū gé lán
de*

scratched *adj* 刮擦的 *guā cā de*

> **scratched surface** 有刮痕的表
> 面 *yǒu guā hén de biǎo miàn*

scuba dive, to scuba dive *v* 水
肺潜水 *shuǐ fèi qián shuǐ*

sculpture *n* 雕刻 *diāo kè*

seafood *n* 海鲜 *hǎi xiān*

search *n* 搜查 *sōu chá*

> **hand search** 手工搜查 *shǒu
> gōng sōu chá*

search, to search *v* 搜查 *sōu
chá*

seasick *adj* 晕船的 *yùn chuán
de*

> **I am seasick.** 我晕船。*wǒ yùn
> chuán。* **seasickness pill** *n* 晕
> 船药 *yùn chuán yào*

seat *n* 座位 *zuò wèi*

> **child seat** 儿童座位 *ér tóng
> zuò wèi*

second *adj* 第二的 *dì èr de*

security *n* 安全 *ān quán*

security checkpoint 安检处 ān jiān chǔ

security guard 保安 bǎo ān

sedan n 箱式小轿车 xiāng shì xiǎo jiào chē

see, to see v 看见 kàn jiàn

May I see it? 我可以看一下吗? wǒ kě yǐ kàn yī xià ma?

self-serve adj 自助的 zì zhù de

sell, to sell v 销售 xiāo shòu

seltzer n 苏打水 sū dǎ shuǐ

send, to send v 发送 fā sòng

separated (marital status) adj 分居的（婚姻状态）fēn jū de (hūn yīn zhuàng tài)

September n 九月 jiǔyuè

serve, to serve v 服务 fú wù

service n 服务 fú wù

out of service 超出服务范围 chāo chū fú wù fàn wéi

services (religious) n 仪式 yí shì

service charge n 服务费 fú wù fèi

seven adj 七 qī

seventy adj 七十 qī shí

seventeen adj 十七 shí qī

seventh adj 第七 dì qī

sew, to sew v 缝制 féng zhì

sex (gender) n 性别 xìng bié

sex, to have (intercourse) v 性交 xìng jiāo

shallow adj 浅薄的 qiǎn báo de

sheet (bed linen) n 床单 chuáng dān

shellfish n 贝 bèi

ship n 轮船 lún chuán

ship, to ship v 载运 zǎi yùn

How much to ship this to ____? 把这运到_____多少钱? bǎ zhè yùn dào _____ duō shǎo qián?

shipwreck n 船只失事 chuán zhī shī shì

shirt n 衬衫 chèn shān

shoe n 鞋子 xié zǐ

shop n 商店 shāng diàn

shop v 选购 xuǎn gòu

I'm shopping for mens' clothes. 我在选购男士衣服。 wǒ zài xuǎn gòu nán shì yī fu.

I'm shopping for womens' clothes. 我在选购女式衣服。 wǒ zài xuǎn gòu nǚ shì yī fu.

I'm shopping for childrens' clothes. 我在选购童装。 wǒ zài xuǎn gòu tóng zhuāng.

short adj 短的 duǎn de

shorts n 短裤 duǎn kù

shot (liquor) n 口杯 kǒu bēi

shout v 喊叫 hǎn jiào

show (performance) n 表演 biǎo yǎn

What time is the show? 表演几点开始? biǎo yǎn jǐ diǎn kāi shǐ?

show, to show v 指示 zhǐshì

Would you show me? 您能指给我看吗? nín néng zhǐ gěi wǒ kàn ma?

shower n 淋浴 lín yù

Does it have a shower? 有淋浴吗? yǒu lín yù ma?

shower, to shower v 淋浴 lín yù

shrimp n 小虾 xiǎo xiā

shuttle bus n 机场大巴 jī chǎng dà bā

sick adj 不舒服的 bù shū fú de

I feel sick. 我感觉不舒服。 wǒ gǎn jué bù shū fú.

side n 边缘 biān yuán

on the side (e.g., salad dressing) 在边上（例如，沙拉油）zài biān shàng (lìrú, shā lā yóu)

sidewalk n 人行道 rén xíng dào

sightseeing n 观光 guān guāng

sightseeing bus n 观光车 guān guāng chē

sign, to sign v 签署 qiān shǔ

Where do I sign? 我签在哪里? wǒ qiān zài nǎ lǐ?

silk n 丝 sī

silver adj 银质的 yín zhì de

sing, to sing v 歌唱 gē chàng

single (unmarried) adj 单身的（未婚）dān shēn de (wèi hūn)

Are you single? 您是单身吗? nín shì dān shēn ma?

single (one) adj 单一的 dān yī de

single bed 单人床 dān rén chuáng

sink n 水池 shuǐ chí

sister n 姐妹 jiě mèi

sit, to sit v 坐 zuò

six adj 六 liù

sixteen adj 十六 shí liù

sixty adj 六十 liù shí

size (clothing, shoes) n 尺码 chǐ mǎ

skin n 皮肤 pí fū

sleeping berth n 卧铺 wò pù

slow adj 慢的 màn de

slow, to slow v 减慢 jiǎn màn

Slow down! 慢点开! màn diǎn kāi!

slow(ly) adv 慢慢地 màn màn de

Speak more slowly. 请慢点说。 qǐng màn diǎn shuō.

slum n 贫民窟 pín mín kū

small adj 小的 xiǎo de

smell, to smell v 闻 wén

smoke, to smoke v 抽烟 chōu yān

smoking n 吸烟 xī yān

smoking area 吸烟区 xī yān qū

No Smoking 禁止吸烟 jìn zhǐ xī yān

snack n 小吃 xiǎo chī

Snake eyes! n 蛇眼 shé yǎn

snorkel n 浮潜 fú qián

soap n 肥皂 féi zào

sock n 短袜 duǎn wà

soda n 苏打水 sū dǎ shuǐ

diet soda 减肥苏打水 jiǎn féi sū dǎ shuǐ

soft adj 软的 ruǎn de

software n 软件 ruǎn jiàn

sold out adj 售完的 shòu wán de

some adj 一些 yī xiē

someone n 某人 mǒu rén

something n 某事物 mǒu shì wù

son n 儿子 ér zǐ

song n 歌曲 gē qǔ

sorry adj 抱歉的 bào qiàn de

I'm sorry. 很抱歉。 hěn bào qiàn.

soup n 汤 tāng

spa n 水疗 shuǐ liáo

Spain n 西班牙 xī bān yá

Spanish adj 西班牙的 xī bān yá de

spare tire n 备用轮胎 bèi yòng lún tāi

speak, to speak v 说出 shuō chū

Do you speak English? 您说英语吗？ nín shuō yīng yǔ ma？

Would you speak louder, please? 您能大声点说吗？ nín néng dà shēng diǎn shuō ma？

Would you speak slower, please? 您能说慢点吗？ nín néng shuō màn diǎn ma？

special (featured meal) n 特色菜（特色套餐）tè sè cài (tè sè tào cān)

specify, to specify v 详细说明 xiáng xì shuō míng

speed limit n 限速 xiàn sù

What's the speed limit? 限速是多少？ xiàn sù shì duō shǎo？

speedometer n 里程计 lǐ chéng jì

spell, to spell v 写出 xiě chū

How do you spell that? 请问它怎么写？ qǐng wèn tā zěn me xiě？

spice n 调味品 tiáo wèi pǐn

spill, to spill v 溢出 yì chū

split (gambling) n 平局（赌博）píng jú (dǔ bó)

sports n 运动 yùn dòng

spring (season) n 春天（季节）chūn tiān (jì jié)

stadium n 体育场 tǐ yù chǎng

staff (employees) n 员工 yuán gōng

stamp (postage) n 邮票 yóu piào

stair n 楼梯 lóu tī

> **Where are the stairs?** 楼梯在哪里? lóu tī zài nǎ lǐ?
>
> **Are there many stairs?** 有许多级楼梯吗? yǒu xǔ duō jí lóu tī ma?

stand, to stand v 站起 zhàn qǐ

start, to start (commence) v 开始 kāi shǐ

start, to start (a car) v 发动 fā dòng

state n 状态 zhuàng tài

station n 车站 chē zhàn

> **Where is the nearest_____?** 最近的_____在哪里? zuì jìn de _____ zài nǎ lǐ?
>
> **gas station** 加油站 jiā yóu zhàn
>
> **bus station** 公共汽车站 gōng gòng qì chē zhàn
>
> **subway station** 地铁站 dì tiě zhàn
>
> **train station** 火车站 huǒ chē zhàn

stay, to stay v 停留 tíng liú

> **We'll be staying for _____ nights.** 我们将停留_____晚。wǒ mén jiāng tíng liú _____ wǎn。 See p7 for numbers.

steakhouse n 牛排餐厅 niú pái cān tīng

steal, to steal v 偷窃 tōu qiè

stolen adj 被偷的 bèi tōu de

stop n 站 zhàn

> **Is this my stop?** 这是我要下车的站吗? zhè shì wǒ yào xià chē de zhàn ma?
>
> **I missed my stop.** 我坐过站了。wǒ zuò guò zhàn le。.

stop, to stop v 停止 tíng zhǐ

> **Please stop.** 请停下来。qǐng tíng xià lái。
>
> **STOP (traffic sign)** 停车（交通标志）tíng chē (jiāo tōng biāo zhì)
>
> **Stop, thief!** 抓小偷! zhuā xiǎo tōu!

store n 商店 shāng diàn

straight adj 直的 zhí de（头发）(tóu fa)

> **straight ahead** 一直向前 yī zhí xiàng qián
>
> **straight (drink)** 纯喝（饮料）chún hē (yǐn liào)
>
> **Go straight.** (给出方向)（gěi chū fāng xiàng) 直走 zhí zǒu

straight (gambling) n 顺子（赌博）shùn zǐ (dǔ bó)

street n 街道 jiē dào

across the street 街道对面 jiē dào duì miàn

down the street 沿着街道 yán zhe jiē dào

Which street? 哪条街? nǎ tiáo jiē?

How many more streets? 多少街道? duō shǎo jiē dào?

stressed adj 有压力的 yǒu yā lì de

striped adj 有斑纹的 yǒu bān wén de

stroller n 婴儿车 yīng ér chē

Do you rent baby strollers? 您租婴儿手推车吗? nín zū yīng ér shǒu tuī chē ma?

substitution n 替代品 tì dài pǐn

suburb n 郊区 jiāoqū

subway n 地铁 dì tiě

subway line 地铁线 dì tiě xiàn

subway station 地铁站 dì tiě zhàn

Which subway do I take for ____? 到____应乘地铁几号线? dào ____ yīng chéng dì tiě jǐ hào xiàn?

subtitle n 字幕 zì mù

suitcase n 手提箱 shǒu tí xiāng

suite n 套间 tào jiān

summer n 夏季 xià jì

sun n 太阳 tài yáng

sunburn n 晒斑 shai bān

I have a bad sunburn. 我有很严重的晒斑. wǒ yǒu hěn yán zhòng de shai bān.

Sunday n 星期天 xīng qī tiān

sunglasses n 太阳镜 tài yáng jìng

sunny adj 晴朗的 qíng lǎng de

It's sunny out. 外边天气很晴朗. wài biān tiān qì hěn qíng lǎng.

sunroof n 天窗 tiān chuāng

sunscreen n 遮光剂 zhē guāng jì

Do you have sunscreen SPF ____? 有 SPF____ 的遮光剂吗? yǒu SPF____ de zhē guāng jì ma? **参见第七页的数字。** See p7 for numbers.

supermarket n 超市 chāo shì

surf v 冲浪 chōng làng

surfboard n 冲浪板 chōng làng bǎn

suspiciously adv 令人怀疑地 lìng rén huái yí de

swallow, to swallow v 吞咽 tūn yàn

sweater n 套衫 tào shān

swim, to swim v 游泳 yóu yǒng

Can one swim here? 可以在这里游泳吗? kě yǐ zài zhè lǐ yóu yǒng ma?

swimsuit *n* 泳衣 *yǒng yī*

swim trunks *n* 泳裤 *yǒng kù*

symphony *n* 交响乐 *jiāo xiǎng yuè*

T

table *n* 桌子 *zhuō zi*

table for two 两人餐桌 *liǎng rén cān zhuō*

tailor *n* 裁缝 *cái feng*

Can you recommend a good tailor? 能推荐一位好的裁缝吗? *néng tuī jiàn yī wèi hǎo de cái feng ma?*

take, to take *v* 带领 *dài lǐng*

Take me to the station. 带我到车站吧。*dài wǒ dào chē zhàn bā。*

How much to take me to _____? 到_____需要多少钱? *dào _____ xū yào duō shǎo qián?*

takeout menu *n* 外卖菜单 *wài mài cài dān*

talk, to talk *v* 谈论 *tán lùn*

tall *adj* 高的 *gāo de*

tanned *adj* 茶色的 *chá sè de*

taste (flavor) *n* 风味 *fēng wèi*

taste *n* (discernment) 品位 *pǐn wèi*

taste, to taste *v* 品尝 *pǐn cháng*

tax *n* 税 *shuì*

ENGLISH—CHINESE

value-added tax (VAT) 增值税 *zēng zhí shuì*

taxi *n* 出租车 *chū zū chē*

Taxi! 出租车! *chū zū chē!*

Would you call me a taxi? 您能帮我叫辆出租车吗? *nín néng bāng wǒ jiào liàng chū zū chē ma?*

tea *n* 茶 *chá*

team *n* 队 *duì*

Techno *n* 电子音乐 *diàn zǐ yīn yuè*

television *n* 电视 *diàn shì*

temple *n* 寺庙 *sì miào*

ten *adj* 十 *shí*

tennis *n* 网球 *wǎng qiú*

tennis court 网球场 *wǎng qiú chǎng*

tent *n* 帐篷 *zhàng péng*

tenth *adj* 第十 *dì shí*

terminal *n* (airport) 候机楼 (机场) *hòu jī lóu (jī chǎng)*

Thank you. 谢谢您。*xiè xiè nín*

that (near) *adj* 那个 *nà gè*

that (far away) *adj* 那个 *nà gè*

theater *n* 剧院 *jù yuàn*

them (m / f) 他们 *tā mén*

there (demonstrative) *adv* 那里 *nà lǐ* (nearby), *allí* (far)

Is / Are there? 有? *yǒu?*

over there 在那里 *zài nà lǐ*

these *adj* 这些 *zhè xiē*

thick adj 厚的 hòu de

thin adj 瘦的 shòu de

third adj 第三 dì sān

thirteen adj 十三 shí sān

thirty adj 三十 sān shí

this adj 这个 zhè gè

those adj 那些 nà xiē

thousand 千 qiān

three 三 sān

Thursday n 星期四 xīng qī sì

ticket n 票 piào

> **ticket counter** 售票台 shòu piào tái

> **one-way ticket** 单程票 dān chéng piào

> **round-trip ticket** 往返票 wǎng fǎn piào

tight adj 紧的 jǐn de

time n 时间 shí jiān

> **Is it on time?** 准时吗? zhǔn shí ma?

> **At what time?** 在几点? zài jǐ diǎn?

> **What time is it?** 现在几点了? xiàn zài jǐ diǎn le?

timetable n (train) 时刻表 shí kè biǎo

tip (gratuity) n 小费 xiǎo fèi

tire n 轮胎 lún tāi

> **I have a flat tire.** 爆胎了。 bào tāi le.

tired adj 疲惫的 pí bèi de

today n 今天 jīn tiān

toilet n 马桶 mǎ tǒng

> **The toilet is overflowing.** 马桶溢水了。 mǎ tǒng yì shuǐ le.

> **The toilet is backed up.** 马桶堵上了。 mǎ tǒng dǔ shàng le.

toilet paper n 卫生纸 wèi shēng zhǐ

> **You're out of toilet paper.** 您的卫生纸用完了。 nín de wèi shēng zhǐ yòng wán le.

toiletries n 化妆品 huà zhuāng pǐn

toll n 通行费 tōng xíng fèi

tomorrow n 明天 míng tiān

ton n 吨 dūn

too (excessively) adv 太 (过分) tài (guò fēn)

too (also) adv 也 yě

tooth n 牙 yá

> **I lost my tooth.** 我的牙掉了。 wǒ de yá diào le.

toothache n 牙痛 yá tòng

> **I have a toothache.** 我牙疼。 wǒ yá téng.

total n 总数 zǒng shù

> **What is the total?** 总数是多少? zǒng shù shì duō shǎo?

tour n 旅游 lǚ yóu

> **Are guided tours available?** 有配导游的旅游吗? yǒu pèi dào yóu de lǚ yóu ma?

Are audio tours available?
有用英文解说的语音导览设备吗? yǒu yòng yīng wén jiě shuō de yǔ yīn dǎo lǎn shè bèi ma?

towel n 毛巾 máo jīn

May we have more towels?
可以多给我们几条毛巾吗? kě yǐ duō gěi wǒ mén jǐ tiáo máo jīn ma?

toy n 玩具 wán jù

toy store n 玩具店 wán jù diàn

Do you have any toys for the children? 您有儿童玩具吗? nín yǒu ér tóng wán jù ma?

traffic n 交通 jiāo tōng

How's traffic? 交通怎么样? jiāo tōng zěn me yàng?

traffic rules 交通规则 jiāo tōng guī zé

trail n 小径 xiǎo jìng

Are there trails? 有些小径吗? yǒu xiē xiǎo jìng ma?

train n 火车 huǒ chē

express train 特快火车 tè kuài huǒ chē

local train 普通火车 pǔ tōng huǒ chē

Does the train go to _____? 这列火车到_____吗? zhè liè huǒ chē dào _____ ma?

May I have a train schedule? 可以给我一份火车时刻表吗? kě yǐ gěi wǒ yī fèn huǒ chē shí kè biǎo ma?

Where is the train station? 火车站在哪里? huǒ chē zhàn zài nǎ lǐ?

train, to train v 训练 xùn liàn

transfer, to transfer v 转移 zhuǎn yí

I need to transfer funds. 我需要转帐。wǒ xū yào zhuǎn zhàng。

transmission n 传输 chuán shū

automatic transmission 自动传输 zì dòng chuán shū

standard transmission 标准传输 biāo zhǔn chuán shū

travel, to travel v 旅行 lǚxíng

travelers' check n 旅行支票 lǚ xíng zhī piào

Do you cash travelers' checks? 您兑现旅行支票吗? nín duì xiàn lǚ xíng zhī piào ma?

trim, to trim (hair) v 修剪(头发) xiū jiǎn (tóu fa)

trip n 旅程 lǚ chéng

triple adj 三倍的 sān bèi de

trumpet n 喇叭 lǎ ba

trunk n 大衣箱 dà yī xiāng

try, to try (attempt) v 试 shì

try, to try on (clothing) v 试穿 shì chuān

try, to try (food) v 尝试 cháng shì

Tuesday n 星期二 xīng qī èr

turkey *n* 火鸡 huǒ jī

turn, to turn *v* 转动 zhuàn dòng

> **to turn left / right** 左 / 右转 zuǒ / yòu zhuǎn

> **to turn off / on** 关 / 开 guān / kāi

twelve *adj* 十二 shí èr

twenty *adj* 二十的 èr shí de

twine *n* 细绳 xì shéng

two *adj* 两个的 liǎng gè de

U

umbrella *n* 伞 sǎn

uncle *n* 叔叔 shū shū

undercooked *adj* 未做熟的 wèi zuò shú de

understand, to understand *v* 理解 lǐ jiě

> **I don't understand.** 我不理解。 wǒ bù lǐ jiě 。

> **Do you understand?** 您理解吗? nín lǐ jiě ma?

underwear *n* 内衣裤 nèi yī kù

university *n* 大学 dà xué

up *adv* 向上 xiàng shàng

update, to update *v* 更新 gēng xīn

upgrade *n* 升级 shēng jí

upload, to upload *v* 上传 shàng chuán

upscale *adj* 最高级的 zuì gāo jí de

Uruguayan *adj* 乌拉圭的 wū lā guī de

us *pron* 我们 wǒ mén

USB port *n* USB 接口 USB jiē kǒu

use, to use *v* 使用 shǐ yòng

V

vacation *n* 假期 jià qī

> **on vacation** 在休假 zài xiū jiǎ

> **to go on vacation** 去度假 qù dù jià

vacancy *n* 空房 kōng fáng

van *n* 面包车 miàn bāo chē

VCR *n* 录像机 lù xiàng jī

> **Do the rooms have VCRs?** 房间有录像机吗? fáng jiān yǒu lù xiàng jī ma?

vegetable *n* 蔬菜 shū cài

vegetarian *n* 素食主义者 sù shí zhǔ yì zhě

vending machine *n* 自动售货机 zì dòng shòu huò jī

Venezuelan *adj* 委内瑞拉的 wěi nèi ruì lā de

version *n* 版本 bǎn běn

very 很 hěn

video n 录像 lù xiàng

Where can I rent videos or DVDs? 哪里可以租到录像带或 DVD？nǎ lǐ kě yǐ zū dào lù xiàng dài huò DVD?

view n 风景画 fēng jǐng huà

beach view 海滩景观 hǎi tān jǐng guān

city view 城市景观 chéng shì jǐng guān

vineyard n 葡萄园 pú tao yuán

vinyl n 乙烯树脂 yǐ xī shù zhī

violin n 小提琴 xiǎo tí qín

visa n 签证 qiān zhèng

Do I need a visa? 我需要签证吗？wǒ xū yào qiān zhèng ma?

vision n 视觉 shì jué

visit, to visit v 参观 cān guān

visually-impaired adj 视障的 shì zhàng de

vodka n 伏特加酒 fú tè jiā jiǔ

voucher n 优惠券 yōu huì quàn

W

wait, to wait v 等待 děng dài

Please wait. 请等一下。qǐng děng yī xià.

How long is the wait? 要等多长时间？yào děng duō cháng shí jiān?

waiter n 服务员 fú wù yuán

waiting area n 等候区 děng hòu qū

wake-up call n 电话叫醒服务 diàn huà jiào xǐng fú wù

wallet n 钱夹 qián jiā

I lost my wallet. 我的钱夹丢了。wǒ de qián jiā diu le.

Someone stole my wallet. 有人偷了我的钱夹。yǒu rén tōu le wǒ de qián jiā.

walk, to walk v 走 zǒu

walker (ambulatory device) n 助行器（助行设备）zhù xíng qì (zhù xíng shèbèi)

walkway n 人行道 rén xíng dào

moving walkway 自动人行道 zì dòng rén xíng dào

want, to want v 想要 xiǎng yào

war n 战争 zhàn zhēng

warm adj 温暖的 wēn nuǎn de

watch, to watch v 观看 guān kàn

water n 水 shuǐ

Is the water potable? 这水可以饮用吗？zhè shuǐ kě yǐ yǐn yòng ma?

Is there running water? 有自来水吗？yǒu zì lái shuǐ ma?

wave, to wave *v* 摇动 *yáo dòng*

waxing *n* 去毛 *qù máo*

weapon *n* 武器 *wǔ qì*

wear, to wear *v* 穿 *chuān*

weather forecast *n* 天气预报 *tiān qì yù bào*

Wednesday *n* 星期三 *xīng qī sān*

week *n* 周 *zhōu*

this week 这周 *zhè zhōu*

last week 上周 *shàng zhōu*

next week 下周 *xià zhōu*

weigh *v* 重 *zhòng*

I weigh ____. 我的体重是____. *wǒ de tǐ zhòng shì ____.*

It weighs ____. 它重____. *tā zhòng ____. See p7 for numbers.*

weights *n* 重量 *zhòng liàng*

welcome *adv* 欢迎 *huān yíng*

You're welcome. 不用谢。 *bù yòng xiè.*

well *adv* 好 *hǎo*

well done (meat) 煮熟的（肉） *zhǔ shú de (ròu)*

well done (task) 做的很好（任务） *zuò de hěn hǎo (rènwù)*

I don't feel well. 我感觉不舒服。 *wǒ gǎn jué bù shū fú.*

western *adj* 西方的 *xī fāng de*

whale *n* 鲸 *jīng*

what *adv* 什么 *shén me*

What sort of ____? 哪种____? *nǎ zhǒng ____ ?*

What time is ____? 什么时间____? *shén me shí jiān ____ ?*

wheelchair *n* 轮椅 *lún yǐ*

wheelchair access 轮椅通道 *lún yǐ tōng dào*

wheelchair ramp 轮椅坡道 *lún yǐ pō dào*

power wheelchair 电轮椅 *diàn lún yǐ*

wheeled (luggage) *adj* 带轮的（行李） *dài lún de (xíng li)*

ENGLISH–CHINESE

when *adv* 何时 *hé shí*

where *adv* 哪里 *nǎ lǐ*

Where is it? 这是哪里? *zhè shì nǎ lǐ?*

which *adv* 哪个 *nǎ gè*

Which one? 哪一个? *nǎ yī gè?*

white *adj* 白色的 *bái sè de*

who *adv* 谁 *shuí*

whose *adj* 谁的 *shuí de*

wide *adj* 宽的 *kuān de*

widow, widower *n* 寡妇, 鳏夫 *guǎ fù, guān fū*

wife *n* 妻子 *qī zǐ*

wi-fi *n* 无线保真 *wú xiàn bǎo zhēn*

window *n* 窗户 *chuāng hu*

drop-off window 邮件投入窗口 *yóu jiàn tóu rù chuāng kǒu*

pickup window 领取窗口 *lǐng qǔ chuāng kǒu*

windshield *n* 挡风玻璃 *dǎng fēng bō li*

windshield wiper *n* 挡雨雪刷 *fēng dàng yǔ xuě shuā*

windy *adj* 有风的 *yǒu fēng de*

wine *n* 葡萄酒 *pú tao jiǔ*

winter *n* 冬天 *dōng tiān*

wiper *n* 雨刷 *yǔ shuā*

with *prep* 和 *hé*

withdraw *v* 提款 *tí kuǎn*

I need to withdraw money. 我需要取钱。*wǒ xū yào qǔ qián.*

without *prep* 没有 *méi yǒu*

woman *n* 妇女 *fù nǚ*

work, to work *v* 工作 *gōng zuò*

This doesn't work. 它坏了。*tā huài le.*

workout *n* 测验 *cè yàn*

worse 更坏 *gèng huài*

worst 最坏 *zuì huài*

write, to write *v* 写出 *xiě chū*

Would you write that down for me? 您能给我写下那个吗? *nín néng gěi wǒ xiě xià nà gè ma?*

writer *n* 作家 *zuò jiā*

X

x-ray machine *n* x 射线机 *x shè xiàn jī*

Y

yellow *adj* 黄色的 *huáng sè de*

Yes. *adv* 是 *shì*

yesterday *n* 昨天 *zuó tiān*

  the day before yesterday
    前天 *qián tiān*

yield sign *n* 避让标志 *bì ràng biāo zhì*

you *pron* 您 *nín*

  you (singular, informal) 你 *nǐ*
  you (singular, formal) 您 *nín*
  you (plural informal) 你们 *nǐ mén*
  you (plural formal) 你们 *nǐ mén*

your, yours *adj* 您的 *nín de*

young *adj* 年轻的 *nián qīng de*

Z

zoo *n* 动物园 *dòng wù yuán*

A

阿根廷的 **ā gēn tíng de** Argentinian adj

阿司匹林 **ā sī pǐ lín** aspirin n

哎唷！ **āi yō!** Ouch! interj

哎唷！很痛！ **āi yō! hěn tòng!** Ouch! That hurts!

爱 **ài** love n

爱 **ài** to love v

爱尔兰 **ài ěr lán** Ireland n

爱尔兰的 **ài ěr lán de** Irish adj

爱好 **ài hào** hobby n

安静的 **ān jìng de** quiet adj

安全 **ān quán** security n

> 安检处 **ān jiǎn chù** security checkpoint
>
> 保安 **bǎo ān** security guard

安全的 **ān quán de** safe (secure) adj

按摩 **àn mó** to massage v

昂贵的 **áng guì de** expensive adj

盎司 **àng sī** ounce n

凹陷 **āo xià** dent n

澳大利亚 **ào dà lì yà** Australia n

澳大利亚的 **ào dà lì yà de** Australian adj

B

八 **bā** eight n adj

八十 **bā shí** eighty n adj

八月 **bā yuè** August n

巴拉圭的 **bā lā guī de** Paraguayan adj

巴拿马的 **bā ná mǎ de** Panamanian adj

吧台 **bā tái** counter (in bar) n

利口酒 **lì kǒu jiǔ** liqueur, liquor n

白兰地 **bái lán dì** brandy n

白色的，黄白的 **bái sè de, huáng bái de** white, off-white adj

百 **bǎi** hundred n adj

版本 **bǎn běn** version n

办登机手续 **bàn dēng jī shǒu xù** check-in n

> 电子登机服务 **diàn zǐ dēng jī fú wù** electronic check-in
>
> 快办登机手续服务 **kuài bàn dēng jī shǒu xù fú wù** express check-in
>
> 路边办理登机服务 **lù biān bàn lǐ dēng jī fú wù** curbside check-in

半磅 **bàn bàng** half-pound

半个 **bàn gè** half n

帮帮我！ **bāng bāng wǒ!** Help!

搬运工人 **bān yùn gōng rén** porter n

帮助 **bāng zhù** help n

帮助 **bāng zhù** to help v

磅 **bàng** pound n

包（交通工具）bāo (jiāo tōng gōng jù) to charter (transportation) v

包裹 bāo guǒ package n

包厢 bāo xiāng box (seat) n

保安 bǎo ān security guard n

保持 bǎo chí to keep v

保卫 bǎo wèi guard n

保险 bǎo xiǎn insurance n

碰撞险 pèng zhuàng xiǎn collision insurance

责任险 zé rèn xiǎn liability insurance

保险丝 bǎo xiǎn sī fuse n

保险箱（存储贵重物品）bǎo xiǎn xiāng (cún chǔ guì zhòng wù pǐn) safe (for storing valuables) n

报亭 bào tíng newsstand n

报纸 bào zhǐ newspaper n

杯（饮用）bēi (yǐn yòng) glass (drinking) n

贝 bèi shellfish n

贝司（乐器）bèi sī (yuè qì) bass (instrument) n

背 bèi back n

被偷的 bèi tōu de stolen adj

本地 běn dì local adj

泵 bèng pump n

鼻子 bí zi nose n

比萨 bǐ sà pizza n

比赛 bǐ sài to match v

比赛（运动）bǐ sài (yùn dòng) match (sport) n

笔记本电脑 bǐ jì běn diàn nǎo laptop n

避让标志 bì ràng biāo zhì yield sign n

避孕 bì yùn birth control n

避孕套 bì yùn tào condom n

避孕中的 bì yùn zhōng de birth control adj

我没有避孕药丸了。wǒ méi yǒu bì yùn yào wán le. I'm out of birth control pills.

边缘 biān yuán side n

在边上（例如，沙拉油）zài biān shàng (lì rú, shā lā yóu) on the side (e.g., salad dressing)

编辑，出版商 biān jí, chū bǎn shāng editor, publisher n

变色 biàn sè to color v

表哥 / 弟 / 姐 / 妹 biǎo gē / dì / jiě / mèi cousin n

表演 biǎo yǎn show (performance) n

冰 bīng ice n

冰咖啡 bīng kā fēi iced coffee n

浓咖啡 nóng kā fēi espresso n

拨（电话）bō (diàn huà) to dial (a phone number) v

直拨 zhí bi to dial direct

波多黎各的 bō duō lí gè de Puerto Rican adj

波尔图葡萄酒 **bō ěr tú pú táo jiǔ** *port (beverage)* n

玻利维亚的 **bō lì wéi yà de** *Bolivian* adj

博物馆 **bó wù guǎn** *museum* n

不 **bù** *no* adj adv

不叫牌（赌博）**bù jiào pái (dǔ bó)** *to pass (gambling)* v

不可知论 **bù kě zhī lùn** *agnostic* n adj

不舒服的 **bù shū fú de** *sick* adj

不同的（其它的）**bù tóng de (qí tā de)** *different (other)* adj

不用谢。**bù yòng xiè。** *You're welcome.*

不准进入。**bù zhǔn jìn rù。** *Do not enter.*

美国盲人 **měi guó máng rén** *braille (American)* n

C

CD 播放器 **CD bō fàng qì** *CD player* n

裁缝 **cái feng** *tailor* n

菜单 **cài dān** *menu* n

> 儿童菜单 **ér tóng cài dān** *children's menu*

> 糖尿病人菜单 **táng niào bìng rén cài dān** *diabetic menu*

> 外卖菜单 **wài mài cài dān** *takeout menu*

参观 **cān guān** *to visit* v

参加、协助 **cān jiā , xié zhù** *to attend* v / *to assist* v

餐后甜点 **cān hòu tián diǎn** *dessert* n

> 餐后甜点菜单 **cān hòu tián diǎn cài dān** *dessert menu*

残疾 **cán ji** *disability* n

苍白的 **cāng bái de** *pale* adj

舱内 **cāng nèi** *board* n

层 **céng** *floor* n

> 底层 **dǐ céng** *ground floor, first floor*

插上 **chā shàng** *to plug* v

插头 **chā tóu** *plug* n

查号服务 **chá hào fú wù** *directory assistance* n

茶 **chá** *tea* n

> 草药茶 **cǎo yào chá** *herbal tea*

> 加了牛奶和糖的茶 **jiā le niú nǎi hé táng de chá** *tea with milk and sugar*

> 加了柠檬的茶 **jiā le níng méng de chá** *tea with lemon*

茶色 **chá sè** *tanned* adj

产品 **chǎn pǐn** *product* n

长笛 **cháng dí** *flute* n

长的 **cháng de** *long* adj

> 更长 **gèng cháng** *longer*

> 最长 **zuì cháng** *longest*

尝试 **cháng shì** *to taste v, to try (food)* v

场地（运动）**chǎng dì (yùn dòng)** *court (sport)* n

敞篷汽车 **chǎng péng qì chē** *convertible* n

超大的 **chāo dà de** *extra-large* adj

超市 **chāo shì** *supermarket* n

潮湿的 **cháo shī de** *humid* adj

车站 **chē zhàn** *station* n

最近的加油站在哪里？**zuì jìn de jiā yóu zhàn zài nǎ lǐ?** *Where is the nearest gas station?*

衬衫 **chèn shān** *shirt* n

成员 **chéng yuán** *member* n

城市 **chéng shì** *city* n

乘客 **chéng kè** *passenger* n

橙、橙色的 **chéng, chéng sè de** *orange* n, *orange (color)* adj

橙汁 **chéng zhī** *orange juice* n

吃 **chī** *to eat* v

持续 **chí xù** *to last* v

尺码 **chǐ mǎ** *size (clothing, shoes)* n

齿冠（牙科）**chǐ guàn (yá kē)** *crown (dental)* n

充电 **chōng diàn** *to charge (a battery)* v

充血（窦）**chōng xuè (dòu)** *congestion (sinus)* n

冲浪 **chōng làng** *to surf* v

冲浪板 **chōng làng bǎn** *surfboard* n

冲刷 **chōng shuā** *to flush* v

重复 **chóng fù** *to repeat* v

抽烟 **chōu yān** *smoking* n *to smoke* v

出租车 **chū zū chē** *taxi* n

出租车！**chū zū chē!** *Taxi!*

出租车停靠点 **chū zū chē tíng kào diǎn** *taxi stand*

初中/高中 **chū zhōng/gāo zhōng** *junior high / middle school*

厨房 **chú fáng** *kitchen* n

储藏柜 **chǔ cáng guì** *storage locker*

处方 **chǔ fāng** *prescription* n

轻拿轻放。**qīng ná qīng fàng.** *Handle with care.*

处理 **chǔ lǐ** *to process (a transaction)* v

处于 **chǔ yú** *to be (temporary state, condition, mood)* v

触及、演奏 **chù jí, yǎn zòu** *to touch* v / *to play (an instrument)* v

穿衣 **chuān yī** *to dress* v

传输 **chuán shū** *transmission* n

标准传输 **biāo zhǔn chuán shū** *standard transmission*

自动传输 **zì dòng chuán shū** *automatic transmission*

传送带 **chuán sòng dài** *conveyor belt n*

传真 **chuán zhēn** *fax n*

船只失事 **chuán zhī shī shì** *shipwreck n*

窗口 **chuāng kǒu** *window n*

领取窗口 **lǐng qǔ chuāng kǒu** *pickup window*

邮件投入窗口 **yóu jiàn tóu rù chuāng kǒu** *drop-off window*

窗口 **chuāng kǒu** *window n*

床 **chuáng** *bed n*

床单 **chuáng dān** *sheet (bed linen) n*

床铺加早餐 **chuáng pù jiā zǎo cān** *bed-and-breakfast (B & B) n*

吹风机 **chuī fēng jī** *hair dryer n*

春天（季节） **chūn tiān (jì jié)** *spring (season) n*

词典 **cí diǎn** *dictionary n*

匆忙 **cōng máng** *to hurry v*

存物柜 **cún wù guì** *locker n*

存物室 **cún wù shì** *locker room n*

痤疮 **cuó chuāng** *acne n*

错过 **cuò guò** *to lose v / to miss (a flight) v*

错误 **cuò wù** *mistake n*

D

DVD *DVD n*

答案 **dá àn** *answer n*

打（电话） **dǎ (diàn huà)** *to call (to phone) v*

打赌 **dǎ dǔ** *to bet v*

打断 **dǎ duàn** *to break v*

打高尔夫球 **dǎ gāo ěr fū qiú** *to go golfing v*

打火机 **dǎ huǒ jī** *light (for cigarette) n*

我能帮您点火吗？ **wǒ néng bāng nín diǎn huǒ ma?** *May I offer you a light?*

打火机 **dǎ huǒ jī** *lighter (cigarette) n*

打扫 **dǎ sǎo** *to clean v*

打印 **dǎ yìn** *to print v*

大的 **dà de** *big adj, large adj*

更大的 **gèng dà de** *bigger, larger*

最大的 **zuì dà de** *biggest, largest*

大使馆 **dà shǐ guǎn** *embassy n*

大蒜 **dà suàn** *garlic n*

大象 **dà xiàng** *elephant n*

大学 **dà xué** *university n*

大衣箱（行李） **dà yī xiāng (xíng li)** *trunk (luggage) n*

带 **dài** *belt* n

带领 **dài lǐng** *to take* v

这将用多长时间? **zhè jiāng yòng duō cháng shí jiān?** *How long will this take?*

带轮的（行李） **dài lún de (xíng li)** *wheeled (luggage)* adj

袋子 **dài zǐ** *bag* n

单程票 **dān chéng piào** *one-way ticket* n

单个的、简单的 **dān gè de, jiǎn dān de** *single* n adj / *simple* adj

纯喝（饮料） **chún hē (yǐn liào)** *straight up (drink)*

单身的（未婚）**dān shēn de (wèi hūn)** *single (unmarried)* adj

您是单身吗? **nín shì dān shēn ma?** *Are you single?*

单身酒吧 **dān shēn jiǔ bā** *singles bar* n

单行线（交通标志）**dān xíng xiàn (jiāo tōng biāo zhì)** *one way (traffic sign)* n

淡紫色的 **dàn zǐ sè de** *lavender* adj

挡雨雪刷 **dǎng fēng bō li** *windshield wiper* n

导游 **dǎo yóu** *guide (of tours)* n

倒下 **dǎo xià** *to fall* v

到_____应乘地铁几号线? **dào _____ yīng chéng dì tiě jǐ hào xiàn?** *Which subway do I take for ____?*

到达 **dào dá** *arrivals* n *to arrive* v

道路 **dào lù** *road* n

道路封闭标志 **dào lù fēng bì biāo zhì** *road closed sign* n

得分 **dé fēn** *score* n

得分（运动）**dé fēn (yùn dòng)** *goal (sport)* n

德国人、德国的 **dé guó rén, dé guó de** *German* n adj

灯 **dēng** *light (lamp)* n

灯 **dēng** *light (on car dashboard)*

机油灯 **jī yóu dēng** *oil light*

前灯 **qián dēng** *headlight*

刹车灯 **shā chē dēng** *brake light*

引擎检验灯 **yǐn qíng jiǎn yàn dēng** *check engine light*

登机牌 **dēng jī pái** *boarding pass* n

等待 **děng dài** *wait* n

等候 **děng hòu** *to hold (to pause)* v, *to wait* v

等候区 **děng hòu qū** *waiting area* n

等级 **děng jí** *class* n

低的 **dī de** *low* adj

滴下 **dī xià** *to drip* v

迪士高 **dí shì gāo** *disco* n

地铁 **dì tiě** *subway* n

地铁线 **dì tiě xiàn** *subway line*

地图 dì tú *map n*

> 车载地图 chē zǎi dì tú
> *onboard map*

地址 dì zhǐ *address n*

> 地址是什么? dì zhǐ shì shén
> me? *What's the address?*

第八 dì bā *eighth n adj*

> 八分之三 bā fēn zhī sān
> *three eighths*

第二的 dì èr de *second adj*

第九的 dì jiǔ de *ninth n adj*

第七的 dì qī de *seventh n adj*

第三的 dì sān de *third n adj*

第十的 dì shí de *tenth adj*

第四的 dì sì de *fourth n adj*

第五的 dì wǔ de *fifth adj*

第一的 dì yī de *first adj*

点钟 diǎn zhōng *o'clock adv*

> 两点钟 liǎng diǎn zhōng
> *two o'clock*

电池（手电筒使用的）diàn chí
(shǒu diàn tǒng shǐ yòng
de) *battery (for flashlight) n*

电动扶梯 diàn dòng fú tī
escalator n

电话 diàn huà *phone adj*

> 电话号码簿 diàn huà hào
> mǎ bù *phone directory*

电话 diàn huà *phone, phone
call n*

> 长途电话 cháng tú diàn huà
> *long-distance phone call*

> 对方付费电话 duì fāng fù fèi
> diàn huà *collect phone call*

> 国际电话 guó jì diàn huà
> *international phone call*

电话机 diàn huà jī *phone n*

> 电话接线员 diàn huà jiē xiàn
> yuán *phone operator*

> 可以给我您的电话号码吗? kě
> yǐ gěi wǒ nín de diàn huà
> hào mǎ ma? *May I have
> your phone number?*

> 移动电话 yí dòng diàn huà
> *cell phone*

> 预付费电话 yù fù fèi diàn
> huà *prepaid phones*

电话叫醒服务 diàn huà jiào xǐng
fú wù *wake-up call n*

电视 diàn shì *television n*

> 有线电视 yǒu xiàn diàn shì
> *cable television*

> 卫星电视 wèi xīng diàn shì
> *satellite television*

电梯 diàn tī *elevator n*

电线板 diàn xiàn bǎn *electrical
hookup n*

电影 diàn yǐng *movie n*

电影院 diàn yǐng yuàn *cinema n*

电子音乐 diàn zǐ yīn yuè
techno n (music)

电子邮件 diàn zǐ yóu jiàn
e-mail n

> 电子邮件消息 diàn zǐ yóu jiàn
> xiāo xi *e-mail message*

可以给我您的电子邮件地址吗？**kě yǐ gěi wǒ nín de diàn zǐ yóu jiàn dì zhǐ ma?** *May I have your e-mail address?*

雕刻 **diāo kè** *sculpture n*

顶部 **dǐng bù** *roof n*

天窗 **tiān chuāng** *sunroof*

顶楼房间 **dǐng lóu fáng jiān** *penthouse n*

丢失的 **diū shī de** *missing adj, lost adj*

冬天 **dōng tiān** *winter n*

动物 **dòng wù** *animal n*

动物园 **dòng wù yuán** *zoo n*

斗鸡 **dòu jī** *cockfight n*

斗牛 **dòu niú** *bullfight n*

斗牛士 **dòu niú shì** *bullfighter n*

读 **dú** *to read v*

赌 **dǔ** *bet n*

我看你押。**wǒ kàn nǐ yā.** *I'll see your bet.*

赌场 **dǔ chǎng** *casino n*

杜松子酒 **dù sōng zǐ jiǔ** *gin n*

短的 **duǎn de** *short adj*

短袜 **duǎn wà** *sock n*

断开连接 **duàn kāi lián jiē** *to disconnect v*

锻炼 **duàn liàn** *workout n*

队、设备 **duì、shè bèi** *team n / equipment n*

对不起 **duì bù qǐ** *sorry adj*

我很抱歉。**wǒ hěn bào qiàn.** *I'm sorry.*

兑现 **duì xiàn** *to cash v*

兑现（赌博）**duì xiàn (dǔ bó)** *to cash out (gambling) v*

吨 **dūn** *ton n*

多长时间？**duō cháng shí jiān?** *For how long?*

多少 **duō shǎo** *how (many) adv*

多少 **duō shǎo** *how (much) adv*

多少钱？**duō shǎo qián?** *How much?*

多雨的 **duō yǔ de** *rainy adj*

多云的 **duō yún de** *cloudy adj*

E

额外的 **é wài de** *extra adj*

厄瓜多尔的 **è guā duō ěr de** *Ecuadorian adj*

儿科医师 **ér kē yī shī** *pediatrician n*

儿童 **ér tóng** *children n pl*

儿子 **ér zi** *son n*

耳机 **ěr jī** *headphones n*

饵 **ěr** *bait n*

二 **èr** *two n adj*

二分之一的 **èr fēn zhī yī de** *adj, one-half adj*

二十的 **èr shí de** *twenty n adj*

二月 **èr yuè** *February n*

F

发辫 **fā biàn** *braid n*

发动 **fā dòng** *to start (a car) v, to turn on v*

发牌 **fā pái** *to deal (cards) v*

让我参加。**ràng wǒ cān jiā.** *Deal me in.*

发送 **fā sòng** *to send v*

发送电子邮件 **fā sòng diàn zǐ yóu jiàn** *to send e-mail v*

发现 **fā xiàn** *to find v*

罚款（交通违规）**fá kuǎn (jiāo tōng wéi guī)** *fine (for traffic violation) n*

法国的 **fǎ guó de** *French adj*

法律 **fǎ lǜ** *law n*

法学院 **fǎ xué yuàn** *law school n*

法院 **fǎ yuàn** *court (legal) n*

帆 **fān** *reef n*

帆布（纤维）**fān bù (xiān wéi)** *canvas (fabric) n*

返回 **fǎn huí** *to return (to a place) v*

饭店 **fàn diàn** *restaurant n*

牛排餐厅 **niú pái cān tīng** *steakhouse*

方向 **fāng xiàng** *direction*

放置 **fàng zhì** *to place v*

非裔美国人 **fēi yì měi guó rén** *African American adj*

非洲的 **fēi zhōu de** *afro adj*

肥皂 **féi zào** *soap n*

费 **fèi** *fee n*

费用 **fèi yòng** *fare n / rate n*

分居的（婚姻状态）**fēn jū de (hūn yīn zhuàng tài)** *separated (marital status) adj*

分钟 **fēn zhōng** *minute n*

马上 **mǎ shàng** *in a minute*

粉红的 **fěn hóng de** *pink adj*

风帆冲浪 **fēng fān chōng làng** *to windsurf v*

风景画 **fēng jǐng huà** *landscape (painting) n*

风景 **fēng jǐng** *view n / vision n*

城市景观 **chéng shì jǐng guān** *city view*

海滩景观 **hǎi tān jǐng guān** *beach view*

风味 **fēng wèi** *taste, flavor n*

巧克力味 **qiǎo kè lì wèi** *chocolate flavor*

缝制 **féng zhì** *to sew v*

佛教徒 **fó jiào tú** *Buddhist n*

伏特加酒 **fú tè jiā jiǔ** *vodka n*

服务 **fú wù** *service n*

超出服务范围 **chāo chū fú wù fàn wéi** *out of service*

服务 **fú wù** *to serve v*

服务费 **fú wù fèi** *service charge n*

服务员 **fú wù yuán** *waiter n*

服装 **fú zhuāng** *dress (garment) n*

浮潜（呼吸管）fú qián (hū xī guǎn) snorkel (breathing tube) n

抚慰者 fǔ wèi zhě pacifier n

父亲 fù qīn father, parent n

妇科医生 fù kē yī shēng gynecologist n

妇女 fù nǚ woman n

附近的 fù jìn de near, nearby adj

G

该死！gāi sǐ! Damn! expletive

干的 gān de dried adj

干的 gān de dry adj

干净的 gān jìng de clean, neat (tidy) adj

干洗 gān xǐ dry cleaning n

干洗店 gān xǐ diàn dry cleaner n

尴尬的 gān gà de embarrassed adj

干邑酒 gān yì jiǔ cognac n

感冒 gǎn mào cold (illness) n

橄榄色 gǎn lǎn sè olive n

钢琴 gāng qín piano n

钢琴酒吧 gāng qín jiǔ bā piano bar

港口 gǎng kǒu port (for ship mooring) n

高的 gāo de high adj

更高的 gèng gāo de higher

高尔夫球 gāo ěr fū qiú golf n

高尔夫球场 gāo ěr fū qiú chǎng golf course

高尔夫球练习场 gāo ěr fū qiú liàn xí chǎng driving range n

高级的 gāo jí de upscale adj

高速公路 gāo sù gōng lù highway n

高兴的 gāo xìng de delighted adj

高中 gāo zhōng high school n

哥伦比亚的 gē lún bǐ yà de Colombian adj

哥斯达黎加的 gē sī dá lí jiā de Costa Rican n adj

胳膊 gē bo arm n

歌唱 gē chàng to sing v

歌剧 gē jù opera n

歌剧院 gē jù yuàn opera house n

歌曲 gē qǔ song n

格式 gé shi format n

给 gěi to give v

更便宜 gèng pián yi cheaper adj

更低 gèng dī adj lower

更好的 gèng hǎo de better adj See good

更坏 gèng huài worse adj See bad

更近 gèng jìn closer adj

更近的（对比）gèng jìn de (duì bǐ) nearer (comparative) adj

更适宜的 **gèng shì yí de** *preferably adj*

更喜欢 **gèng xǐ huān** to *prefer v*

更新 **gēng xīn** *to update v*

更衣室 **gēng yī shì** *changing room n*

工程师 **gōng chéng shī** *engineer n*

工作 **gōng zuò** *to work v*

我为＿＿＿工作。**wǒ wèi ＿＿＿ gōng zuò.** *I work for ＿＿＿.*

公共汽车 **gōng gòng qì chē** *bus n*

公共汽车站 **gōng gòng qì chē zhàn** *n bus stop*

机场大巴 **jī chǎng dà bā** *shuttle bus*

公牛 **gōng niú** *bull n*

公顷 **gōng qǐng** *hectare n*

公文包 **gōng wén bāo** *briefcase n*

公园 **gōng yuán** *park n*

狗 **gǒu** *dog n*

帮助犬 **bāng zhù quǎn** *service dog*

购物 **gòu wù** *to shop v*

购物 **gòu wù** *to shop v*

购物中心 **gòu wù zhōng xīn** *mall n*

姑妈 **gū mā** *aunt n*

古典的（音乐）**gǔ diǎn (yīn yuè)** *classical (music) adj*

鼓 **gǔ** *drum n*

雇员 **gù yuán** *employee n*

雇主 **gù zhǔ** *employer n*

刮擦 **guā cā** *to scratch v*

刮擦的 **guā cā de** *scratched adj*

刮痕 **guā hén** *scratch mark n*

刮水片 **guā shuǐ piàn** *wiper blade n*

寡妇 **guǎ fù** *widow n*

挂断电话（结束通话）**guà duàn diàn huà (jié shù tōng huà)** *hang up (to end a phone call) v*

关掉（灯）**guān diào (dēng)** *to turn off (lights) v*

观光 **guān guāng** *sightseeing n*

观光车 **guān guāng chē** *n sightseeing bus*

观看 **guān kàn** *to look (observe) v*

看这里！**kàn zhè lǐ!** *Look here!*

观看 **guān kàn** *to watch v*

鳏夫 **guān fū** *widower n*

罐头 **guàn tóu** *can n*

光盘 **guāng pán** *CD n*

逛街（热闹的市区）**guàng jiē (rè nào de shì qū)** *hangout (hot spot) n*

逛街（休息）**guàng jiē (xiū xi)** *to hang out (relax) v*

果汁 **guǒzhī** *fruit juice n*

过错 **guòcuò** *fault n*

过道（商店）**guò dào (shāng diàn)** *aisle (in store) n / hallway n*

过敏 **guò mǐn** *allergy n*

过敏的 **guò mǐn de** *allergic adj*

过热 **guò rè** *to overheat v*

H

海拔 **hǎi bá** *altitude n*

海关 **hǎi guān** *customs n*

海滩 **hǎi tān** *beach n*

海鲜 **hǎi xiān** *seafood n*

喊叫 **hǎn jiào** *to call (shout) v*

喊叫 **hǎn jiào** *to shout v*

航班 **háng bān** *flight n*

航班乘务员 **háng bān chéng wù yuán** *flight attendant*

航空邮件 **háng kōng yóu jiàn** *n air mail*

第一类邮件 **dì yī lèi yóu jiàn** *first class mail*

挂号邮件 **guà hào yóu jiàn** *certified mail*

挂号邮件 **guà hào yóu jiàn** *registered mail*

邮局在哪里？**yóu jú zài nǎ lǐ?** *Where is the post office?*

邮政特快 **yóu zhèng tè kuài** *express mail*

航行 **háng xíng** *sail n*

毫米 **háo mǐ** *millimeter n*

毫升 **háo shēng** *milliliter n*

豪华大巴 **háo huá dà bā** *limo n*

好 **hǎo** *fine, good, Okay adj / well, Okay adv*

喝 **hē** *to drink v*

何时 **hé shí** *when adv*

和 **hé** *with prep*

和蔼的 **hé ǎi de** *kind (nice) n*

和解（抱歉）**hé jiě (bào qiàn)** *to make up (apologize) v*

河 **hé** *river n*

黑暗 **hēi àn** *darkness n*

黑发的 **hēi fā de** *brunette n*

黑暗 **hēi sè de** *black adj*

黑色的 **hēi àn de** *dark adj*

很 **hěn** *very adv*

很少的 **hěn shǎo de** *little adj*

红发人 **hóng fā rén** *redhead n adj*

红色的 **hóng sè de** *red adj*

洪都拉斯的 **hóng dū lā sī de** *Honduran adj*

后来 **hòu lái** *later adv*

回见。**huí jiàn。** *See you later.*

后面的 **hòu miàn de** *behind adj*

候机楼（机场）**hòu jī lóu (jī chǎng)** *terminal (airport) n*

呼叫（某人）**hū jiào (mǒu rén)** *to page (someone) v*

护士 **hù shì** *nurse n*

护照 **hù zhào** *passport n*

花 **huā** *flower n*

花费 **huā fèi** *to cost v*

花生 **huā shēng** *peanut n*

化妆（用化妆品）**huà zhuāng (yòng huà zhuāng pǐn)** *to make up (apply cosmetics) v*

化妆品 **huà zhuāng pǐn** *toiletries n*

怀孕的 **huái yùn de** *pregnant adj*

环境 **huán jìng** *environment n*

换钱／衣服 **huàn qián / yī fu** *to change (money) v / to change (clothes) v*

患便秘症的 **huàn biàn bì zhèng de** *constipated adj*

黄白的 **huáng bái de** *off-white adj*

黄金 **huáng jīn** *gold n*

黄色的 **huáng sè de** *yellow adj*

黄油 **huáng yóu** *butter n*

灰色的 **huī sè de** *gray adj*

汇率 **huì lǜ** *exchange rate n*

会员 **huì yuán** *membership n*

绘画（活动）**huì huà (huó dòng)** *to paint, drawing (activity) v*

混杂种族人 **hùn zá zhǒng zú rén** *biracial adj*

火 **huǒ** *fire n*

火柴 **huǒ chái** *match (fire) n*

火车 **huǒ chē** *train n*

普通火车 **pǔ tōng huǒ chē** *local train*

特快火车 **tè kuài huǒ chē** *express train*

火鸡 **huǒ jī** *turkey n*

伙伴 **huǒ bàn** *partner n*

货币兑换处 **huò bì duì huàn chù** *currency exchange n*

J

机场 **jī chǎng** *airport n*

机构 **jī gòu** *agency n*

机器 **jī qì** *machine n*

x 射线机 **x shè xiàn jī** *x-ray machine*

自动售货机 **zì dòng shòu huò jī** *vending machine*

鸡肉 **jī ròu** *chicken n*

吉他 **jí tā** *guitar n*

极瘦的 **jí shòu de** *thin (skinny) adj*

急速的 **jí sù de** *express adj*

快速登机 **kuài sù dēng jī** *express check-in*

脊椎指压治疗者 **jǐ zhuī zhǐ yā zhì liáo zhě** *chiropractor n*

计算机 **jì suàn jī** *computer n*

忌乳糖的 **jì rǔ táng de** *lactose-intolerant adj*

继续 **jì xù** *to continue v*

加冰块 **jiā bīng kuài** *on the rocks*

加仑 **jiā lún** *gallon n*

加拿大 **jiā ná dà** *Canada n*

加拿大的 **jiā ná dà de** *Canadian adj*

夹克衫 **jiā kè shān** *jacket n*

家 **jiā** *home n*

家禽 **jiā qín** *poultry n*

家人 **jiā rén** *family n*

家庭的 **jiā tíng de** *home adj*

家庭地址 **jiā tíng dì zhǐ** *home address*

家庭电话号码 **jiā tíng diàn huà hào mǎ** *home telephone number*

家庭主妇 **jiā tíng zhǔ fù** *homemaker n*

价格 **jià gé** *price n*

价格适中的 **jià gé shì zhōng de** *moderately priced*

门票 **mén piào** *admission fee n*

驾驶 **jià shǐ** *to drive v*

驾驶执照 **jià shǐ zhí zhào** *driver's license*

假期 **jià qī** *holiday n*

假期 **jià qī** *vacation n*

在休假 **zài xiū jiǎ** *on vacation*

去度假 **qù dù jià** *to go on vacation*

坚果 **jiān guǒ** *nut n*

间断 **jiàn duàn** *intermission n*

减慢 **jiǎn màn** *to slow v*

慢点开！**màn diǎn kāi!** *Slow down!*

减慢 **jiǎn màn** *to slow v*

健身房 **jiàn shēn fáng** *fitting room n*

健身中心 **jiàn shēn zhōng xīn** *fitness center n*

交际舞 **jiāo jì wǔ** *ballroom dancing n*

交通 **jiāo tōng** *traffic n*

交通怎么样? **jiāo tōng zěn me yàng?** *How's traffic?*

交通很糟。**jiāo tōng hěn zāo。** *Traffic is terrible.*

交通 **jiāo tōng** *traffic n*

交通规则 **jiāo tōng guī zé** *traffic rules*

交通法庭 **jiāo tōng fǎ tíng** *traffic court n*

交响乐 **jiāo xiǎng yuè** *symphony n*

交易 **jiāo yì** *deal (bargain), transaction n*

郊区 **jiāo qū** *suburb n*

焦虑的 **jiāo lù de** *anxious adj*

角 **jiǎo** *horn n*

角落 **jiǎo luò** *corner n*

脚、尺 **jiǎo、chǐ** *foot (body part) n, foot (unit of measurement) n*

教堂 **jiào táng** *church n*

教育工作者 **jiào yù gōng zuò zhě** *educator n*

接（电话），回答（问题）**jiē (diàn huà), huí dá (wèn tí)** to answer (phone call) v, to answer (respond to a question) v

接受 **jiē shòu** to accept v

接线员 **jiē xiàn yuán** operator (phone) n

街道 **jiē dào** street n

街道对面 **jiē dào duì miàn** across the street n

街舞 **jiē wǔ** hip-hop n

节目单 **jié mù dān** program n

节日 **jié rì** festival n

结婚 **jié hūn** to marry v

睫毛 **jié máo** eyelash n

她 **tā** she pron

她的 **tā de** hers adj

姐妹 **jiě mèi** sister n

解释 **jiě shì** to explain v

介绍 **jiè shào** to introduce v

我想把您介绍给＿＿＿。**wǒ xiǎng bǎ nín jiè shào gěi ＿＿＿.** I'd like to introduce you to ___.

今天 **jīn tiān** today n

金发的 **jīn fā de** blond(e) n adj

金钱 **jīn qián** money n

金色的 **jīn sè de** gold (color), golden adj

金属探测器 **jīn shǔ tàn cè qì** metal detector n

紧的 **jǐn de** tight adj

紧急联络人 **jǐn jí lián luò rén** emergency contact n

紧急情况 **jǐn jí qíng kuàng** emergency n

紧邻地 **jǐn lín dì** next prep

靠近 **kào jìn** next to

近的 **jìn de** near adj

进入 **jìn rù** to enter v

进行比赛 **jìn xíng bǐ sài** to play (a game) v

禁止进入。**jìn zhǐ jìn rù.** Entry forbidden.

禁止停车 **jìn zhǐ tíng chē** no parking v

禁止吸烟的 **jìn zhǐ xī yān de** non-smoking adj

禁烟车 **jìn yān chē** non-smoking car

禁烟房间 **jìn yān fáng jiān** non-smoking room

禁烟区 **jìn yān qū** non-smoking area

经济 **jīng jì** economy n

经济舱 **jīng jì cāng** economy class n

经理 **jīng lǐ** manager n

警察 **jǐng chá** police n

警察局 **jǐng chá jú** police station n

纠正 **jiū zhèng** to correct v

九 **jiǔ** nine n adj

九十 **jiǔ shí** ninety n adj

九月 **jiǔ yuè** September n

酒吧 **jiǔ bā** *bar n*

酒店 **jiǔ diàn** *hotel n*

酒精 **jiǔ jīng** *alcohol n*

救护车 **jiù hù chē** *ambulance n*

救生用具 **jiù shēng yòng jù** *life preserver n*

居住 **jū zhù** *to live v*

> 您住在哪里? **nín zhù zài nǎ lǐ?** *Where do you live?*

举动 **jǔ dòng** *to behave v*

拒付的 **jù fù de** *declined adj*

> 您的信用卡被拒付了。**nín de xìn yòng kǎ bèi jù fù le.** *Your credit card was declined.*

剧院 **jù yuàn** *theater n*

卷发 **juàn fà** *curly hair n, adj*

爵士乐 **jué shì yuè** *jazz n*

军官 **jūn guān** *officer n*

军事 **jūn shì** *military n*

K

咖啡 **kā fēi** *coffee n*

卡 **kǎ** *card n*

> 可以用信用卡吗? **kě yǐ yòng xìn yòng kǎ ma?** *Do you accept credit cards?*
>
> 名片 **míng piàn** *business card*
>
> 信用卡 **xìn yòng kǎ** *credit card*

卡里普索(音乐) **kǎ lǐ pǔ suǒ (yīn yuè)** *calypso (music) n*

卡普契诺咖啡 **kǎ pǔ qì nuò kā fēi** *cappuccino n*

开放时间(博物馆) **kāi fàng shí jiān (bó wù guǎn)** *hours (at museum) n*

开始 **kāi shǐ** *to begin v, to start (commence) v*

开帐单 **kāi zhàng dān** *to bill v*

看见 **kàn jiàn** *to see v*

> 我可以看一下吗? **wǒ kě yǐ kàn yī xià ma?** *May I see it?*

看起来 **kàn qǐ lái** *to look (appear) v*

抗生素 **kàng shēng sù** *antibiotic n*

抗组胺剂 **kàng zǔ àn jì** *antihistamine n*

烤焦的(肉) **kǎo jiāo de (ròu)** *charred (meat) adj*

靠近 **kào jìn** *to close v*

靠近的 **kào jìn de** *close, near adj*

靠近的 **kào jìn de** *closed adj*

咳嗽 **ké sou** *cough n to cough v*

可得的 **kě dé de** *available adj*

可以用信用卡。**kě yǐ yòng xìn yòng kǎ.** *Credit cards accepted.*

克 **kè** *gram n*

客房(酒店) **kè fáng (jiǔ diàn)** *room (hotel) n*

客人 **kè rén** *guest n*

课程 **kè chéng** *lesson n*

空调 **kōng tiáo** *air conditioning n*

空房 **kōng fáng** *vacancy n*

没有空房 **méi yǒu kōng fáng** *no vacancy*

口杯 **kǒu bēi** *shot (liquor) n*

口译人员 **kǒu yì rén yuán** *interpreter n*

裤子 **kù zi** *pair of pants n*

短裤 **duǎn kù** *shorts*

泳裤 **yǒng kù** *swim trunks n*

夸脱 **kuā tuō** *quart n*

快的 **kuài de** *fast adj*

快乐的 **kuài lè de** *happy adj*

宽带 **kuān dài** *broadband n*

宽的 **kuān de** *wide adj*

宽松上衣 **kuān sōng shàng yī** *blouse n*

困惑的 **kùn huò de** *confused adj*

困难的 **kùn nán de** *difficult adj*

L

拉 **lā** *to pull v*

喇叭 **lǎ ba** *trumpet n*

蓝色的 **lán sè de** *blue adj*

朗姆酒 **lǎng mǔ jiǔ** *rum n*

浪漫的 **làng màn de** *romantic adj*

牢固的 **láo gù de** *hard (firm) adj*

老板 **lǎo bǎn** *boss n*

老的 **lǎo de** *old adj*

老年人折扣 **lǎo nián rén zhé kòu** *senior discount n*

老鼠 **lǎo shǔ** *mouse n*

乐队 **yuè duì** *band n*

冷的 **lěng de** *cold adj*

冷水 **lěng shuǐ** *cold water n*

厘米 **lí mǐ** *centimeter n*

离开 **lí kāi** *to leave (depart) v*

离异的 **lí yì de** *divorced adj*

黎明 **lí míng** *dawn n*

礼服 **lǐ fú** *dress (general attire) n*

礼物 **lǐ wù** *gift n*

里边的 **lǐ biān de** *inside adj*

里程计 **lǐ chéng jì** *speedometer n*

理发 **lǐ fà** *haircut n*

理发师 **lǐ fà shī** *barber n*

理发师 **lǐ fà shī** *hairdresser n*

理解 **lǐ jiě** *to understand v*

您理解吗? **nín lǐ jiě ma?** *Do you understand?*

我不理解。 **wǒ bù lǐ jiě。** *I don't understand.*

历史 **lì shǐ** *history n*

历史的 **lì shǐ de** *historical adj*

立体派 **lì tǐ pài** *Cubism n*

利率 **lì lǜ** *interest rate n*

痢疾 **lì jí** *diarrhea n*

连接速度 lián jiē sù dù *connection speed* n

脸 liǎn *face* n

裂缝（玻璃品上）liè féng (bō li pǐn shàng) *crack (in glass object)* n

邻居 lín jū *neighbor* n

临时照顾幼儿者 lín shí zhào gù yòu ér zhě *babysitter* n

淋浴 lín yù *shower* n to *shower* v

零钱 líng qián *change (money)* n

令人怀疑地 lìng rén huái yí dì *suspiciously* adv

另一个 lìng yī gè *another* adj

流（水）liú (shuǐ) *current (water)* n

六 liù *six* n adj

六十 liù shí *sixty* n adj

六月 liù yuè *June* n

龙头 lóng tóu *faucet* n

聋的 lóng de *deaf* adj

露营 lù yíng *to camp* v to go *camping* v

露营地 lù yíng dì *campsite* n

露营者 lù yíng zhě *camper* n

录像 lù xiàng *video* n

录像机 lù xiàng jī *VCR* n

驴子 lǘ zǐ *donkey* n

旅程 lǚ chéng *trip* n

旅社 lǚ shè *hostel* n

旅行 lǚ xíng *to travel* v

旅行支票 lǚ xíng zhī piào *travelers' check* n

旅游 lǚ yóu *tour* n

铝 lǚ *aluminum* n

律师 lǜ shī *lawyer* n

绿色的 lǜ sè de *green* adj

轮胎 lún tāi *tire* n

备用轮胎 bèi yòng lún tāi *spare tire* n

轮椅 lún yǐ *wheelchair* n

电轮椅 diàn lún yǐ *power wheelchair*

轮椅通道 lún yǐ tōng dào *wheelchair access*

轮椅坡道 lún yǐ pō dào *wheelchair ramp*

M

妈妈 mā ma *mom* n, *mommy* n

马 mǎ *horse* n

马桶 mǎ tǒng *toilet* n

满堂彩！mǎn táng cǎi! *Full house!* n

慢 màn *slowly* adv *slow* adj

忙碌的（饭店）máng lù de (fàn diàn) *busy (restaurant)* adj

盲的 máng de *blind* adj

猫 māo *cat* n

毛巾 máo jīn *towel* n

毛毯 máo tǎn *blanket* n

毛衣 máo yī *sweater* n

帽子 mào zi *hat* n

没人 **méi rén** *none n*

没油了 **méi yóu le** *out of gas*

没有 **méi yǒu** *without prep*

没有避孕套不行 **méi yǒu bì yùn tào bù xíng** *not without a condom*

玫瑰 **méi guī** *rose n*

眉毛 **méi mao** *eyebrow n*

美国的 **měi guó de** *American adj*

美好的 **měi hǎo de** *nice adj*

美元 **měi yuán** *dollar n*

门 **mén** *door n*

登机口（在机场）**dēng jī kǒu (zài jī chǎng)** *gate (at airport)*

弥补 **mí bǔ** *to make up (compensate) v*

迷你酒吧 **mí nǐ jiǔ bā** *minibar n*

秘鲁人、秘鲁的 **mì lǔ rén、mì lǔ de** *Peruvian n adj*

密码 **mì mǎ** *password n*

蜜蜂 **mì fēng** *bee n*

棉布 **mián bù** *cotton n*

免费赠送的饮料 **miǎn fèi zèng sòng de yǐn liào** *complimentary drink n*

免税 **miǎn shuì** *duty-free adj*

面包 **miàn bāo** *bread n*

面包车 **miàn bāo chē** *van n*

民事权利 **mín shì quán lì** *civil rights n*

民主 **mín zhǔ** *democracy n*

民族 **mín zú** *nationality n*

名字 **míng zi** *name n*

我叫＿＿＿。**wǒ jiào ＿＿＿。** *My name is ＿＿＿.*

明亮的 **míng liàng de** *bright adj*

明天 **míng tiān** *tomorrow n adv*

明信片 **míng xìn piàn** *postcard n*

模糊的 **mó hu de** *blurry adj*

摩托车 **mó tuō chē** *motorcycle n*

墨西哥的 **mò xī gē de** *Mexican adj*

某人 **mǒu rén** *someone n*

某事物 **mǒu shì wù** *something n*

母牛 **mǔ niú** *cow n*

母亲 **mǔ qīn** *mother n*

母乳喂养 **mǔ rǔ wèi yǎng** *to breastfeed v*

木块 **mù kuài** *block n*

目的地 **mù dì dì** *destination n*

沐浴 **mù yù** *to bathe v*

穆斯林教 **mù sī lín jiào** *Muslim n adj*

N

哪个 **nǎ ge** *which adv*

哪里 **nǎ lǐ** *where adv*

内衣裤 **nèi yī kù** *underwear n*

那个 **nà ge** that *adj*

那里 **nà lǐ** there (far) *adv* (demonstrative)

那里 **nà lǐ** there (nearby) *adv* (demonstrative)

那些 **nà xiē** those *adj*

奶酪 **nǎi lào** cheese *n*

奶油 **nǎi yóu** cream *n*

男朋友 **nán péng yǒu** boyfriend *n*

男人 **nán rén** man *n*

男洗手间 **nán xǐ shǒu jiān** men's restroom *n*

男性（人） **nán xìng (rén)** male (person) *n*

男性的 **nán xìng de** male *adj*

难题 **nán tí** problem *n*

能够 **néng gòu** to be able to (can) *v*, may *v aux*

我可以＿＿＿吗? **wǒ kě yǐ ＿＿＿ ma?** May I ＿＿＿?

尼加拉瓜的 **ní jiā lā guā de** Nicaraguan *adj*

你 **nǐ** you *pron sing* (informal)

你的 **nǐ de** your, yours *adj sing* (informal)

你们 **nǐ mén** you *pron pl* (informal)

年 **nián** year *n*

您多大了? **nín duō dà le?** What's your age?

年级（学校） **nián jí (xué xiào)** grade (school) *n*

年龄 **nián líng** age *n*

年轻的 **nián qīng de** young *adj*

尿布 **niào bù** diaper *n*

布尿布 **bù niào bù** cloth diaper

一次性尿布 **yī cì xìng niào bù** disposable diaper

您 **nín** you *pron* (formal)

您的 **nín de** your, yours *adj* (formal)

您的年龄多大? **nín de nián líng duō dà?** What's your age?

您好 **nín hǎo** hello *n*

您还好吗? **nín hái hǎo ma?** Are you okay?

您叫什么名字? **nín jiào shén me míng zi?** What's your name?

名字 **míng zi** first name

您们 **nǐn mén** you *pron pl* (formal)

您有避孕套吗? **nín yǒu bì yùn tào ma?** Do you have a condom?

您在哪里长大? **nín zài nǎ lǐ zhǎng dà?** Where did you grow up?

柠檬水 **níng méng shuǐ** lemonade *n*

牛奶 **niú nǎi** milk *n*

奶昔 **nǎi xī** milk shake *n*

浓的 **nóng de** thick *adj*

女儿 **nǚ ér** daughter *n*

女孩 **nǔ hái** *girl* n

女朋友 **nǔ péng yǒu** *girlfriend* n

女仆（酒店）**nǔ pú (jiǔ diàn)** *maid (hotel)* n

女洗手间 **nǔ xǐ shǒu jiān** *women's restroom*

P

爬楼梯 **pá lóu tī** *to climb stairs* v

爬山 **pá shān** *mountain climbing* n, *to climb a mountain* v

攀登 **pān dēng** *climbing* n *to climb* v

攀登的 **pān dēng de** *climbing* adj

攀登设备 **pān dēng shè bèi** *climbing gear*

攀岩 **pān yán** *rock climbing*

盘子 **pán zǐ** *dish* n

胖的 **pàng de** *fat* adj

跑 **pǎo** *to run* v

跑步机 **pǎo bù jī** *treadmill* n

配导游的旅游 **pèi dǎo yóu de lǚ yóu** *guided tour* n

配方 **pèi fāng** *formula* n

烹饪 **pēng rèn** *to cook* v

朋友 **péng yǒu** *friend* n

皮肤 **pí fū** *skin* n

皮革 **pí gé** *leather* n

疲惫的 **pí bèi de** *tired* adj

啤酒 **pí jiǔ** *beer* n

便宜的 **pián yi de** *cheap, inexpensive* adj

漂白剂 **piāo bái jì** *bleach* n

漂亮的 **piào liàng de** *beautiful* adj

票 **piào** *ticket* n

贫民窟 **pín mín kū** *slum* n

品尝室 **pǐn cháng shì** *tasting room* n

品脱 **pǐn tuō** *pint* n

品位（识别力）**pǐn wèi (shí bié lì)** *taste (discernment)* n

平衡 **píng héng** *to balance* v

平局（赌博）**píng jú (dǔ bó)** *split (gambling)* n

瓶子 **píng zǐ** *bottle* n

葡萄 **pú tao** *grape* n

葡萄酒 **pú tao jiǔ** *wine* n

葡萄园 **pú tao yuán** *vineyard* n

Q

七 **qī** *seven* n adj

七分熟的（肉）**qī fēn shú de (ròu)** *medium well (meat)* adj

七十 **qī shí** *seventy* n adj

七月 **qī yuè** *July* n

妻子 **qī zǐ** *wife* n

启航 **qǐ háng** *to sail* v

我们什么时候启航？ **wǒ mén shén me shí hou qǐ háng?** *When do we sail?*

汽车 **qì chē** car n

汽车牌照 **qì chē pái zhào** *automobile license plate*

汽车租赁公司 **qì chē zū lìn gōng sī** *car rental agency*

汽油 **qì yóu** gas n

器官 **qì guān** organ n

千 **qiān** kilo n

千 **qiān** thousand n adj

千米 **qiān mǐ** kilometer n

签署 **qiān shǔ** to sign v

在这里签字。**zài zhè lǐ qiān zì.** Sign here.

前灯 **qián dēng** headlight n

前额 **qián é** forehead n

前面的 **qián miàn de** front adj

前台 **qián tái** front desk n

前天 **qián tiān** the day before yesterday adv

钱包 **qián bāo** purse n

钱包 **qián bāo** purse n, wallet n

钱夹 **qián jiā** wallet n

潜水 **qián shuǐ** to dive v

浅薄的 **qiǎn báo de** shallow adj

抢夺、偷窃 **qiǎng duó 、tōu qiè** to rob v, to steal v

桥（横跨河两岸，牙齿结构）**qiáo (héng kuà hé liǎng àn, yá chǐ jié gòu)** bridge (across a river) n / bridge (dental structure) n

切 **qiē** to cut v

切口 **qiē kǒu** cut (wound) n

亲属 **qīn shǔ** relative n

青铜色的 **qīng tóng sè de** bronze (color) adj

清澈的 **qīng chè de** clear adj

清晰的 **qīng xī de** to clear v

清真寺 **qīng zhēn sì** mosque n

情况 **qíng kuàng** condition n

情形很好 / 差 **qíng xíng hěn hǎo / chà** in good / bad condition

晴朗的 **qíng lǎng de** sunny adj

请（礼貌的请求）**qǐng (lǐ mào de qǐng qiú)** please (polite entreaty) adv

请回答我。**qǐng huí dá wǒ.** Answer me, please.

请快点！**qǐng kuài diǎn**! Hurry, please!

庆祝 **qìng zhù** to celebrate v

秋季 **qiū jì** autumn (fall season) n

球（运动）**qiú (yùn dòng)** ball (sport) n

取消 **qǔxiāo** to cancel v

去 **qù** to go v

去馆子吃饭 **qù guǎn zǐ chī fàn** to eat out v

去毛 **qù máo** waxing n

权利 **quán lì** rights n pl

雀斑 **què bān** freckle n

确认 **què rèn** confirmation n to confirm v

R

热的，温暖的 **rè de，wēn nuǎn de** *hot adj, warm adj*

热巧克力 **rè qiǎo kè lì** *hot chocolate n*

热情的 **rè qíng de** *enthusiastic adj*

热水 **rè shuǐ** *hot water n*

人 **rén** *person n*

视障人士 **shì zhàng rén shì** *visually-impaired person*

人行道 **rén xíng dào** *sidewalk n*

人行道 **rén xíng dào** *walkway n*

自动人行道 **zì dòng rén xíng dào** *moving walkway*

认识（某人） **rèn shí (mǒu rén)** *to know (someone) v*

任何的 **rèn hé de** *any adj*

任何地方 **rèn hé dì fāng** *anywhere adv*

任何事 **rèn hé shì** *anything n*

日本的 **rì běn de** *Japanese adj*

日晒 **rì shài** *sunburn n*

揉背 **róu bèi** *back rub n*

肉 **ròu** *meat n*

肉丸子 **ròu wán zǐ** *meatball n*

如何 **rú hé** *how adv*

入场最低消费（酒吧） **rù chǎng zuì dī xiāo fèi (jiǔ bā)** *cover charge (in bar) n*

入口 **rù kǒu** *entrance n*

软的 **ruǎn de** *soft adj*

软件 **ruǎn jiàn** *software n*

瑞格舞 **ruì gé wǔ** *reggae n*

S

萨尔瓦多的 **sà ěr wǎ duō de** *Salvadoran adj*

三 **sān** *three n adj*

三倍的 **sān bèi de** *triple adj*

三分熟的 **sān fēn shú de** *rare (meat) adj, undercooked adj*

三十 **sān shí** *thirty n adj*

三月 **sān yuè** *March (month) n*

伞 **sǎn** *umbrella n*

散步 **sàn bù** *walk n*

扫描 **sǎo miáo** *to scan (document) v*

色彩 **sè cǎi** *color n*

杀虫剂 **shā chóng jì** *insect repellent n*

沙拉 **shā lā** *salad n*

沙司 **shā sī** *sauce n*

刹车 **shā chē** *brake n to brake v*

山 **shān** *mountain n*

爬山 **pá shān** *mountain climbing*

山羊 **shān yáng** *goat n*

扇子（手握的） **shàn zi (shǒu wò de)** *fan (hand-held) n*

膳食 **shàn shí** *meal n*

伤害 **shāng hài** *injury n*

伤害（感到痛苦）**shāng hài (gǎn dào tòng kǔ)** to hurt (to feel painful) v

伤心的 **shāng xīn de** sad adj

商店 **shāng diàn** shop n, store n

帐篷 **zhàng péng** tent n

商务舱 **shāng wù cāng** business class n

商业 **shāng yè** business n, business adj

商业中心 **shāng yè zhōng xīn** business center

上传 **shàng chuán** to upload v

上飞机 **shàng fēi jī** to board v

上面的 **shàng miàn de** above adj

烧制 **shāo zhì** to burn v

少量 **shǎo liàng** bit (small amount) n

蛇眼！**shé yǎn!** Snake eyes! n

设计师 **shè jì shī** designer n

社会主义 **shè huì zhǔ yì** socialism n

申报 **shēn bào** to declare v

深的 **shēn de** deep adj

升 **shēng** liter n

升级 **shēng jí** upgrade n

生活 **shēng huó** life n

您是做什么工作的？**nín shì zuò shén me gōng zuò de?** What do you do for a living?

生气的 **shēng qì de** angry adj

生育 **shēng yù** to mother v

十 **shí** ten n adj

十八 **shí bā** eighteen n adj

十二 **shí èr** twelve n adj

十二月 **shí èr yuè** December n

十九 **shí jiǔ** nineteen n adj

十六 **shí liù** sixteen n adj

十七 **shí qī** seventeen n adj

十三 **shí sān** thirteen n adj

十四 **shí sì** fourteen n adj

十五 **shí wǔ** fifteen n adj

十一 **shí yī** eleven n adj

十一月 **shí yī yuè** November n

十月 **shí yuè** October n

什么 **shén me** what adv

怎么了？**zěn me le?** What's up?

时间 **shí jiān** hour n, time n

时刻表 **shí kè biǎo** schedule n, timetable (train) n

实际的 **shí jì de** actual adj

食品 **shí pǐn** groceries n

食物 **shí wù** food n

使干燥 **shǐ gān zào** to dry v

使合身（衣服）**shǐ hé shēn (yī fu)** to fit (clothes) v

使愉快 **shǐ yú kuài** to please v, to be pleasing to v

市场 **shì chǎng** market n

露天市场 **lù tiān shì chǎng** open-air market

跳蚤市场 tiào zǎo shì chǎng flea market

市区 shì qū downtown n

事故 shì gù accident n

事件 shì jiàn matter, affair

别多管闲事。bié duō guǎn xián shì。 Mind your own business.

试 shì to try (attempt) v

试穿 shì chuān to measure v / to try on (clothing) v

是 shì to be (permanent quality) v

的 shì de yes adv

是他的过错。shì tā de guò cuò。 It was his fault.

是用玻璃杯喝吗？shì yòng bō li bēi hē ma? Do you have it by the glass?

请给我来一杯。qǐng gěi wǒ lái yī bēi。 I'd like a glass please.

适配器插头 shì pèi qì chā tóu adapter plug n

收到 shōu dào to receive v

收费计划（移动电话）shōu fèi jì huà (yí dòng diàn huà) rate plan (cell phone) n

有收费计划吗？yǒu shōu fèi jì huà ma? Do you have a rate plan?

收回 shōu huí to withdraw v, withdrawal n

收集 shōu jí to collect v

收据 shōu jù receipt n

收钱 shōu qián to charge (money) v

手 shǒu hand n

手册 shǒu cè manual (instruction booklet) n

手工搜索 shǒu gōng sōu suǒ hand search v

手套 shǒu tào glove n

手提箱 shǒu tí xiāng suitcase n

守门员 shǒu mén yuán goalie n

受欢迎的 shòu huān yíng de popular adj, welcome adj

售票处 shòu piào chù box office n

售票台 shòu piào tái ticket counter n

瘦的（苗条）shòu de (miáo tiáo) thin (fine) adj

瘦的（苗条）shòu de (miáo tiáo) thin (slender) adj

书 shū book n

书店 shū diàn bookstore n

叔叔 shū shū uncle n

蔬菜 shū cài vegetable n

竖笛 shù dí clarinet n

数量 shù liàng amount n

数字 shù zì number n

双倍的 shuāng bèi de double adj

双语的 shuāng yǔ de bilingual adj

谁 **shéi** who adv

_____是谁的？ _____**shì shuí de?** Whose is _____?

水 **shuǐ** water n

水池 **shuǐ chí** sink n

水肺潜水 **shuǐ fèi qián shuǐ** to scuba dive v

水果 **shuǐ guǒ** fruit n

水疗 **shuǐ liáo** spa n

税 **shuì** tax n

增值税 **zēng zhí shuì** value-added tax (VAT)

顺子 **shùn zǐ** stair n / flush, straight (gambling) n

说出 **shuō chū** to say v

丝 **sī** silk n

司机 **sī jī** driver n

四 **sì** four n adj

四分熟的（肉）**sì fēn shú de (ròu)** medium rare (meat) adj

四分之一 **sì fēn zhī yī** one quarter, one fourth

四十 **sì shí** forty n adj

四月 **sì yuè** April n

寺庙 **sì miào** temple n

松的 **sōng de** loose adj

搜索 **sōu suǒ** search n

苏打水 **sū dǎ shuǐ** seltzer, soda n

减肥苏打水 **jiǎn féi sū dǎ shuǐ** diet soda

苏格兰的 **sū gé lán de** Scottish adj

素餐 **sù cān** vegetarian meal

素食者、素食的 **sù shí zhě、sù shí de** vegetarian n adj

塑料 **sù liào** plastic n

损坏的 **sǔn huài de** damaged adj

所有的 **suǒ yǒu de** all adj

索赔 **suǒ péi** claim n

锁 **suǒ** lock n

锁上 **suǒ shàng** to lock v

T

他 **tā** him pron

他的 **tā de** his adj

他们 **tā mén** them pron pl

踏板 **tà bǎn** scooter n

这是哪里？ **tā zài nar?** Where is it?

台球（游戏）**tái qiú (yóu xì)** pool (the game) n

太（过分）**tài (guò fèn)** too (excessively) adv

太阳 **tài yáng** sun n

太阳镜 **tài yáng jìng** sunglasses n

谈论 **tán lùn** to speak v, to talk v

这里说英语。 **zhè lǐ shuō yīng yǔ.** English spoken here.

汤 **tāng** soup n

糖尿病的 **táng niào bìng de** *diabetic adj*

糖尿病人餐 **táng niào bìng rén cān** *diabetic meal n*

烫（头发）**tàng (tóu fa)** *permanent (hair) n*

套间 **tào jiān** *suite n*

特色菜（特色套餐）**tè sè cài (tè sè tào cān)** *special (featured meal) n*

提供 **tí gōng** *to offer v*

提前 **tí qián** *advance n, in advance adv*

体育场 **tǐ yù chǎng** *stadium n*

体育馆 **tǐ yù guǎn** *gym n*

体育馆存物柜 **tǐyù guǎn cún wù guì** *gym locker*

替代品 **tì dài pǐn** *substitution n*

天 **tiān** *day n*

天鹅 **tiān é** *swan n*

天气预报 **tiān qì yù bào** *weather forecast n*

天主教的 **tiān zhǔ jiào de** *Catholic n adj*

挑染（头发）**tiāo rǎn (tóu fa)** *highlights (hair) n*

调味品 **tiáo wèi pǐn** *spice n*

调味品（沙拉）**tiáo wèi pǐn (shā lā)** *dressing (salad) n*

听 **tīng** *to listen v*

听见 **tīng jiàn** *to hear v*

听障的 **tīng zhàng de** *hearing-impaired adj*

停泊 **tíng bó** *berth n*

停车（交通标志）**tíng chē (jiāo tōng biāo zhì)** *STOP (traffic sign) n*

停车的 **tíng chē de** *parking adj*

停放 **tíng fàng** *to park v*

停留 **tíng liú** *to stay v*

停止 **tíng zhǐ** *to stop v*

请停下来。**qǐng tíng xià lái。** *Please stop.*

通行费 **tōng xíng fèi** *toll n*

同花大顺 **tóng huā dà shùn** *royal flush n*

铜的 **tóng de** *copper adj*

桶装啤酒，生啤 **tǒng zhuāng pí jiǔ, shēng pí** *beer on tap, draft beer n*

头等舱 **tóu děng cāng** *first class*

头发 **tóu fa** *hair n*

头痛 **tóu tòng** *headache n*

投票 **tóu piào** *to vote v*

图画（艺术品）**tú huà (yì shù pǐn)** *drawing (work of art) n*

徒步的 **tú bù de** *pedestrian adj*

步行购物区 **bù xíng gòu wù qū** *pedestrian shopping district*

兔子 **tù zǐ** *rabbit n*

团体 **tuán tǐ** *group n*

推 **tuī** *to push v*

推荐 **tuī jiàn** *to recommend v*

腿 tuǐ *leg* n

退房 tuì fáng *check-out* n / departure n / exit n

非出口 fēi chū kǒu *not an exit*

紧急出口 jǐn jí chū kǒu *emergency exit*

退房时间 tuì fáng shí jiān *check-out time*

退房（酒店）tuì fáng (jiǔ diàn) *to check out (of hotel)* v

退还（某物）tuì huán (mǒu wù) *to return (something)* v

吞咽 tūn yān *to swallow* v

托儿所 tuō ér suǒ *nursery* n

托牙板 tuō yá bǎn *dentures, denture plate* n

托运 tuō yùn *to check* v

拖上岸 tuō shàng àn *to beach* v

脱销的 tuō xiāo de *sold out (thing)* adj

U

USB 接口 USB jiē kǒu *USB port* n

V

签证 qiān zhèng *visa* n

W

外面 wài miàn *outside* n

外套 wài tào *coat* n

完全的 wán quán de *full* adj

玩具 wán jù *toy* n

玩具店 wán jù diàn *toy store* n

晚安 wǎn ān *good night*

晚的 wǎn de *late* adj

请不要晚了。qǐng bù yào wǎn le。 *Please don't be late.*

晚饭 wǎn fàn *dinner* n

晚上好 wǎn shàng hǎo *good evening*

网吧 wǎng bā *Internet café* n

网络 wǎng luò *Internet* n

哪里有网吧？nǎ lǐ yǒu wǎng bā？ *Where can I find an Internet café?*

网络 wǎng luò *network* n

网球 wǎng qiú *tennis* n

往返票 wǎng fǎn piào *round-trip ticket*

危地马拉的 wēi dì mǎ lā de *Guatemalan* adj

危险 wēi xiǎn *danger* n

围栏 wéi lán *curb* n

委内瑞拉的 wěi nèi ruì lā de *Venezuelan* adj

卫生间 wèi shēng jiān *bathroom, restroom* n

卫生纸 wèi shēng zhǐ *toilet paper* n

卫星 wèi xīng *satellite* n

卫星跟踪 wèi xīng gēn zōng *satellite tracking*

卫星广播 **wèi xīng guǎng bō**
satellite radio

未婚夫（妇）**wèi hūn fū (fù)**
fiancé(e) n

闻 **wén** *to smell v*

吻 **wěn** *kiss n*

问 **wèn** *to ask v*

问讯台 **wèn xùn tái**
information booth n

我 **wǒ** *I pron*

我保留娘家姓。**wǒ bǎo liú
niáng jia xìng.** *I kept my
maiden name.*

我的钱包丢了。**wǒ de qián
bāo diū le.** *I lost my wallet.*

我对＿＿过敏。**wǒ duì
＿＿＿guò mǐn.** *I'm allergic
to ＿＿. See p74 and p153
for common allergens.*

我很好。**wǒ hěn hǎo.** *I'm fine.*

我们 **wǒmén** *we, us pron pl*

我是过错方。**wǒ shì guò cuò
fāng.** *I'm at fault.*

我想要杯饮料。**wǒ xiǎng yào
bēi yǐn liào.** *I'd like a drink.*

我需要抗生素。**wǒ xū yào
kàng shēng sù.** *I need an
antibiotic.*

我要进行水肺潜水。**wǒ yào jìn
xíng shuǐ fèi qián shuǐ.** *I
scuba dive.*

浮潜 **fú qián** *to snorkel v*

我有哮喘。**wǒ yǒu xiào
chuǎn.** *I have asthma.*

我在避孕。**wǒ zài bì yùn.** *I'm
on birth control.*

卧铺车 **wò pù chē** *sleeping
car n*

握着 **wò zhe** *to hold v*

牵手 **to hold hands**

握着（赌博）**wò zhe (dǔ bó)** *to
hold (gambling) v*

乌拉圭人 **wū lā guī rén**
Uruguayan n

无神论 **wú shén lùn** *atheist adj*

无线保真 **wú xiàn bǎo zhēn**
wi-fi n

无线广播 **wú xiàn guǎng bō**
radio n

卫星广播 **wèi xīng guǎng bō**
satellite radio

五 **wǔ** *five n adj*

五十 **wǔ shí** *fifty n adj*

五月 **wǔyuè** *May (month) n*

午餐 **wǔ cān** *lunch n*

午夜 **wǔyè** *midnight adv*

武器 **wǔqì** *weapon n*

武装力量 **wǔ zhuāng lì liàng**
armed forces n pl

侮辱 **wǔrǔ** *to insult v*

X

西班牙（的）**xī bān yá (de)**
Spanish n adj

西方的 **xī fāng de** *western adj*

西方的（电影）**xī fāng de (diàn
yǐng)** *western adj (movie)*

吸烟区 **xī yān qū** *smoking area*

禁止吸烟 **jìn zhǐ xī yān** *no smoking*

希腊的 **xī là de** *Greek adj*

希腊正教的 **xī là zhèng jiào de** *Greek Orthodox adj*

袭击 **xí jī** *to mug (assault) v*

洗衣店 **xǐ yī diàn** *laundry n*

喜欢参见（关于喜欢的解释）**xǐhuān cān jiàn (guān yú xǐ huān de jiě shì)** *to please v*

戏剧 **xì jù** *drama n*

细绳 **xì shéng** *rope n, twine n*

狭窄的 **xiá zhǎi de** *narrow adj*

下面的 **xià miàn de** *below adj*

下午 **xià wǔ** *afternoon n*

在下午 **zài xià wǔ** *in the afternoon*

下午好 **xià wǔ hǎo** *Good afternoon!*

下一站 **xià yī zhàn** *the next station*

下雨 **xià yǔ** *to rain v*

下载 **xià zǎi** *to download v*

夏季 **xià ji** *summer n*

纤维 **xiān wéi** *fabric n*

闲荡 **xián dàng** *to lounge v*

现金 **xiàn jīn** *cash n*

只收现金 **zhǐ shōu xiàn jīn** *cash only*

现在 **xiàn zài** *now adv*

限速 **xiàn sù** *speed limit n*

乡村音乐 **xiāng cūn yīn yuè** *country-and-western music adj*

香烟 **xiāng yān** *cigarette n*

箱式小轿车 **xiāng shì xiǎo jiào chē** *sedan n*

详细说明 **xiáng xì shuō míng** *to specify v*

享受 **xiǎng shòu** *to enjoy v*

想法 **xiǎng fǎ** *thought n*

想要 **xiǎng yào** *to want v*

向 **xiàng** *toward prep*

向前的 **xiàng qián de** *forward adj*

向上 **xiàng shàng** *up adv*

向下 **xiàng xià** *down adv*

消耗 **xiāo hào** *drain n*

消化不良 **xiāo huà bù liáng** *indigestion n*

消失 **xiāo shī** *to disappear v*

销售 **xiāo shòu** *to sell v*

销售人员 **xiāo shòu rén yuán** *salesperson n*

街头小贩 **jiē tóu xiǎo fàn** *street vendor*

小吃 **xiǎo chī** *snack n*

小虫 **xiǎo chóng** *bug n*

小厨房 **xiǎo chú fáng** *kitchenette n*

小船 **xiǎo chuán** *boat n, ship n*

小的、短的 **xiǎo de, duǎn de** *small adj, short adj, little adj*

更小的 gèng xiǎo de *smaller, littler*

最小的 zuì xiǎo de *smallest, littlest*

小费 xiǎo fèi *tip (gratuity)*

包含小费 bāo hán xiǎo fèi *tip included*

小孩 xiǎo hái *boy n, kid n*

小径 xiǎo jìng *trail n*

小鸟 xiǎo niǎo *bird n*

小女孩 xiǎo nǚhái *little girl n*

小跑 xiǎo pǎo *jogging n*

小说 xiǎo shuō *novel n*

爱情小说 ài qíng xiǎo shuō *romance novel*

神秘故事 shén mì gù shì *mystery novel*

小提琴 xiǎo tí qín *violin n*

小甜饼 xiǎo tián bǐng *cookie n*

小虾 xiǎo xiā *shrimp n*

小学 xiǎo xué *primary school n*

肖像 xiào xiàng *portrait n*

哮喘 xiào chuǎn *asthma n*

鞋子 xié zi *shoe n*

写出 xiě chū *to spell v*

请问它怎么写? qǐng wèn tā zěn me xiě? *How do you spell that?*

写出 xiě chū *to write v*

您能给我写下那个吗? nín néng gěi wǒ xiě xià nà ge ma? *Would you write that down for me?*

谢谢您 xiè xiè nín *thank you*

心脏 xīn zàng *heart n*

心脏病 xīn zàng bìng *heart attack n*

新的 xīn de *new adj*

新教 xīn jiào *Protestant n adj*

新西兰 xīn xī lán *New Zealand n*

新西兰的 xīn xī lán de *New Zealander adj*

新鲜的 xīn xiān de *fresh adj*

信封 xìn fēng *envelope n*

信息 xìn xī *information n*

信用局 xìn yòng jú *credit bureau n*

星期二 xīng qī èr *Tuesday n*

星期六 xīng qī liù *Saturday n*

星期三 xīng qī sān *Wednesday n*

星期四 xīng qī sì *Thursday n*

星期天 xīng qī tiān *Sunday n*

星期五 xīng qī wǔ *Friday n*

星期一 xīng qī yī *Monday n*

行李 xíng lǐ *baggage, luggage n*

行李丢了 xíng lǐ diū le *lost baggage*

行李车 xíng lǐ chē *trunk (of car) n*

行李领取处 xíng lǐ lǐng qǔ chù *baggage claim*

姓 xìng *last name*

幸会 xìng huì *charmed adj*

性别 **xìng bié** *sex (gender)* n

性交 **xìng jiāo** *intercourse (sexual)* n

兄弟 **xiōng dì** *brother* n

休息室 **xiū xī shì** *lounge* n

修剪（头发）**xiū jiǎn (tóu fa)** *to trim (hair)* v

需要 **xū yào** *to need* v

许多 **xǔ duō** *a lot* n *many* adj

许多的 **xǔ duō de** *much* adj

许可证 **xǔ kě zhèng** *permit* n

续处方 **xù chǔ fāng** *refill (of prescription)* n

蓄电池（汽车使用的）**xù diàn chí (qì chē shǐ yòng de)** *battery (for car)* n

选举 **xuǎn jǔ** *election* n

选中的（样式）**xuǎn zhōng de (yàng shì)** *checked (pattern)* adj

学生折扣 **xué shēng zhé kòu** *student discount*

学校 **xué xiào** *school* n

学院，高中 **xué yuàn, gāo zhōng** *college* n, *high school* n

雪茄 **xuě jiā** *cigar* n

寻找 **xún zhǎo** *to look for (to search)* v

训练 **xùn liàn** *to train* v

Y

押注（赌博）**yā zhù (dǔ bó)** *to put (gambling)* v

放在红色 / 黑色上！**fàng zài hóng sè / hēi sè shàng!** *Put it on red / black!*

鸭子 **yā zǐ** *duck* n

牙 **yá** *tooth* n

牙痛 **yá tòng** *toothache* n

我牙疼。**wǒ yá téng。** *I have a toothache.*

牙医 **yá yī** *dentist* n

亚洲的 **yà zhōu de** *Asian* adj

延误 **yán wù** *delay* n

岩石 **yán shí** *rock* n

沿着街道 **yán zhe jiē dào** *down the street*

盐 **yán** *salt* n

低盐 **dī yán** *low-salt*

眼睛 **yǎn jīng** *eye* n

眼镜 **yǎn jìng** *eyeglasses, glasses (spectacles)* n

验光师 **yàn guāng shī** *optometrist* n

羊绒衫 **yáng róng shān** *cashmere* n

阳台 **yáng tái** *balcony* n

氧气罐 **yǎng qì guàn** *oxygen tank* n

摇滚 **yáo gǔn** *rock and roll* n

药草 **yào cǎo** *herb* n

药片 **yào piàn** *pill* n

晕船药 **yùn chuán yào** seasickness pill

药物 **yào wù** medicine n, medication n

要求 **yāo qiú** to order, request, demand v

也 **yě** too (also) adv

夜晚 **yè wǎn** night n

每夜 **měi yè** per night
在夜晚 **zài yè wǎn** at night

夜总会 **yè zǒng huì** nightclub n

一 **yī** one n adj

一包香烟 **yī bāo xiāng yān** pack of cigarettes

一打 **yī dá** dozen n

一份 **yī fèn** portion (of food) n

一些 **yī xiē** some adj

一月 **yī yuè** January n

一直 **yī zhí** all the time

就那些。**jiù nà xiē.** That's all.

衣架 **yī jià** hanger n

医生 **yī shēng** doctor n

医生办公室 **yī shēng bàn gōng shì** doctor's office n

医学院 **yī xué yuàn** medical school n

仪式 **yí shì** service (religious) n

移动 **yí dòng** to move, to remove v

乙烯基 **yǐ xī jī** vinyl n

已婚的 **yǐ hūn de** married adj

艺术 **yì shù** art n

艺术展 **yì shù zhǎn** exhibit of art

艺术博物馆 **yì shù bó wù guǎn** art museum n

手艺人 **shǒu yì rén** craftsperson / artisan n

艺术的 **yì shù de** art adj

艺术家 **yì shù jiā** artist n

易碎的 **yì suì de** fragile adj

溢出 **yì chū** to spill v

音乐 **yīn yuè** music n

流行音乐 **liú xíng yīn yuè** pop music

音乐的 **yīn yuè de** musical adj

音乐会 **yīn yuè huì** concert n

音乐家 **yīn yuè jiā** musician n

音乐厅 **yīn yuè tīng** coliseum n

音乐喜剧（音乐流派）**yīn yuè xǐ jù (yīn yuè liú pai)** musical (music genre) n

音频 **yīn pín** audio n

音频的 **yīn pín de** audio adj

银 **yín** silver n

银色的 **yín sè de** silver (color) adj

银行 **yín háng** bank n

银行卡 **yín háng kǎ** bank card n

银行账户 **yín háng zhàng hù** bank account n

银质的 yín zhì de *silver adj*

引擎 yǐn qíng *engine n*

饮料 yǐn liào *drink n*

隐形眼镜 yǐn xíng yǎn jìng *contact lens n*

印度教教徒 yìn dù jiào jiào tú *Hindu n*

印象流派 yìn xiàng liú pài *Impressionism n*

英寸 yīng cùn *inch n*

英格兰 yīng gé lán *England n*

英俊的 yīng jùn de *handsome adj*

英里 yīng lǐ *mile n*

英语的 yīng yǔ de *English adj*

婴儿 yīng ér *baby n*

婴儿车 yīng ér chē *stroller n*

婴儿床 yīng ér chuáng *crib n*

婴儿的 yīng ér de *infantile adj*

婴儿食品 yīng ér shí pǐn *baby food*

婴儿推车 yīng ér tuī chē *baby stroller*

鹰 yīng *eagle n*

营业中 yíng yè zhōng *open (business) adj*

影印 yǐng yìn *to photocopy v*

硬币 yìng bì *coin n*

拥挤的 yōng jǐ de *congested adj*

拥塞（交通）yōng sāi (jiāo tōng) *congestion (traffic) n*

泳衣 yǒng yī *swimsuit n*

用 yòng *to use v*

优惠券 yōu huì quàn *voucher n*

就餐优惠券 jiù cān yōu huì quàn *meal voucher*

住宿优惠券 zhù sù yōu huì quàn *room voucher*

由对方付费的 yóu duì fāng fù fèi de *collect adj*

犹太教的 yóu tài jiào de *Jewish adj Judaism n*

犹太教的 yóu tài jiào de *kosher adj*

犹太教食品 yóu tài jiào shí pǐn *kosher meal n*

邮件 yóu jiàn *mail*

邮局 yóu jú *post office n*

邮票 yóu piào *stamp (postage) n*

油 yóu *oil n*

油表 yóu biǎo *gas gauge n*

油画 yóu huà *painting n*

疣 yóu *wart n*

游戏 yóu xì *play n*

游戏控制台 yóu xì kòng zhì tái *game console n*

游行 yóu xíng *parade n*

游泳 yóu yǒng *to swim v*

禁止游泳。 jìn zhǐ yóu yǒng。 *Swimming prohibited.*

游泳池 **yóu yǒng chí** *pool (swimming)* n

有 **yǒu** *to have* v

性交 **xìng jiāo** *to have sex (intercourse)*

有_____吗? **yǒu _____ ma?**
Is / Are there _____?

有斑纹的 **yǒu bān wén de** *striped* adj

有风的 **yǒu fēng de** *windy* adj

有公共洗手间吗? **yǒu gōng gòng xǐ shǒu jiān ma?** *Do you have a public restroom?*

有机的 **yǒu jī de** *organic* adj

有礼貌的 **yǒu lǐ mào de** *courteous* adj

有人偷了我的钱包。 **yǒu rén tōu le wǒ de qián bāo** *Someone stole my wallet.*

有压力的 **yǒu yā lì de** *stressed* adj

幼儿 **yòu ér** *infant* n

鱼竿 **yú gān** *fishing pole* n

愉快 **yú kuài** *pleasure* n

见到您很愉快。 **jiàn dào nín hěn yú kuài.** *It's a pleasure.*

羽绒枕 **yǔ róng zhěn** *down pillow*

语言 **yǔ yán** *language* n

浴缸 **yù gāng** *bathtub* n

预定 **yù dìng** *reservation* n

预算 **yù suàn** *budget* n

员工 **yuán gōng** *staff (employees)* n

原谅 **yuán liàng** *to excuse (pardon)* v

对不起。 **duì bù qǐ。** *Excuse me.*

援助 **yuán zhù** *assistance* n

远的 **yuǎn de** *far* adj

更远的 **gèng yuǎn de** *farther*

最远的 **zuì yuǎn de** *farthest*

远足 **yuǎn zú** *to hike* v

约会 **yuē huì** *appointment* n

月 **yuè** *month* n

允许 **yǔn xǔ** *to permit* v

运动 **yùn dòng** *sports* n

运动场 **yùn dòng chǎng** *playground* n

运行 **yùn xíng** *to ride* v / *to run* v

晕车 **yùn chē** *carsickness* n

晕船 **yùn chuán** *nausea* n

晕倒 **yūn dǎo** *to faint* v

晕眩的/晕船 **yūn xuàn de/yùn chuán** *dizzy* adj / *seasick* adj

Z

杂志 **zá zhì** *magazine* n

载运 **zǎi yùn** *to ship* v

再见 **zài jiàn** *goodbye* n

再斟满 **zài zhēn mǎn** *refill (of beverage)* n

在飞机上 **zài fēi jī shàng** on board

在角落 **zài jiǎo luò** on the corner

在黎明 **zài lí míng** at dawn

在那边 **zài nà biān** over there adv

遭袭击 **zāo xí jī** to get mugged

早餐 **zǎo cān** breakfast n

早晨 **zǎo chén** morning n

在早晨 **zài zǎo chén** in the morning

早的 **zǎo de** early adj

早上好 **zǎo shàng hǎo** Good morning!

噪杂的 **zào zá de** loud, noisy adj

增长 **zēng zhǎng** to grow (get larger) v

炸弹 **zhà dàn** bomb n

展览 **zhǎn lǎn** exhibit n

占线的，占用的 **zhàn xiàn de, zhàn yòng de** busy adj (phone line), occupied adj

战争 **zhàn zhēng** war n

站 **zhàn** stop n

公共汽车站 **gōng gòng qì chē zhàn** bus stop

站起 **zhàn qǐ** to stand v

丈夫 **zhàng fū** husband n

账户 **zhàng hù** account n

障碍 **zhàn gài** handicap n

遮光剂 **zhē guāng jì** sunscreen n

折扣 **zhé kòu** discount n

儿童折扣 **ér tóng zhé kòu** children's discount

这个 **zhè gè** this adj this n

这里 **zhè lǐ** here adv

这是哪一种? **zhè shì nǎ yī zhǒng?** What kind is it?

这些 **zhè xiē** these n adj pl

真棒! **zhēn bàng!** Great! interj

真的 **zhēn de** really adj

枕头 **zhěn tóu** pillow n

正确的 **zhèng què de** correct adj

证明 **zhèng míng** identification n

政党 **zhèng dǎng** political party n

支付 **zhī fù** to pay v

支票 **zhī piào** check n

汁 **zhī** juice n

知道（某事）**zhī dao (mǒu shì)** to know (something) v

执照 **zhí zhào** license n

侄女 **zhí nǚ** niece n

侄子 **zhí zi** nephew n

直 **zhí** straight adv

在拐角处右转。**zài guǎi jiǎo chù yòu zhuǎn.** Turn right at the corner.

在右侧。**zài yòu cè.** It is on the right.

直走（指示方向）. zhí zǒu
(zhǐ shì fāng xiàng) Go
straight. (giving directions)

直 zhí straight adj

直（头发）zhí (tóu fa) straight
(hair) adj

纸 zhǐ paper n

餐巾纸 cān jīn zhǐ paper
napkin

纸盘 zhǐ pán paper plate

纸币（货币）zhǐ bì (huò bì) bill
(currency) n

纸巾 zhǐ jīn napkin n

指出 zhǐ chū to point v

指南（出版物）zhǐ nán (chū
bǎn wù) guide
(publication) n

指示 zhǐ shì to show v

您能指给我吗? nín néng zhǐ
gěi wǒ ma? Would you
show me?

至少 zhì shǎo at least n

制冰机 zhì bīng jī ice machine

制造 zhì zào to make v

痣（脸部特征）zhì (liǎn bù
tè zhēng) mole (facial
feature) n

中（号）zhōng (hào) medium
adj (size)

中国的 zhōng guó de Chinese
adj

中间的 zhōng jiān de middle
adj

中午 zhōng wǔ noon n

钟 zhōng clock n, watch n

闹钟 nào zhōng alarm clock

种类 zhǒng lèi kind (type) n

重 zhòng to weigh v

请您再重复一遍好吗? qǐng
nín zài chóng fù yī biàn
hǎo ma? Would you
please repeat that?

重量 zhòng liàng weights n

周 zhōu week n

从现在起一周 cóng xiàn
zài qǐ yī zhōu a week
from now

上周 shàng zhōu last week

下周 xià zhōu next week

一周 yī zhōu one week

这周 zhè zhōu this week

猪 zhū pig n

煮得过久的 zhǔ dé guò jiǔ de
overcooked adj

助行器（助行设备）zhù xíng qì
(zhù xíng shè bèi) walker
(ambulatory device) n

蛀洞（牙洞）zhù dòng (yá
dòng) cavity (tooth cavity) n

抓小偷! zhuā xiǎotōu! Stop,
thief!

专业的 zhuān yè de
professional adj

转动 zhuàn dòng to turn v

左/右转. zuǒ/yòu zhuǎn.
Turn left / right.

转移 zhuǎn yí to transfer v
transfer n

转帐 zhuǎn zhàng money transfer

装入 zhuāng rù to bag v

装束 zhuāng shù costume n

状态 zhuàng tài state n

准备好的 zhǔn bèi hǎo de prepared adj

桌子 zhuō zǐ table n

啄木鸟 zhuó mù niǎo woodpecker n

着陆 zhuó lù to land v

紫色的 zǐ sè de purple adj

字幕 zì mù subtitle n

自动取款机 zì dòng qǔ kuǎn jī ATM n

自助餐 zì zhù cān buffet n

自助的 zì zhù de self-serve adj

自助形式的 zì zhù xíng shì de buffet-style adj

棕色的 zōng sè de brown adj

总数 zǒng shù total n

总数是多少? zǒng shù shì duō shǎo? What is the total?

走 zǒu to walk v

租赁 zū lìn to rent v

租用中的 zū yòng zhōng de charter adj

包机 bāo jī charter flight

阻塞 zǔsè to block v

组成 zǔ chéng makeup n

组成的 zǔ chéng de made of adj

祖父 zǔ fù grandfather n

祖母 zǔ mǔ grandmother n

嘴 zuǐ mouth n

最便宜 zuì pián yi cheapest

最低 zuì dī lowest

（银行账户上的）余额 (yín háng zhàng hù shàng de) yú é balance (on bank account) n

最高的 zuì gāo de highest

最好的 zuì hǎo de best See good

最后 zuì hòu last adv

最后这些日子 zuì hòu zhè xiē rì zǐ these last few days

最坏 zuì huài worst See bad adj

最近 zuì jìn closest adj

最近的（最高级）zuì jìn de (zuì gāo jí) nearest (superlative)

最少的 zuì shǎo de least See little

昨天 zuó tiān yesterday adv

左边的 zuǒ biān de left adj

作家 zuò jiā writer n

坐 **zuò** *to sit v*

座位 **zuò wèi** *seat n*

做预算 **zuò yù suàn** *to budget v*

前排座位 **qián pái zuò wèi** *orchestra seat*

NOTES

NOTES

NOTES

NOTES

NOTES

NOTES

NOTES